The Trials and Joys of Marriage

Middle English Texts

General Editor
Russell A. Peck
University of Rochester

Associate Editor
Alan Lupack
University of Rochester

Assistant Editor
Dana M. Symons
University of Rochester

Advisory Board
Rita Copeland
University of Pennsylvania

Thomas G. Hahn
University of Rochester

Lisa Kiser
Ohio State University

Thomas Seiler
Western Michigan University

R. A. Shoaf
University of Florida

Bonnie Wheeler
Southern Methodist University

The Middle English Texts Series is designed for classroom use. Its goal is to make available to teachers and students texts that occupy an important place in the literary and cultural canon but have not been readily available in student editions. The series does not include those authors, such as Chaucer, Langland, or Malory, whose English works are normally in print in good student editions. The focus is, instead, upon Middle English literature adjacent to those authors that teachers need in compiling the syllabuses they wish to teach. The editions maintain the linguistic integrity of the original work but within the parameters of modern reading conventions. The texts are printed in the modern alphabet and follow the practices of modern capitalization, word formation, and punctuation. Manuscript abbreviations are silently expanded, and *u/v* and *j/i* spellings are regularized according to modern orthography. Yogh is transcribed as *g*, *gh*, *y*, or *s*, according to the letter in modern English spelling to which it corresponds. Distinction between the second person pronoun and the definite article is made by spelling the one *thee* and the other *the*, and final -*e* that receives full syllabic value is accented (e.g., *charité*). Hard words, difficult phrases, and unusual idioms are glossed on the page, either in the right margin or at the foot of the page. Explanatory and textual notes appear at the end of the text, along with a glossary. The editions include short introductions on the history of the work, its merits and points of topical interest, and also contain briefly annotated bibliographies.

The Trials and Joys of Marriage

Edited by
Eve Salisbury

Published for TEAMS
(The Consortium for the Teaching of the Middle Ages)
in Association with the University of Rochester

by

Medieval Institute Publications

WESTERN MICHIGAN UNIVERSITY

Kalamazoo, Michigan — 2002

Library of Congress Cataloging-in-Publication Data

The trials and joys of marriage / edited by Eve Salisbury.
      p. cm. -- (Middle English texts)
"Published for TEAMS (The Consortium for the Teaching of the Middle
Ages) in Association with the University of Rochester."
Includes bibliographical references.
   ISBN 1-58044-035-5 (alk. paper)
  1. English literature--Middle English, 1100-1500. 2.
Marriage--Literary collections. I. Salisbury, Eve. II. Consortium for
the Teaching of the Middle Ages. III. Middle English texts (Kalamazoo,
Mich.)
  PR1120 .T74 2002
  820.9'3543'0902--dc21

                        2002004298

ISBN 1-58044-035-5

For David and Meghan

Contents

Acknowledgments

The ultimate satisfaction in putting together a volume such as this, at least for me, resides in the daily commiseration and decision-making, the working together with many people — readers, commentators, editors, friends, and associates — all of whom deserve full recognition and much gratitude.

Special thanks go first to Russell A. Peck whose careful reading and active engagement with every detail at every stage of production renders the editing process satisfying and pleasurable, even as he insists upon the highest standards possible. Likewise, Alan Lupack's rigorous reading upholds that high standard while his good natured commentary makes receiving a thoroughly red-marked text far less daunting than it can be. I would also like to thank Mara Amster for her valuable suggestions on revisions of various sorts; Ronald B. Herzman for his feedback on an early draft of the introduction; Dana M. Symons, whose editing savvy and continuous vigilance in preparing camera-ready copy are nothing short of heroic; John Sutton for reading texts against manuscripts and other editions; Rose Paprocki for locating and procuring often obscure library materials; Tom Seiler, Julie Scrivener, and the editorial staff at the Medieval Institute for scrutinizing final copy; Clifford Davidson for his scholarly expertise; and Douglas Moffat and Mary Elizabeth Ellzey for their work on a preliminary version of *Prohemy of a Mariage Betwixt an Olde Man and a Yonge Wife, and the Counsail*, including many explanatory notes and glosses; also Paul Shaffner whose original suggestion for a volume on medieval marriage set the work in motion. Of course, none of this would be possible without the continued support of TEAMS (Consortium for the Teaching of the Middle Ages), a grant from the National Endowment for the Humanities, and the cooperation of many holding libraries in the UK as well as the Robbins Library at the University of Rochester.

Finally, I would like to acknowledge and dedicate this book to the two people in my life whose sardonic wit and perpetual sense of irony continue to make me laugh.

The Trials and Joys of Marriage

Introduction

> Who koude telle, but he hadde wedded be,
> The joye, the ese, and the prosperitee
> That is bitwixe an housbonde and his wyf?
> The Franklin's Tale, *CT* V(F)803–05

Marriage and Society

The works presented in this anthology bridge generic categories — satire, fabliaux, secular lyrics, didactic treatises, homiletic matter — and range from the late thirteenth century to the emergence of the English Renaissance in the late fifteenth and early sixteenth centuries. Some of these texts are obscure, written by anonymous authors, while others are by well-known authors, such as John Lydgate, England's first poet laureate, and the fifteenth-century Scots writer William Dunbar. Yet the theme of marriage links these seemingly disparate texts together to provide an illuminating view of a social institution with a long and complex history. We might expect notions of medieval marriage to be unified and cohesive given the fact that marriage became a sacrament in the twelfth century and was increasingly recognized as a viable social arrangement by ecclesiastical and secular authorities. However, as some of the texts in this volume suggest, heterosexual marriage as an institution was not always a stabilizing and orderly social force. These texts challenge and, in some cases, parody, satirize, and critique the institution of marriage. In so doing they allow us to interrogate the traditional assumptions that shape the idea of the medieval household. The trials of marriage seem to outweigh its joys at times and, as some of these texts suggest, maintaining a sense of humor in the face of what must have been great difficulty could have been no easy task.

The Middle Ages inherited a set of assumptions from classical and biblical sources that helped shape its understandings of nuptial commitment. Depictions on Greek and Roman pottery, murals and friezes, cultural artifacts and some of the most poignant epic and lyric poetry ever written indicate the honor with which marital union was held. Who could forget the pathos of Homer's Odysseus weeping on the island of Kalypso, pining for Penelope and his homeland, or the abjection of Andromache as she mourns the death of her beloved Hector, or the passion of Virgil's Dido whose union with Aeneas she calls "marriage," or Sappho's lyrical exhortation to "raise the roof" for the bridegroom rendered godlike by his impending nuptials? Neither gods nor poets could deny the power of the fusion of two bodies into one soul, two souls into one body; nor could they deny the pain and loss of separation.

Scriptural texts of the Hebrew Bible parallel the high regard of the Greeks and Romans by underwriting marriage in religious traditions in compelling tales of marital love and burgeoning family life. The Hebrew stories of Genesis place marital union at the very center of creation — "Wherefore a man shall leave father and mother, and shall cleave to his wife: and they shall be two in one flesh" (Genesis 2:24). Moreover, the scriptural edict to "[i]ncrease and multiply" (Genesis 1:28) endorses marital procreation as practiced by the first married couple and carried on by their sons and countless generations thereafter, a genealogy that traces humanity back to an original progenitor. The idea of marriage as a central feature of the mythology of these ancient societies could be used to explain the literal relation between men and women as well as to explicate a metaphorical relation between human and divine, form and matter, and the inexplicable mysteries of Nature. One of the most stunning of Old Testament texts — *The Song of Songs* — could be interpreted in many ways: as the erotic longing between bride and bridegroom, as the mystical marriage of the human soul and its maker, as the conjoining of God and his people, or as the sublime fusion within the Godhead itself. Perhaps the most famous commentator on *The Song of Songs* in the Middle Ages, Bernard of Clairvaux, wrote eighty-six sermons in which he eloquently described an intense erotic longing not for the pleasures of the flesh but for the pleasures of God's embrace. Using the imagery of the Bride and Bridegroom as set forth by earlier writers such as Origen[1] (e.g., the Bride's ardent desire to kiss the mouth of her beloved), Bernard speaks to his monastic audience of the soul's yearning for spiritual ecstasy: "We do not hesitate boldly to proclaim that every soul, if it is vigilant and careful in the practice of all the virtues, can arrive at this holy repose and enjoy the embraces of the Bridegroom."[2] Bernard's desire is to inspire the transformation of the souls of his initiates, men who may well have tasted the delights of erotic experience, to encourage the sublimation of their sexual energy into impassioned religious devotion.[3]

Marriage, in the story of the Wedding at Cana in the Gospel of John, also functions as a metaphor for transformation according to Augustine of Hippo:

---

[1] See, for instance, *Origin, The Song of Songs: Commentary and Homilies*, trans. R. P. Lawson (Westminster, MD: Newman Press, 1957). For a comprehensive discussion of the tradition, see also Ann W. Astell, *The Song of Songs in the Middle Ages* (see Select Bibliography for full reference) and E. Ann Matter, *"The Voice of My Beloved": The Song of Songs in Western Medieval Christianity*.

[2] Bernard of Clairvaux, *On the Song of Songs*, trans. Kilian Walsh (Kalamazoo: Cistercian Publications, 1981), p. x. For Bernard's theology of love, see Etienne Gilson, *The Mystical Theology of St. Bernard*, trans. A. H. C. Downes (Kalamazoo: Cistercian Publications, 1940; rpt. 1955, 1990).

[3] See Jean LeClerq, *Monks on Marriage: A Twelfth-Century View.*

Introduction

> For the Word was the Bridegroom and human flesh the bride: and both one, the Son of God, the same also being Son of man. The womb of the Virgin Mary, in which He became head of the Church, was His bridal chamber. . . . From His chamber He came forth as a bridegroom, and being invited [to the Wedding at Cana] came to the marriage.[4]

Marriage imagery also appears in Augustine's explication of the meeting between Christ and the Samaritan woman who is transformed into a figure for the wayward human soul in the absence of Truth; the Samaritan woman's five husbands become the five senses over which she has no control. When Christ commands her to "call her husband" it is for the purpose of provoking reason, the higher human faculty, into governing a soul mired in the materiality of life. The Samaritan woman's "true" husband is announced when she recognizes the Truth of what is being said to her.[5]

Other New Testament teachings emphasize the literal union between man and woman as advocated in Christ's teaching: "What therefore God hath joined together, let no man put asunder" (Matthew 19:6), which became the Christian ideal of marriage. According to Michael M. Sheehan, Christian marriage was to be understood as a "sacred relationship" that "provided the ordinary means to the full Christian life . . . [T]he ideal sought in the full Christian life was one in which there would be no erotic activity outside marriage."[6] Given the historical context of early Christianity and the social systems it opposed — the polygamy of Celtic societies and the persistent concubinage of the Romans — this endorsement of a new nuptial ideal must have been very attractive, particularly to women. Nonetheless, the presence of a deep ambivalence about marriage, articulated in Pauline theology and reiterated thereafter, subordinates the matrimonial state of human existence to a life of chastity. In his compelling letter to the Corinthians, Paul says:

> He that is without a wife is solicitous for the things that belong to the Lord: how he may please God. But he that is with a wife is solicitous for the things of the world: how he may please his wife. And he is divided. And the unmarried woman and the virgin thinketh on the things of the Lord: that she may be holy both in body and in spirit. But she that is married thinketh on the things of the world: how she may please her husband. (1 Corinthians 7:32b–34)

As Katharina M. Wilson and Elizabeth M. Makowski point out, Paul's view was shaped in large part by his expectation of an imminent second coming and the spiritual readiness such

---

[4] St. Augustine, "Homilies on the Gospel of John; Homilies on the First Epistle of John Tractate VIII," in *The Nicene and Post-Nicene Authors*, vol. VII, ed. Philip Schaff (Grand Rapids, MI: Wm. B. Eerdmans Publishing Co., 1991), p. 58.

[5] St. Augustine, "Homilies," p. 59.

[6] Michael M. Sheehan, *Marriage, Family, and Law in Medieval Europe*, p. 78.

an occasion required.[7] But added to other comments made by Paul, i.e., "It is good for a man not to touch a woman" and "it is better to marry than to be burnt" (1 Corinthians 7:1, 9), this statement and the theology it underwrites prove too much for early Christian writers to ignore. What St. Paul preached under a particular set of historical circumstances initiated interpretations that became part of the Latin exegetical tradition.

Despite the fact that the institutional church supported marriage, the conflict Paul introduced was never very far from intense internal debate. The earliest Latin writings of influential patristic thinkers, like Tertullian, John Chrysostom, Origen, and Jerome, all of whom cited Paul as their authoritative source, subordinated the married state to an ascetic lifestyle and urged the sublimation of sexual desire into religious devotion. Perhaps what might be described as the most notorious opposition to marriage appears in Jerome's *Adversus Jovinianus*, which argues vehemently for the superiority of virginity. The argument initiates a debate on marriage that remains a contentious issue surfacing hundreds of years later, among other places, in Chaucer's The Wife of Bath's Prologue.

However influential Jerome might have been, it was Augustine's ambivalence about marital sexuality that ultimately had the most profound effect on clerical views of marriage. Called by at least one scholar "the architect of spiritual marriage in the West," Augustine upheld the "goods" of marriage, i.e., procreation, marital fidelity, and the sacramental bond, in his treatise on the subject. At the same time, however, he proposed that there could be a perfectly valid marriage without sex like that of Mary and Joseph, whose relation endorsed marital affection, the sacramental bond.[8] As Elizabeth A. Clark puts it,

> Augustine argues thus: because Joseph acted in the role of Jesus's father, he can be named Mary's *husband*, and this despite their failure ever to have intercourse. They can be called *husband and wife* because 'intercourse of the mind is more intimate than that of the body.' Fleshly intercourse is *not* the chief element in marriage, he asserts; a couple can be husband and wife without it.[9]

Not only did some Christian writers emphasize companionate marriage and encourage metaphorical familial ties rather than actual family bonding, but there is a similar trend in the philosophical tradition as well. Athena and Lady Philosophy could become surrogate wives or mothers for seekers of wisdom just as readily as the Virgin Mary or Christ could be understood as parents or spouses. Both religious and philosophical asceticism carried over into

---

[7] Katharina M. Wilson and Elizabeth M. Makowski, *Wykked Wyves and the Woes of Marriage: Misogamous Literature from Juvenal to Chaucer.*

[8] Dyan Elliott, *Spiritual Marriage: Sexual Abstinence in Medieval Wedlock*, p. 43.

[9] See Elizabeth A. Clark, "'Adam's Only Companion': Augustine and the Early Christian Debate on Marriage," p. 23.

late medieval life, and both those in search of a religious life as well as those in search of a university career were expected to remain celibate and chaste.

When marriage became a sacrament in the twelfth century, an already important social arrangement found endorsement from the church, which stood opposed to secular abuses of marital rights by the upper classes. What evolved from the opposition were two models of marriage — secular and ecclesiastical — whose "radical" differences, according to Georges Duby, were in emphasis and focus. While the lay model of marriage supported by the French aristocracy was intended "to safeguard the social order," the ecclesiastical model was created to "safeguard the divine order."[10] The lay aristocracy, which had operated under customary laws for centuries, sought to protect a patriarchally controlled system of marriage in which young adults had little choice of marriage partner. Instead, marriages were arranged by parents seeking beneficial social and political alliances with other households sometimes not very far removed from their own. The system was designed primarily to control the patrimony and maintain the economic position and legitimacy of children born to wedded couples.

The difference in focus of this secular model of marriage presented a challenge to churchmen seeking to write a comprehensive set of rules and regulations that would protect scriptural edicts and the sanctity of wedlock.[11] The ecclesiastical view of marriage demanded that consent take place between the two principles in the union and that nuptial vows be witnessed in a public place — initially at the church door — rather than arranged and carried out clandestinely; this would help to distinguish legitimate conjugal relations from the sort of concubinage practiced by the Romans. However, because consent of the spouses was a necessary prerequisite to a valid union, many marriages could take place informally and, as long as no one opposed them, could be considered legitimate.[12] To render a marriage "legal" required a simple vow of consent either in the present or the future tense which was usually, but not always, followed by consummation; sanctification by a priest was also desirable but not necessary.[13] Central to the obligations of this marital arrangement was payment of the conjugal debt, which required each spouse to fulfill the other's sexual demands even when one partner was unwilling. Needless to say, the very idea of negotiating sex in marriage becomes a point of contention both to canonists and married couples.[14]

---

[10] Georges Duby, *Medieval Marriage: Two Models from Twelfth-Century France*, p. 3.

[11] See James A. Brundage, *Medieval Canon Law*, especially Chapter 3.

[12] Robert C. Palmer, "Contexts of Marriage in Medieval England," pp. 42–67. See also Brundage, *Law, Sex, and Christian Society in Medieval Europe*, pp. 348–64, and *Medieval Canon Law*, p. 73.

[13] Brundage, *Medieval Canon Law*, p. 73.

[14] The episode in *The Book of Margery Kempe* in which Margery and her husband discuss conjugal relations is one example. See *The Book of Margery Kempe*, ed. Lynn Staley (Kalamazoo: Medieval Institute Publications, 1996), chapter 11, p. 37.

Canon law also supported traditional views of the subordinate status of women in relation to men and endorsed placing women *sub virga et potestate*, literally "under the rod and in the power" of their husbands who had legitimate authority over them in both legal and domestic matters.[15] The expectation was, however, that the male head of the household would exercise reason in the discharge of his family duties. Nonetheless, the church, in an effort to protect the institution, strenuously opposed the easy repudiation of spouses and made marital dissolution extremely difficult. Because marriage was intended to be a lifetime monogamous obligation, neither separation nor annulment (the medieval equivalent of divorce) could be granted without enormous effort since both were considered measures of last resort. Over the course of the next two centuries, marriage ordinances were increasingly clarified and a definitive set of rules and regulations eventually disseminated to the public.[16]

Just at the time marriage was being made into an officially sacred bond between consenting men and women, there were others who opposed its alleged virtues. Heloise, according to Abelard's account in a letter contained in his *Historia Calamitatum,* writes that she would rather be his "whore" than his wife, arguing that a man whose mind was made for the study of philosophy should not be distracted by the daily obligations of marriage and family life.[17] Despite her eloquent and learned protest, however, Abelard arranged a clandestine wedding after which time the already-pregnant Heloise was shipped off to Abelard's sister's house to await the birth of their son. Meanwhile, Abelard was left to face some dire consequences of his own. Ambushed and castrated by thugs hired by Heloise's angry and vengeful uncle, Abelard suffered ignominy and pain thereafter; driven out of the university, he took monastic vows and was exiled from the intellectual community he loved.[18] Not only had he participated in an illicit sexual relation, unsanctioned by church and family, but he had also violated the customary chastity expected of scholars and philosophers.[19] Heloise also took religious vows but remained as devoted to Abelard for the rest of her life as she was to the nuns of the priory he had given to her.[20]

---

[15] Palmer, p. 50n26.

[16] Sheehan, *Marriage, Family, and Law in Medieval Europe*, pp. 118–76.

[17] See J. T. Muckle, trans. *The Story of Abelard's Adversities* (Toronto: Pontifical Institute of Mediaeval Studies, 1982), pp. 31–37.

[18] See M. T. Clanchy, *Abelard: A Medieval Life* (Oxford: Blackwell, 1997).

[19] Not surprisingly Heloise cites Jerome's *Adversus Jovinianus* as one of the authorities on the subject. Heloise's diatribe against marriage was reiterated in the *Roman de la Rose*, which became known throughout Europe.

[20] Peter Dronke, *Abelard and Heloise in Medieval Testimonies*. The authenticity of the letters is still a matter of controversy among scholars. For a sense of this and other recent issues, see Bonnie Wheeler, ed., *Listening to Heloise: The Voice of a Twelfth-Century Woman*, and Barbara Newman, *From Virile*

Introduction

The perception of marriage espoused by Heloise, so obviously influenced by the religious and philosophical validation of asceticism, finds another supporter in Andreas Capellanus, author of *The Art of Courtly Love* (*De Honesti de Amandi*). This time, however, the argument is predicated upon the notion that love and marriage are incompatible. Following in the tradition of the Roman poet, Ovid, whose *Ars Amatoria* created such a scandal in Augustan Rome that he was eventually exiled, Andreas constructs a false assumption of marriage as a loveless relation — "we declare and we hold as firmly established that love cannot exert its powers between two people who are married to each other."[21] He goes on to say that, because there is obligation attached to the fulfillment of conjugal duties, there could be no possibility of mutual affection. The place to find love, Andreas argues, is outside of marriage in the arms of a lover, preferably one who is married to someone else. Most of the book consists of a number of dialogues between men and women of various classes and backgrounds rendered ridiculous in their negotiations. Courtly love or *amour courtois*, as it was coined by Gaston Paris in the nineteenth century, was imagined to have an ennobling effect on the lover; he was somehow transformed into a better person in the attempt to attain a desirable lady, preferably one of a higher social rank. A courtly love relationship, because it was extramarital, entailed secrecy and discretion on the part of the lovers as well as whoever was in their employ as a go-between, a pander to pass their encoded messages back and forth. Of course, the entire treatise, written ostensibly to a naive young man named Walter, is stridently satirical, meant to be a critique of *fin amor* rather than a manual for lovers to be taken seriously; Andreas cleverly reveals none of his satirical intention until the treatise's last section, however:

> Read this little book, then, not as one seeking to take up the life of a lover, but that, invigorated by the theory and trained to excite the minds of women to love, you may, by refraining from so doing, win an eternal recompense and thereby deserve a greater reward from God. For God is more pleased with a man who is able to sin and does not than with a man who has no opportunity to sin.[22]

It is hardly a coincidence that at approximately the same time writers like Chrétien de Troyes and Marie de France were addressing the relation of marriage to courtly love and chivalry. A new demand for chivalric romance encouraged Chrétien's invention of his Lancelot and the many characterizations of Tristan, from Thomas of Britain to Béroul to Gottfried von Strassburg. With the possible exception of Wolfram von Eschenbach's *Parzival*, which encourages both the notion of conjugal love and the compatibility of chivalry with marriage,

---

Woman to WomanChrist: Studies in Medieval Religion and Literature.

[21] Andreas Capellanus, *The Art of Courtly Love*, trans. John Jay Parry (New York: Columbia University Press, 1960), p. 107.

[22] Andreas Capellanus, p. 187.

writers of romance delighted in the plight of illicit lovers. Themes of courtly love and the oftentimes humorous antics of the chivalrous lover even found a place in medieval "histories," such as Wace's *Roman de Brut*, a twelfth-century revision of Geoffrey of Monmouth's *Historia Regum Britanniae*, and Layamon's *Brut*, where they were implicitly validated. In the thirteenth century, the *Roman de la Rose* seemed to glorify the foolish lover once again in his attempts to conquer the beloved rose at the center of a heavily guarded *hortus conclusus*; this time the adventures of the lover exposed the absurdity of love's games and encouraged instead the kind of sublimated desire Bernard of Clairvaux and Augustine had in mind earlier. At least that is how its authors Guillaume de Lorris and Jean de Meun apparently intended it to be read. That reading was soon challenged, however, when Christine de Pizan stripped away the allegory to reveal a disturbing defamation of women.[23] Christine's writings, like Marie de France's before her, contributed an important perspective on the position of women in medieval society: both those subject to difficult marriages and those caught in potentially destructive courtly games.[24]

If the tensions inherent in French chivalric romances suggest that marriage was a vexed institution in late medieval France, then it was no less problematic in late medieval England, where from the thirteenth century onward ecclesiastical officials did their best to regulate in practice what was proposed in theory.[25] The issues were just as unsettled in romance literature such as *Havelok the Dane* and *King Horn*, both of which reflect a concern for dynastic marriage while at the same time revealing an inclination toward the idea of consent between spouses. Later romances move more definitively in the direction of consent; *Bevis of Hampton*, for instance, makes it clear that the heroine desires to marry the hero but must wait patiently until he consents to the relationship. By the fourteenth century, the optimism frequently created by the authors of romances can only come about when marriage is made central to the welfare of the crown. In *Sir Orfeo*, for instance, the stability of the hero's kingdom, jeopardized by the queen's abduction, can be restored only when Orfeo successfully rescues her. In Thomas Chestre's *Sir Launfal* the kingdom is jeopardized when the adulterous Guenevere falsely accuses the hero of rape. Both narratives demonstrate a firm position against high-level adultery and the potential harm it could do to a kingdom — the fall of Camelot is

---

[23] See Natalie Zemon Davis' Foreword to the revised edition of *The Book of the City of Ladies*, trans. Earl Jeffrey Richards (New York: Persea Books, 1998), pp. xv–xxii.

[24] At the end of the *Book of the City of Ladies*, the author directs her attention to married ladies: "And you ladies who are married, do not scorn being subject to your husbands, for sometimes it is not the best thing for a creature to be independent. . . . And those women who have husbands who are cruel, mean, and savage should strive to endure them while trying to overcome their vices and lead them back, if they can, to a reasonable and seemly life" (p. 255).

[25] See Shannon McSheffrey, trans. *Love and Marriage in Late Medieval London*.

the primary *exemplum*. It is probably no coincidence that these two works and others like them were written at a time when members of the English aristocracy engaged in courtly love with great enthusiasm — Edward II's notorious relation with his French male lover and Queen Isabella's courtly liaison with Roger Mortimer actually threatened the kingdom, while the elderly Edward III's antics with the strong-willed Alice Perriers and John of Gaunt's long-term relation with Katherine Swynford caused intense public anxiety. Not only were the practices of courtly love passionately embraced in the private lives of public individuals in the fourteenth century, but they were also engaged by the works of writers such as Chaucer and Gower.

Perhaps these are some of the reasons Chaucer's work is so heavily infused with the complexities of marital relations that a "marriage group," consisting of The Wife of Bath's Prologue, The Clerk's Tale, The Merchant's Tale, and The Franklin's Tale, was identified in *The Canterbury Tales* a century ago by George Lyman Kittredge and continues to be a viable subject for discussion among scholars and students. A marriage debate that addresses all the problems inherited by fourteenth-century England can be traced in these tales — questions raised by Alisoun of Bath's prologue and tale, continued by the Clerk's story of the patient Griselda, and January's troubles with a youthful May, are wishfully resolved by the Franklin's narrative of Dorigen and Arveragus.[26] To that list of eligible marriage narratives might be added The Knight's Tale of two marriages, the Miller's fabliau of the foibles of courtly love, the Reeve's fabliau of domestic life, The Shipman's Tale of cuckoldry and exchange, Melibee's tale of household governance, The Nun's Priest's Tale of a literally henpecked husband, and even The Second Nun's Tale, which could be considered an *exemplum* of spiritual marriage. The underlying assumptions about marriage render the tales and their tellers particularly important guides to this realm of social life.

When cataclysmic changes in the economic, social, and political conditions of society allow aggressive women to challenge authority, as does Chaucer's Wife of Bath, male anxieties about female chastity and cuckoldry, potency and paternity become magnified; male sexual power becomes a metaphor for social power, and a perceived decline in prowess in the bedchamber translates into emasculation and potential ridicule in the public sphere. But in an age without Viagra, male sexual anxiety seems to be not only transferred onto women, who

---

[26] See Russell A. Peck, "Sovereignty and the Two Worlds of The Franklin's Tale," *The Chaucer Review* 1 (1967), 253–71. See also Joan G. Haahr, "Chaucer's 'Marriage Group' Revisited: The Wife of Bath and Merchant in Debate," *Acta* 14 (1990), 105–20; Wolfgang E. H. Rudat, "Gentillesse and the Marriage Debate in the Franklin's Tale: Chaucer's Squires and the Question of Nobility," *Neophilologus* 68 (1984), 451–70; Wolfgang E. H. Rudat, "Aurelius' Quest for Grace: Sexuality and the Marriage Debate in the Franklin's Tale," *CEA Critic* 45 (1982), 16–21; Raymond P. Tripp, Jr., "The Franklin's Solution to the 'Marriage Debate,'" in *New Views on Chaucer: Essays in Generative Criticism*, ed. William C. Johnson and Loren C. Gruber (Denver: Society for New Language Study, 1973), pp. 35–41.

bear the brunt of the blame for diminished performance — witches' curses or overly high expectations — but also directed against the institution that seems to benefit women most — marriage. What results is a marked growth in misogamy, this time in popular literature. According to Wilson and Makowski:

> works of misogamy are a source of entertainment not only for generations of wife-beaters and henpecked husbands but also for the general audience. As in most comedy, so in comic and satiric misogamy, the humor derives from a clear incongruity between what is and what should be; between legal and social models and situational ethics, on the one hand, and actual human behavior, on the other; between institutionalized male superiority and occurrences of marital *mundus inversus.* [27]

The inversion of the marital universe, depicted in scenes of wives beating husbands in church carvings, in the margins of manuscripts, or in fabliaux, plays, and puppet shows,[28] elicited joviality (where there might otherwise be pure misery) by diffusing difficult and unpleasant social realities and providing release for collective anxiety. In this sense the genre of fabliau might be considered carnivalesque in its inversion of social and political hierarchies, operating much in the way of festivals and feast-day celebrations by mocking established institutions without threatening their destruction. Instead, such uninhibited events and imaginative works reinforced the status quo by encouraging an entire culture to laugh at itself.

Fabliau and Satire

Many of Chaucer's tales in the expanded version of the marriage group just enumerated belong to a tradition of fabliau that neither achieves the abundance and rich variety of French fabliau nor comes close to the bawdiness of its sexual humor. The paucity of English works in this genre has prompted medieval scholars to find plausible explanations. Keith Busby, for instance, suggests that French traditions permeated English society so thoroughly that there was no need to fill a void because there was no void to be filled.[29] Moreover, he suggests that

---

[27] Wilson and Makowski, pp. 6–7.

[28] For evidence on medieval puppet shows see George Speaight, *The History of English Puppet Theatre* (London: George G. Harrap & Co., 1955), pp. 27–43; Ian Lancashire, "'Ioly Walte and Malkyng': A Grimsby Puppet Play in 1431," *REED Newsletter* 4.2 (1979), 6–8, and a discussion with illustrations of MS Bodleian 264 in Allardyce Nicoll, *Masks, Mimes, and Miracles: Studies in Popular Theatre* (London: George G. Harrap & Co., 1931), p. 168.

[29] Keith Busby, "*Dame Sirith* and *De Clerico et Puella*," in *Companion to Early Middle English Literature*, ed. N. H. G. E. Weldhoen and H. Aertsen (Amsterdam: Free Press, 1995), pp. 67–78.

Introduction

English audiences simply had no interest in matters of French courtly behavior.[30] Yet it is also the case that, like other medieval genres, the English fabliau is part of a hybridized comic mode of expression integrated into other forms of representation and for that reason difficult to identify.[31] Two fabliau texts preceding those of Chaucer — *Dame Sirith* and the *Interludium de clerico et puella* — suggest the well-established presence of this kind of English fabliau prior to the end of the fourteenth century.

Both *Dame Sirith* and the *Interludium de clerico et puella*, when considered with other comic works in this volume, add up to something more than scholars imagined to have existed outside of Chaucer. Both narratives embody elements of other genres that render them resistant to easy categorization. The brief *Interludium* is written so convincingly in dramatic dialogue that it has been called the "oldest extant secular drama" in Middle English.[32] Announcing itself as it does in Latin, it seems to identify with liturgical drama, but does not follow through with religious themes. Neither would it have been performed in the church at any time during the liturgical year. Instead, it might better be understood as a crossover, hybrid genre that has left the church door behind, even slammed it shut since the interlude's anti-clerical satire clearly imagines a secular audience. As satire the work takes from fabliau its two most prominent motifs — sexual deception and the inversion of social hierarchies, particularly marriage — to target wayward and foolish clerics as well as weak and foolish husbands. In its secularity it also targets the weak and foolish young woman who would fall for the tricks of the older, more cunning people around her. The *Interludium* is the kind of play that might have been performed by minstrels as entertainment during a court feast such as that found in *Sir Gawain and the Green Knight*. Indeed, its themes of cuckoldry and fatuous behavior seem rather appropriate in the fictional court of King Arthur, given the ongoing courtly relation between Lancelot and Guenevere.

Whereas the *Interludium* unveils the underlying absurdity of illicit relations, *Dame Sirith* takes that absurdity to a new level in the intricacy of plot, character development, and the addition of a "weeping bitch."[33] It too has been discussed as drama, yet it is much more

---

[30] Busby, p. 69.

[31] John Hines, *The Fabliau in English* (London: Longman, 1993), outlines the characteristics of French fabliau, tracing its development in England, and its relation to other genres.

[32] See J. A. W. Bennett and G. V. Smithers, eds., *Early Middle English Verse and Prose* (Oxford: Clarendon Press, 1966), pp. 77–79; and Charles W. Dunn and Edward T. Burnes, eds., *Middle English Literature* (New York: Harcourt, Brace, Janovich, 1973), p. 174.

[33] The weeping bitch appears as a complete narrative in the *Disciplina Clericalis* of Petrus Alphonsus. See Dorothea Metlitzki, *The Matter of Araby in Medieval England* (New Haven: Yale University Press, 1977), pp. 99–102. It is also found in *A Thousand and One Arabian Nights* and in the medieval Hebrew *Tales of Sendebar*, a collection which represents extant versions of another series of tales, *The Seven*

11

complex than the *Interludium*, requiring as it does a narrator, three actors, and a performing dog. Dame Sirith, the go-between for a would-be lover, Wilekin, and the lady of his dreams, Margery, devises a trick to convince the reluctant young wife to accept Wilekin's indecent proposal. The trick, which calls for a special preparation of mustard and vinegar to make the dog weep, elicits the desired result — the lover successfully dupes the gullible Margery into an affair with him; Sirith's remedies are proven so efficacious by the end of the narrative that she turns to the audience and offers her professional services to anyone who might want them.[34] If the mental acuity of Margery is thrown into question by her quick accession to Sirith's trickery, the intellectual faculties of Sirith are heightened by comparison. She turns a terrific trick by creating a convincing narrative with a little help from a cunningly prepared canine actor. This is English fabliau at its finest.

Whereas French fabliau is often denigrating to women, English fabliau, according to Melissa Furrow, is frequently marked by a "strong tendency . . . to use trickery to put a stop to illicit behavior rather than to further it."[35] This is certainly true in the case of *The Wright's Chaste Wife*, where a young wife cleverly thwarts attempts on her chastity by three would-be lovers — a knight, a steward, and a proctor. When they appear one by one at her door while her husband is away, she lures them one at a time up the stairs to a trapdoor covering a pit forty feet deep into which they fall. This tale of an attempted seduction of a carpenter's wife differs from the attempts made on Alisoun in Chaucer's The Miller's Tale because it ends not in the ridicule of the gullible husband, his wayward young wife, the hopeful lovers, and the practices of a parodic version of courtly love, but rather in the ridicule of the privileged classes. When the knight, his steward, and the proctor are made to do the work of women during their involuntary incarceration not only are they comically emasculated, but their complete ignorance of how manual labor should be done reveals an utter lack of social conscience. As John DuVal suggests, the tale throws the notion of nobility into question when the measure of a person's value is represented by productivity rather than by birthright.[36] The moral of the story underscores the value of women's work — the beating of flax, the spinning and preparation of raw materials into usable fibers — and demonstrates the capabilities of married women in both household management and personal integrity. The fact that the knight, the first

---

Sages of Rome.

[34] Bruce Moore, "The Narrator within the Performance: Problems with Two Medieval Plays," in *Drama in the Middle Ages: Comparative & Critical Essays*, ed. Clifford Davidson and John H. Stroupe (New York: AMS Press, 1991), p. 165.

[35] Melissa Furrow, "Middle English Fabliaux and Modern Myth," *English Language History* 56 (1989), 13.

[36] John DuVal, "*The Wright's Chaste Wife*: A Satiric Fabliau," *Publications of the Missouri Philological Association* 2 (1977), 8–14.

to take advantage of the wright's absence, genuinely learns something from his experience suggests that the lesson on the value of hard work could be taken back to the aristocratic class to which he belongs; meanwhile, the wright's wife gains recognition as the repository of honor and integrity as she teaches the ignorant fools around her. The miraculous garland of roses, the measure of a young woman's chastity given to her by her mother as a meager dowry, remains untainted; so too does the wife's reputation, a fact that confers nobility upon a woman and benefits her husband as well.

The theme of the value of women's work is also present in the *Ballad of a Tyrannical Husband*, as is a strong feminine voice that undercuts an attempted male critique. In this anonymous, unfinished tale, the tyrannical husband, a ploughman, imagines that his field work is far more demanding than his wife's domestic chores. In a manner echoing present-day criticism of the stereotypical bon-bon eating, soap-opera watching housewife, this husband evokes a masculine ideology that presupposes the lesser value of domestic, and therefore feminine, work. When he demands that they switch places for a day, however, he discovers that the raising of children, the production and preparation of food and clothing, the care of the domestic environment, the feeding of the livestock, and the brewing of ale far exceed his simple agricultural chores.[37] The tyranny that he attempts to impose on his wife is exposed not merely as unjust but as utterly fatuous. The marital hierarchies of this narrative, as in *The Wright's Chaste Wife*, have been broken down into equitable egalitarian arrangements wherein the male characters learn to respect women's contributions to medieval society at large and women defend themselves against the slander typical of fabliau.

If French fabliaux encourage the lingering of a lascivious masculine gaze upon the private parts of women, then English fabliaux, or at least one of them, unveil the heretofore invisible male member and provide women with yet another literary venue for venting frustrations about marital intimacy. *A Talk of Ten Wives on Their Husbands' Ware*, for instance, offers a glimpse into feminine discourses on marital sex. Not unlike the contemporary locker room talk of female athletes or the feminine discourse present at gatherings of women honoring an

---

[37] Barbara A. Hanawalt offers an interesting discussion of women's work that applies to both the *Ballad of a Tyrannical Husband* and *The Wright's Chaste Wife* in *The Ties That Bound: Peasant Families in Medieval England* (Oxford: Oxford University Press, 1986), pp. 147 ff. See also Hanawalt's "Peasant Women's Contribution to the Home Economy in Late Medieval England," in *Women and Work in Preindustrial Europe*, ed. Barbara Hanawalt (Bloomington: Indiana University Press, 1996), pp. 3–19; Shulamith Shahar, *The Fourth Estate: A History of Women in the Middle Ages* (London: Methuen, 1983), especially Chapter 7; Judith M. Bennett, *Women in the Medieval English Countryside: Gender & Household in Brigstock Before the Plague* (New York: Oxford University Press, 1987), especially Chapter 5; Rodney H. Hilton, *The English Peasantry in the Later Middle Ages* (Oxford: Clarendon Press, 1975); and Helena Graham, "'A woman's work. . .': Labour and Gender in the Late Medieval Countryside," in Goldberg, pp. 126–48.

impending birth or wedding, or among adolescent women or women's professional communities, this discourse reverses the norm and directs the feminine gaze to the male body. The discussion, which takes place in a tavern, is the stuff of which masculine anxiety over physique, sexual performance, and masculinity is imagined to derive. In euphemistic language worthy of distinction for the number of words describing but never saying the word "penis," ten married women take turns talking frankly about the shortcomings of their husbands' "merchandise." From size to sexual performance to bedroom behavior, they castigate their spouses freely — the anonymous author is careful to mention that there are no men around to hear them. Despite the fact that this is probably a male-authored text mocking the hubris of an assumed male privilege, it nonetheless provides a venue for married women to identify with what must have been very real frustrations. That many young women were strongly encouraged, even coerced, to marry up the social scale to financially successful, often older, men was a fact of social life in late medieval England.

There is no question about the gender of the voice in *Prohemy of a Mariage Betwixt an Olde Man and a Yonge Wife, and the Counsail*, attributed to John Lydgate,[38] nor that the issue at stake is marriage between an older man and a younger woman. Neither is there any question about the influence of Chaucer — the poem is filled with Chaucerian allusions. The work is cast in terms of an epistle written to the narrator/philosopher by his old friend requesting advice on whether to marry. Using Chaucer's The Merchant's Tale and a fabliau about December and his young wife July, the Philosopher sets about dissuading his friend from taking such a drastic step so late in life. At one point in the narrative he quotes Paul's "it is better to marry than to be burnt" statement (as does Chaucer's Wife of Bath, *CT* III[D]52), perhaps a reason that the work is in the highly personal epistle form. Certainly the misogamous themes are evident in the speaker's advice as he lists the negative views of women held by Jerome, Tertullian, and others also listed in The Wife of Bath's Prologue. If we consider this work as an extension of the marriage debate reiterated so entertainingly by Chaucer's Wife of Bath, the Philosopher argues against everything that Alisoun claims about marriage to such

---

[38] James Orchard Halliwell, in the only modern edition of the poem (see Select Bibliography for *Prohemy*, p. 126), refers to it as "one of the best specimens of Lydgate's composition" (p. 27). Julius Hugo Lange, "Zur Verfasserschaft dis *Advice*," *Englissche Studien* 30 (1902), 346, also ascribes the poem to Lydgate. But Henry Noble MacCracken, *The Minor Poems of John Lydgate*, Pt. I, EETS e.s. 107 (London: Oxford University Press, 1911), p. xlviii, suggests that the *Prohemy*, "a clever poem something after Mapes's poem against marriage, which Lydgate put into English at this time and made popular," is more akin to Hoccleve in its attack on women, its pleasure in talking about unsatisfactory marriage, and its fondness for Chaucer. But, McCracken argues, the rhymes are equally against authorship by either Hoccleve or Lydgate, concluding: "There were certainly more poets at work in this period than we know about." Caroline F. E. Spurgeon, *Five Hundred Years of Chaucer Criticism and Allusion, 1357–1900*, vol. 1 (Cambridge: Cambridge University Press, 1925), p. 36, places composition of the poem at about 1430.

an extent that his misogamy approaches misogyny as he proceeds to discredit women as a group. The Philosopher's *exempla* include a wife who has married seven times, a recapitulation of what happened to old January, unwittingly cuckolded by Damian, and a similar narrative about an old man (December) and a young woman (July) who persuades him to marry, only to prove untrustworthy in the end. When December tells July frankly before they wed that he is impotent, she agrees to live with his condition, at least temporarily. When he discovers the intensity of her desire in bed on their wedding night and asks her to recall their conversation, she reveals another plan: that his impotence should be remedied by procuring a younger and more virile surrogate lover. December is not only threatened with cuckoldry, but he is even expected to pay for it! Like January and all the other dupes of fabliau, the old man is made a fool by his desire, not simple lust, but rather a culturally driven desire for public status bequeathed upon him by this trophy wife. Lydgate ends in a Chaucerian-like palinode, an envoy to all men in the audience who might make the same mistake.

That mistake is taken up again in an anonymous and very brief fabliau called *The Meaning of Marriage*. Not only is the older husband castigated by his young wife, but he is also cuckolded by a willing and able priest, whom the Scottish narrator claims is Irish. The priest comes to the home of the husband and his young wife to act as marriage counselor since the husband has spent most of his time away from home to the neglect of his wife and payment of the conjugal debt. When John seems not to comprehend the reasons for marriage offered to him by the Irish priest, i.e., procreation of children, satisfying Nature, and avoiding fornication, the priest offers to demonstrate. He does so well that the young wife wishes him to repeat the demonstration, claiming that her elderly husband will forget what he has just witnessed.[39]

The case of the neglectful and impotent old husband is further debated by Dunbar in his Middle Scots poem *The Tretis of the Twa Mariit Wemen and the Wedo*. Some see Dunbar's *Tretis* as an extension of the marriage debate initiated by Chaucer: the two married women, under the guidance and encouragement of the more experienced widow, mount a scathing attack on the sexual inadequacies of their decrepit husbands. Dunbar casts his marriage satire in an innovative manner, capturing the flavors of English fabliau, while rendering a distinctly different view of it all. The poet adds a dimension of voyeurism reminiscent of *A Talk of Ten Wives*, but much more explicit and overt. The discussion about men in which the women engage is overheard by Dunbar's persona, a narrative eavesdropping device that allows the author to use the text as a means by which his audience may be instructed against nuptial naiveté. Like the title character in *Dame Sirith*, Dunbar's narrator turns to the audience in the end, but rather than recommending his services, he recommends second thoughts to those

---

[39] For a similarly amusing gulling of a foolish husband by a clever priest, see the French fabliau on the priest who peeked, summarized and discussed at the beginning of Russell A. Peck, "Public Dreams and Private Myths: Perspective in Middle English Literature," *PMLA* 90 (1975), 461–62.

considering marriage. As in the anonymous *A Talk of Ten Wives*, Dunbar constructs a feminine community and a collective female voice that has gained credibility among some scholars.[40] Yet, the very freedom with which these women speak, the social and linguistic liberties performed here, are precisely the factors that mark the text as fabliau. These aggressive and forceful females participate in the carnivalesque by mocking the traditions that define social status and keep women firmly in their place.

Didactic Works

If the fabliau offers us a humorous side to the marriage debate, then its serious side is represented by the many entertaining moralized stories found in the *Gesta Romanorum*, certain works of influential writers like John Lydgate, and conduct treatises such as *How the Goode Wife Taught Hyr Doughter* and *How the Goode Man Taght Hys Sone*. All of these works address matters relating to marital union and family life as ideas about both continued to evolve in the late Middle Ages.

The English version of the *Gesta Romanorum* contains a sampling of the kinds of stories that might be read as well as heard in the sermons of medieval preachers and reformulated in the works of writers such as Boccaccio, Chaucer, Gower, Hoccleve, Lydgate, and Shakespeare. The compilation is a vast repository of moral *exempla* used to convert an entertaining mode of literature into moral lessons for members of the laity who might not otherwise be exposed to them.[41] This has led some scholars to suggest that possible authors may be John Bromyard, author of *Summa Prædicantium*, a well-known, frequently used manual for preachers, or Petrus Berchorius, compiler of *Reductorii Moralis*, or Robert Holcot, whose *Moralitates* also renders him a possible candidate.[42] It is more likely, however, that the English *Gesta Romanorum* will remain known simply as a compilation invented by anonymous monks for fireside recreation and edification.

As the title of the *Gesta Romanorum* suggests, the narratives focus on the deeds of the Romans, but the diverse stories collected therein come from a variety of sources, both oral and

---

[40] See, for instance, Edwina Burness, "Female Language in *The Tretis of the Tua Mariit Wemen and the Wedo*," *Scottish Studies* 4 (1984), 359–68.

[41] Larry Scanlon suggests that this particular narrative form was particularly dominant in England. See *Narrative, Authority, and Power: The Medieval Exemplum and the Chaucerian Tradition* (Cambridge: Cambridge University Press, 1994), p. 3.

[42] Other compilations that resemble the *Gesta Romanorum* in form are: Alexander Neckam's *De Natura Rerum*, Bartholomaeus Anglicus' *De Proprietatibus Rerum*, Nicole Bozon's *Les Contes Moralisés*, and Odo de Cheriton's *Parabolae*.

written, some of which may originate well beyond the boundaries of Europe.[43] The vast number of extant manuscripts, approximately one hundred and sixty-five, according to Sir Frederic Madden, renders the *Gesta* something of a medieval bestseller. Compiled first in Latin in the late thirteenth or early fourteenth centuries, it was translated into several European languages. The Middle English versions, which occur sometime in the fifteenth century, pave the way for Wynkyn de Worde's printed edition and many editions thereafter.

As a source of homiletic materials for the parish priest, the *Gesta* must have been invaluable. Any conscientious ecclesiastic seeking to infuse dry didactic homilies with exciting storytelling could look to it for complete narratives. Neither would he have to deduce the moral of the story, since the "moralitee" is explicitly written at the end of each tale. The stories of the *Gesta Romanorum* taught an untutored laity ways in which fictional narratives could be read and interpreted in a manner similar to the traditional exegetical methods used to interpret biblical narratives from Genesis to the Book of Revelation. But they also served to amuse the learned through their often bizarre moralistic ingenuity. Bible stories could be interpreted allegorically, morally, and spiritually, as well as literally, as we have seen demonstrated for The Song of Songs and the Gospel of John. Any number of Old Testament characters and/or events could prefigure Christ or foreshadow the events of the New Testament. Similarly, stock characters in the *Gesta* such as the bawd, the Emperor, the wayward woman, the naive young son, the necromancer, and the cleric could easily be converted into allegorical figures. Shirley Marchalonis' study of one hundred and eighteen *Gesta* stories, for instance, finds that the ruler — king, emperor, knight, or historical figure — is the "most constant symbol," though variation occurs in meaning.[44] In most tales the ruler equates with God or Christ while in others he could be the human soul, the good Christian, or a conscientious prelate.

The three stories from the *Gesta Romanorum* selected for this volume demonstrate how moral *exempla* could be didactic as well as entertaining. Each of the narratives here — "How a Wife Employed a Necromancer to Cause the Death of Her Husband, and How He Was Saved by a Clerk," "Of the Magic Ring, Brooch, and Cloth," and "The Punished of Adulterers" —

---

[43] Three manuscript "families" have been identified by early editors: 1) the Anglo-Latin group from which the five extant manuscripts in Middle English were translated, 2) a group of German and Latin manuscripts, and 3) a Vulgate group compiled around the time of Henry VI. Diane Speed has consolidated the groupings into two major categories: the Anglo-Latin and the continental German and Latin manuscripts. See "Middle English Romance and the *Gesta Romanorum*," in *Tradition and Transformation in Medieval Romance*, ed. Rosalind Field (Rochester: D. S. Brewer, 1999), pp. 45–56. Barbara A. Hanawalt sees some of the stories in the *Gesta Romanorum* as evidence of separation anxiety in late-medieval England. See *'Of Good and Ill Repute': Gender and Social Control in Medieval England* (New York: Oxford University Press, 1998), especially Chapter 6.

[44] Shirley Marchalonis, "Medieval Symbols in the *Gesta Romanorum*," *Chaucer Review* 8 (1974), 311–19.

deals with marriage and family relations in an entertaining yet instructive manner. In fact, because medieval genres often overlap, the resemblances among them are difficult to discern and numerous parallels have been identified between *Gesta* stories and Middle English romances as well as other forms of literary work.[45]

The sins of adultery are the subject of "How a Wife Employed a Necromancer to Cause the Death of Her Husband," where Emperor Felician's wife takes a shine to a knight in her husband's employ. She is so determined to carry out her illicit desire that she employs a magician to murder her husband from afar by means of sorcery; the well-laid plans are thwarted by a cleric with preternatural skills enough to overcome the best any evil sorcerer could conjure. Emperor Felician is ultimately saved, the necromancer dies, and the wife, her heart removed and cut into three pieces, is soon replaced. The moralization immediately following the lively story assigns metaphors to each character and action. The wife becomes the flesh, the necromancer illicit desire, and the clerk the confessor/preacher who saves souls. The divided heart is transformed into the three devotional acts — praying, almsgiving, and fasting — that must be carried out before the fragmented soul can become whole again.

If the first narrative transforms illicit human desires into moral lessons on saving one's soul, then so too does "Of the Magic Ring, Brooch, and Cloth," though in a much more complicated way. This moral tale involves a nuclear family: an emperor, his wife, and their three sons, all of whom receive a share of an inheritance at their father's death. As in folk tales and Bible stories depicting the youngest son as somehow favored, though he appears not to be in the beginning, the third son, Jonathas, receives special magical gifts, while his two older brothers receive property and money. The young boy's acquisitions are given to him one by one by his very wise mother whose plans for this special son include a university education. The magic ring, which brings him the regard of all his professors, helps him get a foothold in his life away from home. The brooch brings him "al thinge that he wolde coveite" (line 60), i.e., worldly goods, while the cloth, a magic carpet, allows him to fly anywhere in the world his heart desires. Complicating his education, perhaps obstructing it, is a seductive and cunning young woman, Felicité, who offers him sex and eventually steals his ring, then his brooch, then his flying carpet, leaving the young man in a state of physical and emotional loss. The resolution includes an extended, gruesome revenge sequence, after which Jonathas undergoes restoration and healing by serving the sick. Eventually he delivers to the betraying woman what she deserves: public humiliation, leprosy, and death. How is a medieval audience to understand

---

[45] Diane Speed has identified parallels in romances such as *Apollonius of Tyre*, *Le Bone Florence of Rome*, *Sir Isumbras*, *Robert of Sicily*, *Awntyrs off Arthure*, *Rauf Coilyear*, *Sir Cleges*, *King Horn*, *Squyr of Lowe Degre*, *Sir Degaré*, *Sir Eglamour of Arois*, *Ywain and Gawain*, *Sir Gowther*, *William of Palerne*, the *Knight of Curtesy*, and *Amys and Amyloun*. Other romances demonstrate minor similarities. See "Middle English Romance and the *Gesta Romanorum*," pp. 45–56.

this? The "moralitee" renders the emperor a figure for Christ; the first son, the angels; the second son, the prophets; and the third son, the Christian man; the ring equals faith, the brooch, the holy spirit, and the magic carpet, "perfite charité" (line 191). Once again, Felicité is equated with the flesh, which must be chastened unto death by penance.

The bawd of "The Punished of Adulterers," reminiscent of Dame Sirith and Chaucer's Alisoun of Bath, introduces a novel approach to the lessons of adultery when she teaches from the afterlife. Having repented and saved her own soul at the last minute, the bawd appears to her husband in a dream to inform him of her new position and to let him know the consequences of illicit sexual behavior. The bawd then performs acts of transformation, becoming first a serpent and then a woman, as she passes through a mysterious stone. When she emerges on the other side she is accompanied by several rowdy demons who proceed to immerse the adulterous couple (or what appears to be the couple) in a cauldron of boiling brass "till the fleshe was sothyn fro the bone" (lines 27–28). Their bones are then taken out and laid beside the cauldron where they are transformed again into the couple whom the bawd identifies as "oure neghbores" (line 33). This is to be their eternal punishment, she explains to her husband, because "they lyvedyn in avoutery, and amendid hem nought" (lines 35–36). Her brief narrative is then transformed into its moral lesson which advocates full repentance and generous almsgiving.

As in the other narratives, the woman becomes a figure of carnality and sin which must be avoided in order for the Christian man's soul to remain whole. The strain of misogamist/anti-feminist thought running throughout these narratives is clearly discernible — carnality is feminine while the loftier spirit is masculine, for instance — but given the ecclesiastical biases of these "Tales of the Romans" and their use as homiletic texts, perhaps these inclinations are less problematic than they might appear to be at first. At the very least, the stories and their moral transformations teach a medieval audience how aptly applied interpretive methods may render almost any text into meaningful doctrine.

The Wycliffite treatise on marriage[46] sounds rather orthodox as it takes another approach to didacticism.[47] Not only does it address theological principles, but it also goes to great lengths

---

[46] Wyclif's authorship of this text remains an unsettled issue. In his edition of Wyclif's works, Thomas Arnold states: "The only known copy of the following tract is in the library of Corpus Christi College, Cambridge MS 296. . . . It is not mentioned even by Bale, and the only reason for ascribing it to Wyclif is that it is found in a volume which Archbishop Parker, in the sixteenth century, believed to contain only tracts of Wyclif's composition, and under that belief bequeathed to the college. St. Augustine's being called here 'Seynt Austyn,' instead of simply 'Austyn,' as in the Homilies, appears a suspicious circumstance, yet capable perhaps of explanation, if we suppose the tract to have been composed by Wyclif in his younger days. But whatever may be thought of its authenticity, it possesses sufficient intrinsic interest to justify its appearing, for the first time, in print" (p. 188).

[47] Shannon McSheffrey argues in *Gender and Heresy: Women and Men in Lollard Communities 1420–1530* that Lollard communities did not offer as much freedom to women as has been supposed.

to address marriage practices — how husbands and wives should treat each other, and how they should raise their children. The treatise begins with the definition of two kinds of marriage: one between Christ and Holy Church, the other between men and women by just consent. Echoing Pauline doctrine, the author, in an ideology close to Wyclif's own, privileges the spiritual over the earthly, since souls, not bodies, are broken by lost faith, a result achieved not only through fornication and adultery, but by worshiping false gods. This loss of faith or "spiritual adultery" is even worse than "brekynge of fleschly matrimonye" (line 16). Following Paul, Augustine of Hippo, and Jerome, the treatise talks about virginity as a higher state of being accessible only by a dedicated few while marriage should be undertaken for procreative purposes or as a preventive measure against fornication — remember: "better to marry than to be burnt." After the children have been born, chaste marriage is the "best kept matrimoyne of all othere" (line 106), for which the *exemplum* is the Virgin Mary and Joseph. Each partner in this conjugal arrangement would be expected to stir the other to charity, righteousness, meekness, patience, and "alle goodnesse" (line 109); moreover, they should not seek divorce for any reason except adultery, since "Crist biddith no man departe atwyn hem that God hath joyned" (lines 110–11).

That the Wycliffite text accepts the traditional hierarchy of marriage, i.e., subordination of wife to husband, goes without saying, though both would be expected to discipline their children. At this point the treatise spends considerable time addressing household governance, reminding husbands to love their wives and to refrain from beating them "withoute resonable cause" (line 171). Fathers are told to raise their children by discipline, learning, and "chastising," without provoking them to indignation that causes them to trespass against God's commandments. Similarly, wives are admonished not to provoke their husbands' wrath, but rather to help them live clean and holy lives. Both husband and wife are advised to avoid the three great pitfalls of marriage and family life: 1) that children prompt parents to seek worldly benefits for them; 2) that wives are inclined to give their husbands' goods to the wrong people; 3) that mothers are too prone to grieve for their dead children and blame God instead of accepting His will. The closing section reminds the audience of the consequences of breaking faith, restating that idleness is the devil's bawd; the husband and wife should pray, live a life of controlled abstinence, feed the hungry, clothe and harbor the sick, and do penance for old sins in order to maintain the bonds of spiritual matrimony.

Though much emphasis is placed on the education of children in the Wycliffite treatise, the issue is more directly addressed in the last three texts in this section. All three — John Lydgate's piece on "evil marriage," *How the Goode Wife Taught Hyr Doughter*, and *How the Goode Man Taght Hys Sone* — convey conduct and courtesy advice in narrative vehicles more

---

Marriage tended to constrain women in part because the movement was clandestine and restricted to the domestic sphere where husbands asserted their authority.

privatized and direct than either a homily or treatise on family life would be. These texts may even mark a discernible social movement in the fifteenth century toward the privatization and domestication of childhood education for both sexes.[48] Many of the manuscripts in which these texts are found have been talked about by scholars as indicators of a rise in literacy among the emerging middle class in late-medieval England. So too may these didactic narratives indicate a concern for leveling the playing field between the upper and lower classes of English feudal society, shifts which are addressed by a number of medieval writers. It is no coincidence that at this time the idea of nobility is undergoing re-definition as a social status to be attained by anyone interested in cultivating and practicing proper etiquette. The emphasis on conduct and matters of social courtesy is evident in the multitude of texts on the subject as is a discernible interest in and acceptance of upward social mobility.

And as in all matters of education, whether medieval or modern, teaching anything worthwhile requires a pleasant pedagogical method and an entertaining approach to the subject matter. These three texts represent a shift from the public rhetoric of homiletic instruction to a more private, personal approach to the education of the young. John Lydgate's *Payne and Sorowe of Evyll Maryage*, for instance, is presented in a light, almost comic tone, which exhorts the "lytell chylde" (line 1) to "[t]hynke on this lesson" (line 7), a short poem on the negative attributes of marriage. The narrator claims that when he was about to marry the woman of his dreams, his friends began to dissuade him. Echoes of the misogamist/anti-feminist inclinations of texts written by other churchmen (he names John Chrysostom, for instance) appear in this poem as the narrator muses over the wiles and waywardness of women. Wedlock, he says, is "an endles penaunce . . . / A martirdome and a contynuaunce / Of sorowe ay lastynge, a deedly violence" (lines 71–74), especially when women try to rule the household. Given all the complaints registered by countless clerics that resonate here — women are fickle, hypocritical, vain, foolish, oversexed, and mean — only fools or martyrs would fall prey to such a snare. Not only is the rhetorical approach effective — after all, who wants to be a fool? — but the tone established by the narrator renders the lesson palatable and persuasive.

Similarly, these didactic addresses to a son and daughter respectively by a parent of the same sex cast within a well-wrought story is rhetorically effective. These lessons are not delivered directly as verbal commands, but rather as tales told by other parents to their children as part of a custom of intergenerational mentorship — from father to son, from mother to daughter — in which the "how" of didactic storytelling is as important as the subject matter. *How the*

---

[48] Felicity Riddy, "Mother Knows Best: Reading Social Change in a Courtesy Text," *Speculum* 71 (1996), 66–86. See also Kathleen M. Ashley, "Medieval Courtesy Literature and Dramatic Mirrors of Female Conduct," in *The Ideology of Conduct: Essays on Literature and the History of Sexuality*, ed. Nancy Armstrong and Leonard Tennenhouse (New York: Methuen, 1987), pp. 25–38.

Goode Man Taght Hys Sone provides a parent with a means by which to convey the importance of good behavior — "in hys langage" (line 15), or "in his own words." It also provides an educational model for the child learning at the feet of an authority figure. Yet its very informality contrasts with official modes of education current in the late Middle Ages which were more emphatically rendered by the rod. The schoolmaster's practice of beating students into submission is not present in either of these didactic texts. Rather, the approach to educating the young is without force or threat of punitive retaliation should the child not learn the lesson in the prescribed manner.[49]

There is a clear gender distinction between the two works, however, that warrants a closer look, since the division of labor, individual responsibilities, and moral obligations not only carry over into future generations, but resonate eerily with some of the recommendations of the Wycliffite treatise. Both begin with an exhortation to listen and an admonition to serve God; both address the avoidance of outspokenness, inappropriate social behavior, the importance of charitable acts, and choosing the right spouse; both advise paying attention to one's health, paying tithes and retiring debts. However, the basic assumptions apparent right from the beginning, i.e., that a girl will almost inevitably become a wife, while a boy retains the option to marry, set up distinctions in social roles defined by sex. Boys are advised to avoid public office, quests, pilgrimages, and vice; girls are advised to cultivate good manners and a modest demeanor and appearance, and to avoid acquiring a bad reputation. If boys should decide to marry they are reminded to govern their wives justly, correcting them by verbal chastisement rather than by corporal punishment. Girls are advised to answer husbands meekly, avoid provocation, manage the household servants, stay at home, bake bread, and, in general, be good housewives. The young girl is admonished not to grieve overly long over the untimely death of a child, and if she has a daughter, her duty is to see to it that she marries. The good wife ends with a stunning proverbial expression: "a child unborn is better than one untaught," while the good man reminds his son that good deeds and fair practices make for a meritorious life.

Secular Lyrics

While the Wycliffite treatise on family relations, the moralized stories of the *Gesta Romanorum*, and the instructional texts focus on a didactic and value-laden view of domestic

---

[49] See Nicholas Orme, *Education and Society in Medieval and Renaissance England* (London: The Hambledon Press, 1989). A grammatical miscellany from Bristol quoted in a chapter on the subject reads: "Good pupils are praised but the bad are beaten with a birch-rod or a whip." Orme explains: "Beating is conceived, here as elsewhere, as a positive aid to education which makes a pupil good and quiet" (p. 96).

relations, the lyrics selected for presentation here move us back into the public realm of popular song. All the anxieties and antipathies toward marriage as well as some of the joys are captured in the carefree, carnivalesque lyrics which mark a convergence between private and public, sacred and profane, official and unofficial spheres of authority. Just as feast day celebrations of late medieval England allowed open mockery of official institutions in a manner carried on in the tradition of Mardi Gras today, these occasions tended to reinforce the status quo rather than to subvert it. In a similar way secular lyrics embody popular sentiment and a proclivity to parody and satirize traditional modes of behavior. What had become conventional stereotypes by the fourteenth and fifteenth centuries — the ideal virtuous woman, the hapless old man, the lusty young wife, the ardent suitor, the befuddled cleric — converge in the lyrics, rendering them comic despite their serious subject matter. "In Praise of Women," for instance, is a tongue-in-cheek defense of women who do valuable domestic work and serve men well rather than an ode to female perfection as its title implies. The various complaints on the tribulations of marriage and the wiles of wayward wives capture the comedy typical of fabliau. And should we be reminded of Chaucer's The Miller's Tale by "Old Hogyn's Adventure," with its motif of the famous misplaced kiss, it is surely no coincidence. The continuing anxieties of husbands over issues of women's domestic power and the consequences of henpecking that resonate in "I Have a Gentle Cock" suggest that concern over masculinity and reputation for prowess among men remains an issue as firmly entrenched as marriage itself.

From the clerical and didactic to the comedy of fabliau and secular lyrics, what the works in this volume suggest is that marriage, as an ancient social institution, has as complicated and controversial a past as the human societies for which it has become a central feature. We may laugh at the antics of the inept cleric, the wily woman, the impotent husband, and the foolish lover in their attempts to subvert marital ideals; yet, however those ideals are besieged and challenged, they remain steadfastly in place. What marriage requires, these texts seem to say, is vigilance, respect, and an extraordinarily well-developed sense of humor.

Select Bibliography

Astell, Ann W. *The Song of Songs in the Middle Ages*. Ithaca: Cornell University Press, 1990.

St. Augustine. *The Good of Marriage*. In *Saint Augustine: Treatises on Marriage and Other Subjects*. Trans. Charles T. Wilcox, et al. Ed. Roy J. Deferrari. Washington, DC: Catholic University of America, 1955.

Blamires, Alcuin, ed., with Karen Pratt and C. W. Marx. *Woman Defamed and Woman Defended: An Anthology of Medieval Texts*. Oxford: Clarendon Press, 1992.

Brooke, Christopher Nugent Lawrence. *Marriage in Christian History: An Inaugural Lecture*. Cambridge: Cambridge University Press, 1978.

———. "Marriage and Society in the Central Middle Ages." In Outhwaite. Pp. 17–34.

———. *The Medieval Idea of Marriage*. Oxford: Oxford University Press, 1989.

Brundage, James A. *Law, Sex, and Christian Society in Medieval Europe*. Chicago: University of Chicago Press, 1987.

———. *Medieval Canon Law*. London: Longman, 1995.

Bullough, Vern L., and James Brundage. *Sexual Practices & the Medieval Church*. Buffalo: Prometheus Books, 1982.

Chaucer, Geoffrey. *The Riverside Chaucer*. Ed. Larry D. Benson. Third ed. Boston: Houghton Mifflin Co., 1987.

Chrysostom, John. *On Marriage and Family Life*. Trans. Catharine P. Roth and David Anderson. Crestwood, NY: St. Vladimir's Seminary Press, 1986.

Clark, Elizabeth A. "'Adam's Only Companion': Augustine and the Early Christian Debate on Marriage." In Edwards and Spector. Pp. 15–31.

Davies, Kathleen M. "Continuity and Change in Literary Advice on Marriage." In Outhwaite. Pp. 58–80.

Introduction

D'Avray, David. "The Gospel of the Marriage Feast of Cana and Marriage Preaching in France." In *The Bible in the Medieval World: Essays in Memory of Beryl Smalley*. Ed. Katherine Walsh and Diana Wood. Oxford: Blackwell, 1985. Pp. 207–24.

Donohue, Charles, Jr. "The Canon Law on the Formation of Marriage and Social Practice in the Later Middle Ages." *Journal of Family History* 8 (1983), 144–58.

Dronke, Peter. *Abelard and Heloise in Medieval Testimonies*. Glasgow: University of Glasgow Press, 1976.

Duby, Georges. *Medieval Marriage: Two Models from Twelfth-Century France*. Trans. Elborg Forster. Baltimore: John Hopkins University Press, 1978.

———. *The Knight, the Lady, and the Priest: The Making of Modern Marriage in Medieval France*. Trans. Barbara Bray. New York: Pantheon Books, 1983.

Edwards, Robert R., and Stephen Spector, eds. *The Olde Daunce: Love, Friendship, Sex and Marriage in the Medieval World*. Albany: State University of New York Press, 1991.

Elliott, Dyan. *Spiritual Marriage: Sexual Abstinence in Medieval Wedlock*. Princeton: Princeton University Press, 1993.

Gies, Frances, and Joseph Gies. *Marriage and the Family in the Middle Ages*. New York: Harper & Row, 1987.

Goldberg, P. J. P., ed. *Woman is a Worthy Wight: Women in English Society c. 1200–1500*. Phoenix Mills: Alan Sutton, 1996.

Helmholz, R. H. *Marriage Litigation in Medieval England*. London: Cambridge University Press, 1974.

Herlihy, David. *Medieval Households*. Cambridge, MA: Harvard University Press, 1985.

Hugo, John J. *St. Augustine on Nature, Sex, and Marriage*. Chicago: Scepter, 1969.

Ingram, Martin. "Spousal Litigation in the English Ecclesiastical Courts c. 1350–c. 1640." In Outhwaite. Pp. 35–57.

Joyce, George Hayward, S. J. *Christian Marriage: An Historical and Doctrinal Study*. Second ed., rev. and enl. London: Sheed & Ward, 1948.

LeClerq, Jean. *Monks on Marriage: A Twelfth-Century View*. New York: The Seabury Press, 1982.

Lee, Francis. *The Crooked Rib: An Analytical Index to the Argument about Women in English and Scots Literature to the End of the Year 1568*. Columbus: Ohio State University Press, 1944.

Leyerle, John, ed. "Marriage in the Middle Ages: Introduction. " *Viator* 4 (1973), 413–18.

Matter, E. Ann. *"The Voice of My Beloved": The Song of Songs in Western Medieval Christianity*. Philadelphia: University of Pennsylvania Press, 1990.

McFarlane, Alan. *Marriage and Love in England: Modes of Reproduction 1300–1840*. Oxford: Basil Blackwell, 1986.

McSheffrey, Shannon, trans. and intro. *Love and Marriage in Late Medieval London*. Kalamazoo: Medieval Institute Publications, 1995.

————. *Gender and Heresy: Women and Men in Lollard Communities 1420–1530*. Philadelphia: University of Pennsylvania Press, 1995.

Newman, Barbara. *From Virile Woman to WomanChrist: Studies in Medieval Religion and Literature*. Philadelphia: University of Pennsylvania Press, 1995.

Noonan, John T., Jr. "Marriage in the Middle Ages: 1. Power to Choose." *Viator* 4 (1973), 419–34.

Outhwaite, R. B., ed. *Marriage and Society: Studies in the Social History of Marriage*. New York: St. Martin's Press, 1981.

Palmer, Robert C. "Contexts of Marriage in Medieval England: Evidence from the King's Court circa 1300." *Speculum* 59 (1984), 42–67.

Reynolds, Philip Lyndon. *Marriage in the Western Church: The Christianization of Marriage During the Patristic and Early Medieval Periods*. Leiden: E. J. Brill, 1994.

Introduction

Sheehan, Michael M. *Marriage, Family, and Law in Medieval Europe: Collected Studies*. Ed. James K. Farge. Toronto: University of Toronto Press, 1996.

Stone, Lawrence. *The Family, Sex and Marriage in England 1500–1800*. Abr. ed. New York: Harper & Row, 1979.

Van Hoecke, Willy, and Andries Welkenhuysen. *Love and Marriage in the Twelfth Century*. Leuven: Leuven University Press, 1981.

Wheeler, Bonnie, ed. *Listening to Heloise: The Voice of a Twelfth-Century Woman*. New York: St. Martin's Press, 2000.

Wilson, Katharina M., and Elizabeth M. Makowski. *Wykked Wyves and the Woes of Marriage: Misogamous Literature From Juvenal to Chaucer*. Albany: State University of New York Press, 1990.

Yarborough, O. Larry. *Not Like the Gentiles: Marriage Rules in the Letters of Paul*. Atlanta: Scholars Press, 1985.

Dame Sirith

Narrator

As I com bi an waie,	*came; way*
Hof on ich herde saie,	*Of one*
Ful modi mon and proud;	*spirited*
Wis he wes of lore,	*Wise; learning*
And gouthlich under gore,	*worthy; garments*
And clothed in fair sroud.	*shroud*

To lovien he bigon	*At love*
On wedded wimmon,	
Therof he hevede wrong;	*did mischief*
His herte hire wes alon,	*was hers alone*
That reste nevede he non,	*had he not any*
The love wes so strong.	

Wel yerne he him bithoute	*longingly he calculated (thought to himself)*
Hou he hire gete moute	*How; her might get*
In ani cunnes wise.	*any way possible*
That befel on an day	*one*
The louerd wend away	*lord went*
Hon his marchaundise.	*On business*

He wente him to then inne	*took himself*
Ther hoe wonede inne,	*Where she lived*
That wes riche won;	*richly decorated dwelling*
And com in to then halle,	
Ther hoe wes srud with palle,	*Where she was dressed; rich fabrics*
And thus he bigon:—	*he began*

Wilekin

"God Almightten be herinne!"

5

10

15

20

25

Margery

  "Welcome, so ich ever bide wenne,"   *feel joy*
  Quod this wif.   *Said*
  "His hit thi wille, com and site,   *[If] it is your will (desire); sit*
  And wat is thi wille let me wite,   *what; know*
30 Mi leve lif.   *dear*
  Bi houre Louerd, hevene king,   *By our Lord*
  If I mai don ani thing
  That thee is lef,   *is dear to you*
  Thou mightt finden me ful fre.   *cooperative*
35 Fol bletheli will I don for thee,   *Full willingly will I do*
  Withhouten gref."   *hesitation*

Wilekin

  "Dame, God thee foryelde,   *reward you*
  Bote on that thou me nout bimelde, *do not denounce me*
  Ne make thee wroth,   *Nor; angry*
40 Min hernde will I to thee bede;   *errand will I tell*
  Bote wraththen thee for ani dede   *anger; any reason*
  Were me loth."   *to me displeasing*

Margery

  "Nai, iwis, Wilekin,   *No, indeed*
  For nothing that ever is min,
45 Thau thou hit yirne,   *Though you yearn for it*
  Houncurteis ne will I be;   *Uncourteous will I never*
  Ne con I nout on vilte, *Nor do I know anything of bad manners*
  Ne nout I nelle lerne.   *Nor will I learn anything*

  "Thou mait saien al thine wille,   *may speak*
50 And I shal herknen and sitten stille,   *listen*
  That thou have told.
  And if that thou me tellest skil, *speak reasonably (put it the right way)*
  I shal don after thi wil,   *do according to*
  That be thou bold.   *Of that you may be sure*

55 "And thau thou saie me ani same, *even though; speak to me of any shameful matter*
  Ne shal I thee nought blame
  For thi sawe.   *Despite whatever you say*

Dame Sirith

"Nou ich have wonne leve,   *Now [that]; given permission*
Yif that I me shulde greve,   *myself should be upset*
60   Hit were hounlawe."   *unlawful*

Wilekin
"Certes, dame, thou seist as hende,   *Truly; speak pleasantly (courteously)*
And I shal setten spel on ende,   *come to the point*
And tellen thee al,
Wat ich wolde, and wi ich com;   *want; why I came*
65   Ne con ich saien non falsdom,   *no falsehood*
Ne non I ne shal.   *Nor shall I [say] none*

"Ich habbe i-loved thee moni yer,   *have*
Thau ich nabbe nout ben her   *Though I have not been [able] here*
Mi love to schowe.
70   Wile thi louerd is in toune,   *While; lord (husband)*
Ne mai no mon with thee holden roune   *have private conversation*
With no thewe.   *Without courtesy*

"Yurstendai ich herde saie,   *Yesterday*
As ich wende bi the waie,   *went*
75   Of oure sire;   *your husband*
Me told me that he was gon   *Someone*
To the feire of Botolfston   *fair; Boston*
In Lincolneschire.

"And for ich weste that he wes houte,   *knew; was gone*
80   Tharfore ich am i-gon aboute   *come here*
To speken with thee.
Him burth to liken wel his lif,   *He has reason*
That mightte welde secc a wif   *have (coerce) as a lover such*
In privité.   *Privately*

85   "Dame, if hit is thi wille,
Both dernelike and stille,   *secretly; discretely*
Ich wille thee love."

Margery
"That wold I don for nothing,   *would I do*

90
Bi houre Louerd, hevene king,   *our Lord*
That ous is bove!   *is above us*

"Ich habe mi louerd that is mi spouse,   *have my husband who*
That maiden broute me to house   *[as a] virgin*
Mid menske inou;   *honor enough*
He loveth me and ich him wel,
95
Oure love is also trewe as stel,   *true as steel*
Withhouten wou.   *sorrow*

"Thau he be from hom on his hernde,   *Though; business trip*
Ich were ounseli, if ich lernede   *I would be unhappy*
To ben on hore,   *be a whore*
100
That ne shal nevere be   *shall*
That I shal don selk falseté,   *such deceit*
On bedde ne on flore,   *[Neither]; nor; floor*

"Nevermore his lif-wile,   *[in] his lifetime*
Thau he were on hondred mile   *a hundred*
105
Biyende Rome,   *Beyond*
For nothing ne shuld I take   *I should not*
Mon on erthe to ben mi make,   *Someone; mate*
Ar his hom come."   *Before; homecoming*

Wilekin
"Dame, dame, torn thi mod: *change your mind*
110
Thi curteisi was ever god,   *courtesy; good*
And yet shal be;   *still*
For the Louerd that ous haveth wrout   *who has made us*
Amend thi mod, and torn thi thout, *Change your mind*
And rew on me."   *have pity*

Margery
115
"We, we! Oldest thou me a fol?   *Whoa! Do you think me a fool*
So ich ever mote biden Yol,   *As sure as Christmas*
Thou art ounwis,   *unwise*
Mi thout ne schalt thou never wende; *You will never change my mind*
Mi louerd is curteis mon and hende, *courteous man; noble*
120
And mon of pris;   *man of excellence*

"And ich am wif bothe god and trewe;   *good; faithful*
Trewer womon ne mai no mon cnowe   *Truer; know*
Then ich am.   *Than*
Thilke time ne shal never bitide   *That; come*
125   That mon for wouing ne thoru prude   *wooing; through pride*
Shal do me scham."   *shame*

Wilekin
"Swete lemmon, merci!   *Sweet beloved, [have] mercy*
Same ne vilani   *Shame nor crudity*
Ne bede I thee non;   *Neither offer; none*
130   Bote derne love I thee bede,   *But secret (discreet); offer*
As mon that wolde of love spede,   *succeed*
And finde won."   *happiness*

Margery
"So bide ich evere mete other drinke,   *As certainly as I eat or drink*
Her thou lesest al thi swinke;   *Here; lose; labor (effort)*
135   Thou might gon hom, leve brother,   *go home, dear*
For ne wille ich thee love, ne non other,   *I will not*
Bote mi wedde houssebonde;   *Except*
To tellen hit thee ne wille ich wonde."   *not hesitate*

[Wilekin]
"Certes, dame, that me forthinketh   *I repent of that*
140   An wo is the mon tha muchel swinketh,   *And; who too much works*
And at the laste leseth his sped!   *in the end loses his reward*
To maken menis his him ned.   *make lament*
Bi me I saie ful iwis,   *truly*
That love the love that I shal mis.   *Who have loved the beloved whom; lose*
145   An, dame, have nou godnedai!   *And; now have a good day*
And thilke Louerd, that al welde mai,   *the same Lord, who; rule*
Leve that thi thout so tourne,   *Grant*
That ich for thee no leng ne mourne."   *I; longer mourn for you*

Narrator
Drerimod he wente awai,   *Sadly*
150   And thoute bothe night and dai   *thought*
Hire al for to wende.   *turn (i.e., make her change her mind)*

	A frend him radde for to fare,	*advised*
	And leven al his muchele kare	*leave (unburden); great woe*
	To Dame Sirith the hende.	*courteous*
155	Thider he wente him anon,	*Thither*
	So suithe so he mightte gon,	*As quickly as*
	No mon he ni mette.	*No man whatsoever did he meet*
	Ful he wes of tene and treie;	*sorrow; grief*
	Mid wordes milde and eke sleie	*also sly*
160	Faire he hire grette.	*Becomingly he greeted her*

Wilekin

	"God thee i-blessi, Dame Sirith!	*God bless you*
	Ich am i-com to speken thee with,	*with you*
	For ful muchele nede.	*great need*
	And ich mai have help of thee	*If*
165	Thou shalt have, that thou shalt se,	
	Ful riche mede."	*reward*

Dame Sirith

	"Welcomen art thou, leve sone;	*dear son*
	And if ich mai other cone	*may or can*
	In eni wise for thee do,	
170	I shal strengthen me therto.	*myself for the task*
	Forthi, leve sone, tel thou me	*tell me*
	Wat thou woldest I dude for thee."	*What I can do for you*

Wilekin

	"Bote, leve nelde, ful evele I fare;	*dear granny; poorly*
	I lede mi lif with tene and kare;	*sorrow*
175	With muchel hounsele ich lede mi lif,	*grief*
	And that is for on swete wif	*for [the sake of] one*
	That heightte Margeri.	*Who is called*
	Ich have i-loved hire moni dai,	*her many [a] day*
	And of hire love hoe seith me nai;	*she tells me no*
180	Hider ich com forthi.	*Here; therefore*
	"Bote if hoe wende hire mod,	*Unless she changes her mind*
	For serewe mon ich wakese wod,	*sorrow; I will go crazy*

Dame Sirith

Other miselve quelle.   *Or kill myself*
Ich hevede i-thout miself to slo;   *had thought; to slay*
185 For then radde a frend me go   *a friend advised me*
To thee mi serewe telle.   *[to] tell my sorrow*

"He saide me, withhouten faille,   *told; doubt*
That thou me couthest helpe and vaile, *could; avail*
And bringen me of wo   *[out] of woe*
190 Thoru thine crafftes and thine dedes; *crafts; conjurings*
And ich wile geve thee riche mede,   *will give; reward*
With that hit be so."   *Provided that*

Dame Sirith
"Benedicité! Be herinne   *Oh my*
Her havest thou, sone, mikel senne.   *Here; great sin*
195 Louerd, for His swete nome,   *name*
Lete thee therfore haven no shome!   *shame*
Thou servest affter Godes grome,   *deserve God's anger*
Wen thou seist on me silk blame. *When; tell such wickedness to me*
For ich am old, and sek and lame;   *sick*
200 Seknesse haveth maked me ful tame. *Sickness; subdued*

Blesse thee, blesse thee, leve knave!   *dear lad*
Leste thou mesaventer have,   *misadventure*
For this lesing that is founden   *lie; visited*
Oppon me that am harde i-bonden. *Upon; who; destitute*
205 Ich am on holi wimon,   *a holy woman*
On wicchecrafft nout I ne con,   *I know nothing*
Bote with gode men almesdede. *Except by; almsdeeds (charity)*
Ilke dai mi lif I fede,   *Each day; sustain*
And bidde mi Pater Noster and mi Crede,   *repeat*
210 That Goed hem helpe at hore nede, *them; in [their] hour of need*
That helpen me mi lif to lede,   *Who*
And leve that hem mote wel spede. *pray God's speed for them*
His lif and his soule worthe i-shend, *[May]; be confounded*

That thee to me this hernde haveth send;   *business*
215 And leve me to ben i-wreken   *avenged*
On him this shome me haveth speken." *shame; spoken*

Wilekin

    "Leve nelde, bilef al this;   *Dear grandmother*
    Me thinketh that thou art onwis.   *mistaken*
    The mon that me to thee taute,   *i.e., who recommended you to me*
220 He weste that thou hous couthest saute. *thought; us could reconcile*
    Help, Dame Sirith, if thou maut,   *might*
    To make me with the sweting saut,   *sweetheart [a] reconciliation*
    And ich wille geve thee gift ful stark,   *great*
    Moni a pound and moni a marke,   *Many; mark*
225 Warme pilche and warme shon,   *fur coat; shoes*
    With that min hernde be wel don.   *Provided that; business*
    Of muchel godlec might thou yelpe,   *much merit; boast*
    If hit be so that thou me helpe."

Dame Sirith

    "Ligh me nout, Wilekin, bi thi leute   *Do not lie to me; honesty*
230 Is hit thin hernest thou tellest me?   *earnest intention*
    Lovest thou wel Dame Margeri?"

[Wilekin]

    "Ye, nelde, witerli.   *Yes, grandmother, surely*
    Ich hire love; hit mot me spille,   *it will kill me*
    Bote ich gete hire to mi wille."   *Unless; bend her*

Dame Sirith

235 "Wat, god Wilekin, me reweth thi scathe,   *Know, good; pity; distress*
    Houre Louerd sende thee help rathe!   *Our; quickly*

    "Weste hic hit mightte ben forholen,   *[If] I knew; utterly concealed*
    Me wolde thunche wel folen   *would think; suited*
    Thi wille for to fullen.   *fulfill*
240 Make me siker with word on honde,   *certain; an oath*
    That thou wolt helen, and I wile fonde   *conceal; try*
    If ich mai hire tellen.   *tell her*
    For al the world ne wold I nout   *I would not*
    That ich were to chapitre i-brout   *chapter (church court) brought*
245 For none selke werkes.   *no such*
    Mi jugement were sone i-given

To ben with shome somer driven *shame [on a] mule*
With prestes and with clarkes." *By; by clerics*

Wilekin
 "Iwis, nelde, ne wold I *Truly, old woman, I would not*
250 That thou hevedest vilani *have [any] trouble*
 Ne shame for mi goed. *Nor; my good (sake)*
 Her I thee mi trouthe plightte, *Here; promise pledge*
 Ich shal helen bi mi mightte, *conceal [it] in every way I can*
 Bi the Holi Roed!" *Cross*

Dame Sirith
255 "Welcome, Wilekin, hiderward;
 Her havest I maked a foreward *contract*
 That thee mai ful wel like.
 Thou maight blesse thilke sith, *this very time*
 For thou maight make the ful blith; *joyous*
260 Dar thou namore sike. *You need sigh no more*

 "To goder hele ever come thou hider, *better fortune*
 For sone will I gange thider, *go*
 And maken hire hounderstonde. *understand*
 I shal kenne hire sulke a lore; *teach her such a lesson*
265 That hoe shal lovien thee mikel more *she; love you much*
 Then ani mon in londe." *Than any man*

Wilekin
 "Al so havi Godes grith, *peace*
 Wel havest thou said, Dame Sirith,
 And Goder-hele shal ben thin. *prosperity (God's health)*
270 Have her twenti shiling, *here*
 This ich geve thee to meding, *reward*
 To buggen thee sep and swin." *buy yourself sheep; swine*

Dame Sirith
 "So ich ever brouke hous other flet, *As ever I have benefit of house or floor*
 Neren never pones beter biset *Never were pence better used*
275 Then thes shulen ben. *Than; shall be*
 For I shal don a juperti, *carry out a cunning plan*

And a ferli maistri,   *masterful trick*
That thou shalt ful wel sen.

[Dame Sirith, speaking to her dog]
"Pepir nou shalt thou eten,   *Pepper; eat*
280   This mustart shal ben thi mete,   *mustard; food*
And gar thin eien to rene;   *make your eyes run*
I shal make a lesing   *trick*
Of thin heie renning,   *eye-running (weeping)*
Ich wot wel wer and wenne."   *know; where; when*

[Wilekin]
285   "Wat! Nou const thou no god?   *can you do no good*
Me thinketh that thou art wod: *crazy*
Gevest thou the welpe mustard?"   *Give you; whelp*

Dame Sirith
"Be stille, boinard!   *fool*
I shal mit this ilke gin   *with this very trick*
290   Gar hire love to ben al thin.   *Make; all yours*
Ne shal ich never have reste ne ro   *peace*
Til ich have told hou thou shalt do.   *what you*
Abid me her til min hom come."   *Wait for me here*
"Yus, bi the somer blome,   *Yes; summer bloom*
295   Hethen null I ben binomen,   *Hence I will not be taken away*
Til thou be agein comen."

[Narrator]
Dame Sirith bigon to go,
As a wrecche that is wo,
That hoe com hire to then inne   *she; dwelling*
300   Ther this gode wif wes inne.   *Where*
Tho hoe to the dore com,   *When she*
Swithe reuliche hoe bigon: *Very pitifully*

[Dame Sirith]
"Louerd," hoe seith, "wo is holde wives,   *woe to old*
That in poverté ledeth ay lives;   *ever lead [their]*
305   Not no mon so muchel of pine   *No one knows; suffering*

38

Dame Sirith

	As poure wif that falleth in ansine.	*into decline*
	That mai ilke mon bi me wite	*each; know*
	For mai I nouther gange ne site.	*walk nor sit down*
	Ded wold I ben ful fain.	*Dead would I be; gladly*
310	Hounger and thurst me haveth nei slain;	*nearly*
	Ich ne mai mine limes on wold,	*limbs control*
	For mikel hounger and thurst and cold.	
	War-to liveth selke a wrecche?	*Why; such*
	Wi nul God mi soule fecche?"	*Why will not; fetch*

[Margery]

315	"Seli wif, God thee hounbinde!	*Good woman; unbind (help you)*
	Todai wille I thee mete finde	*Today; food*
	For love of God.	
	Ich have reuthe of thi wo,	*pity; sorrow*
	For evele i-clothed I se thee go,	*poorly dressed*
320	And evele i-shoed.	*poorly shod*
	Com herin, ich wile thee fede.	
	God Almightten do thee mede,	*give you reward*
	And the Louerd that wes on Rode i-don,	*Cross hung*
	And faste fourti daiis to non,	*fasted; days until the ninth hour (3 p.m.)*
325	And hevene and erthe haveth to welde.	*rule*
	As thilke Louerd thee foryelde,	*redeemed*
	Have her fles and eke bred,	*here meat; also bread*
	And make thee glad, hit is mi red;	*yourself comfortable; counsel*
	And have her the coppe with the drinke;	*here; cup*
330	God do thee mede for thi swinke."	*reward you; efforts*

[Narrator]

	Thenne spac that holde wif,	*old woman*
	Crist awarie hire lif:	*damn*

Dame Sirith

	"Alas! Alas! that ever I live!	*was born*
	Al the sunne ich wolde forgive	*sin*
335	The mon that smite of min heved!	*[Of] the man; cut off; head*
	Ich wolde mi lif me were bireved!"	*wish; were bereft from me*

Margery
    "Seli wif, what eilleth thee?"   *Good woman; ails you*

[Dame Sirith]

    "Bote ethe mai I sori be: *Yet easily*

    Ich hevede a douter feir and fre,   *had; daughter; noble*

340   Feiror ne mightte no mon se.   *Fairer might no man see*

    Hoe hevede a curteis hossebonde;   *She had*

    Freour mon mightte no mon fonde.   *More noble*

    Mi douter lovede him al to wel;   *too*

    Forthi mak I sori del.   *make an unfortunate bargain*

345   Oppon a dai he was out wend,   *One; gone*

    And thar-thoru wes mi douter shend.   *thereby; shamed*

    He hede on ernde out of toune;   *went on errand*

    And com a modi clarc with croune,   *proud cleric; crown (tonsure)*

    To mi douter his love beed,   *offered*

350   And hoe nolde nout folewe his red.   *she would not; counsel*

    He ne mightte his wille have,

    For nothing he mightte crave.   *desire*

    Thenne bigon the clerc to wiche,   *use witchcraft*

    And shop mi douter til a biche.   *transformed; bitch*

355   This is mi douter that ich of speke;

    For del of hire min herte breketh.   *sorrow; breaks*

    Lok hou hire heien greten,   *how her eyes weep*

    On hire cheken the teres meten.   *cheeks; tears flow together*

    "Forthi, dame, were hit no wonder,   *Accordingly; it was*

360   Thau min herte burste assunder.   *That*

    And woseever is yong houssewif,   *whosoever*

    Ha loveth ful luitel hire lif,   *She*

    And eni clerc of love hire bede,   *If; offers*

    Bote hce grante and lete him spede."   *Unless she; succeed*

[Margery]

365   "A! Louerd Crist, wat mai thenne do!

    This enderdai com a clarc me to,   *other day*

    And bed me love on his manere,   *bid*

    And ich him nolde nout i-here.   *would not hear [of it]*

| | Ich trouwe he wolle me forsape. | *trust; transform* |
| 370 | Hou troustu, nelde, ich moue ascape?" | *How do you think; can escape* |

[Dame Sirith]
  "God Almightten be thin help
  That thou ne be nouther bicche ne welp!   *bitch; whelp*
  Leve dame, if eni clerc   *Dear lady*
  Bedeth thee that love werc,   *Offers; work*
375 Ich rede that thou grante his bone,   *advise; request*
  And bicom his lefmon sone.   *lover soon*
  And if that thou so ne dost,   *you do not*
  A worse red thou ounderfost."   *counsel; [may] receive*

[Margery]
  "Louerd Crist, that me is wo,   *woe is me*
380 That the clarc me hede fro,   *went from*
  Ar he me hevede biwonne.   *Before; had won one*
  Me were levere then ani fe   *rather than any money*
  That he hevede enes leien bi me,   *once lain*
  And efftsones bigunne.   *soon afterward*

385 "Evermore, nelde, ich wille be thin,   *will I; yours*
  With that thou feche me Willekin,   *Provided*
  The clarc of wam I telle,   *cleric of whom I speak*
  Giftes will I geve thee
  That thou maight ever the betere be,
390 Bi Godes houne belle!"   *own bell*

[Dame Sirith]
  "Sothliche, mi swete dame,   *Certainly*
  And if I mai withhoute blame,
  Fain ich wille fonde;   *try*
  And if ich mai with him mete,
395 Bi eni wei other bi strete,   *or*
  Nout ne will I wonde.   *hesitate*
  Have goddai, dame! Forth will I go."

[Margery]
  "Allegate loke that thou do so   *In any case*

As ich thee bad;   *requested*

400 Bote that thou me Wilekin bringe,   *Unless*

Ne mai I never lawe ne singe,   *laugh*

Ne be glad."

[Dame Sirith]

"Iwis, dame, if I mai,   *Certainly; [Margery]*

Ich wille bringen him yet todai,

405 Bi mine mightte."

[Narrator]

Hoe wente hire to hire inne,   *She; dwelling*

Ther hoe founde Wilekinne,   *Where she*

Bi houre Drightte!   *our Lord*

[Dame Sirith]

"Swete Wilekin, be thou nout dred,   *afraid*

410 For of thin hernde ich have wel sped. *business; succeeded*

Swithe com forth thider with me,   *Quickly*

For hoe haveth send affter thee.   *she*

Iwis nou maight thou ben above,   *Indeed now*

For thou havest grantise of hire love." *been granted*

[Wilekin]

415 "God the foryelde, leve nelde, *reward, dear old woman*

That hevene and erthe haveth to welde!"

[Narrator]

This modi mon bigon to gon   *proud*

With Sirith to his levemon   *lover*

In thilke stounde.   *that time*

420 Dame Sirith bigon to telle,   *speak*

And swor bi Godes ouene belle,   *swore; own*

Hoe hevede him founde.   *She had found*

[Dame Sirith]

"Dame, so have ich Wilekin sout,   *sought*

For nou have ich him i-brout."   *now*

Dame Sirith

[Margery]

425   "Welcome, Wilekin, swete thing,

       Thou art welcomore then the king.   *more welcome than*

       Wilekin the swete,

       Mi love I thee bihete,   *promise you*

       To don al thine wille.   *your bidding*

430   Turnd ich have mi thout,   *Changed; mind*

       For I ne wolde nout   *would not want*

       That thou thee shuldest spille."   *you should kill yourself*

[Wilekin]

    "Dame, so ich evere bide noen,   *expect the ninth hour*

       And ich am redi and i-boen   *prepared*

435   To don al that thou saie.

       [to Dame Sirith]

       Nelde, par ma fai!   *by my faith*

       Thou most gange awai,   *go*

       Wile ich and hoe shulen plaie."   *While; she*

[Dame Sirith]

    "Goddot so I wille: *God knows*

440   And loke that thou hire tille,   *plow (till)*

       And strek out hir thes.   *stretch; thighs*

       God geve thee muchel kare,

       Yeif that thou hire spare,   *If*

       The wile thou mid here bes.   *As long as you are with her*

445   "And wose is onwis,   *whosoever; unwise*

       And for non pris   *no price*

       Ne con geten his levemon,   *can get*

       I shal, for mi mede,   *reward*

       Garen him to spede,   *Make; succeed*

450   For ful wel I con."   *can*

Select Bibliography and Notes to Dame Sirith

Manuscript

Bodleian Library MS Digby 86 (*SC* 1687), fols. 165a–168a (c. 1275).

Facsimile of Oxford, Bodleian Library, MS Digby 86. Intro. Judith Tschann and M. B. Parkes. EETS s.s. 16. Oxford: Oxford University Press, 1996. [Includes comprehensive introduction.]

Editions

Bennett, J. A. W., and G. V. Smithers, eds. *Early Middle English Verse and Prose*. Oxford: Clarendon Press, 1966. Pp. 77–95.

Benson, Larry D., and Theodore M. Andersson, eds. *The Literary Context of Chaucer's Fabliaux: Texts and Translations*. Indianapolis: The Bobbs-Merrill Co., 1971. Pp. 372–87.

Cook, Albert Stanburrough, ed. *A Literary Middle English Reader*. Boston: Ginn and Company, 1915; rpt. 1943. Pp. 141–58. [Cook draws several parallels between *Dame Sirith* and *Interludium de clerico et puella*, pp. 476–77.]

Dunn, Charles W., and Edward T. Byrnes, eds. *Middle English Literature*. New York: Harcourt Brace Jovanovich, 1973. Pp. 174–87.

Garbáty, Thomas J., ed. *Medieval English Literature*. Lexington, MA: D. C. Heath, 1984. Pp. 442–54.

McKnight. George H., ed. *Middle English Humorous Tales in Verse*. Boston: D. C. Heath & Co., 1913; rpt. New York: Gordian Press, 1972, 1990. Pp. 1–24.

Treharne, Elaine, ed. *Old and Middle English: An Anthology*. Oxford: Blackwell Publishers, 2000. Pp. 338–48.

Select Bibliography to Dame Sirith

Related Studies

Axton, Richard. *European Drama of the Early Middle Ages*. Pittsburgh: University of Pittsburgh Press, 1975. Pp. 17–24.

Boitani, Pietro. *English Medieval Narrative in the Thirteenth and Fourteenth Centuries*. Cambridge: Cambridge University Press, 1982. [Brief discussion of *Sirith* and *De clerico et puella*.]

Busby, Keith. "Conspicuous by Its Absence: The English Fabliau." *Dutch Quarterly Review of Anglo-American Letters* 12 (1981), 30–41.

———. "*Dame Sirith* and *De Clerico et Puella*." In *Companion to Early Middle English Literature*. Ed. N. H. G. E. Veldhoen and H. Aertsen. Amsterdam: Free University Press, 1988. Pp. 69–81.

Canby, Henry Seidel. "The English Fabliau." *PMLA* 21 (1906), 200–14.

Furrow, Melissa. "Middle English Fabliaux and Modern Myth." *English Literary History* 56 (1989), 1–18.

Goodall, Peter. "An Outline History of the English Fabliau after Chaucer." *Journal of Australasian University Language and Literature Association* 57 (1982), 5–23.

Heuser, W. "*Das Interludium de Clerico et Puella* und das Fabliau von *Dame Siriz*." *Anglia* 30 (1907), 306–19.

Hines, John. *The Fabliau in English*. London: Longman, 1993.

Lewis, Robert E. "The English Fabliau Tradition and Chaucer's 'Miller's Tale.'" *Modern Philology* 79 (1982), 241–55.

Robbins, Rossell Hope. "The English Fabliau: Before and After Chaucer." *Moderna Språk* 64 (1970), 231–44.

Swanton, Michael James. *English Literature Before Chaucer*. London: Longman, 1987.

Von Kreisler, Nicholai. "Satire in *Dame Sirith* and the *Weeping Bitch*." In *Essays in Honor of Esmond Linworth Marilla*. Ed. Thomas Austin Kirby and William John Olive. Baton Rouge: Louisiana State University Press, 1970. Pp. 379–87.

Notes

Abbreviations: **B&S**: J. A. W. Bennett and G. V. Smithers; **B&A**: Larry D. Benson and Theodore M. Andersson; **D&B**: Charles W. Dunn and Edward T. Byrnes; **Ga**: Thomas J. Garbáty; **McK**: George H. McKnight; **MS**: Bodleian Library MS Digby 86 (*SC* 1687), fols. 165a–168a; **T**: Elaine Treharne.

The MS begins with a French *incipit*: *Ci comence le fablel et al cointise de dame siriz.*

Narrator   The manuscript includes a number of speech markers: *C* at lines 24, 37, 61, 109, 127, 161, 173, 217, 249, and 267; *V* at lines 26, 43, 88, 115, 133, and 337; *T* at lines 1 and 149; and *F* at lines 167, 193, 229, 235, 255, 273, 288, and 333. B&S, p. 306, identify the capitals as speech markers, suggesting that *C* represents *Clericus* (i.e., Wilekin), with *V* standing for *Vxor* (i.e., Margery), *T* for *Testator* (i.e., the narrator), and *F* for *Femina* (i.e., Dame Sirith). I have placed speech markers throughout the edition, using the names of the characters rather than the Latin equivalents. The brackets indicate that the speech marker is not found in the manuscript, though if the practice were consistently carried through, this would be the designation.

1–6   On the 6-line tale rhyme stanza, see D&B, pp. 32, 174.

1–12   The opening introduces the clerk, who is described in terms of the courtly lover, languishing in lovesickness. The courtly love tradition has a long history, reaching as far back as Ovid's *Ars Amatoria*, a tongue-in-cheek manual for would-be lovers. The challenge to the lover was often to outwit his beloved's husband: marriage thus was an integral feature of the system. The strategies used in this pursuit were often amusing, diversion rather than doctrine. Not everyone in Ovid's time took his love games as harmless entertainment, however, and the Roman poet was soon exiled by Augustus Caesar for promoting adultery. In the twelfth century, courtly love becomes encoded in rules of chivalry for aspiring knights. Andreas Capellanus' *Art of Courtly Love* is another treatise in the spirit of Ovid and just as satirical, a fact not revealed until the last section. Written by the chaplain of Marie de Champagne's court, *The Art of Courtly Love* outlines a series of imaginary dialogues between various kinds of couples distinguished primarily by class. The equally imaginary

46

audience for this treatise on courtly love is a novice lover named Walter. Another influential writer of Marie's court — Chrétien de Troyes — seems at times to have taken the system seriously as a means by which a knight could be induced to courteous behavior and to learn humility by allowing his lady to direct his every action, though this is still a matter of debate. Chrétien's *Lancelot or The Knight of the Cart* illustrates such a "training" procedure. One of Chrétien's other works — *Erec and Enide* — addresses the considerable tensions between chivalry, its courtly codes, and marriage to question whether a knight's wife might also serve as his lady. Marie de France's courtly love stories or Breton lays are also of the same period with emphasis on the repercussions of courtly love for women. *Dame Sirith* reverses the situation, as Margery finds herself (or thinks she does) in jeopardy if she does not play the courtly game.

10–15   Wilekin, the clerk, exhibits lovesickness, the symptoms of which are pallor caused by perpetual yearning, lack of sleep, inability to eat, and general mental confusion.

35   *will I.* MS: *willi.* So too in lines 40, 46, 262, 295 (in negative form, i.e., "nulli") 388, 396, and 397.

43   *Wilekin.* The name is the diminutive form of Will, a name reminiscent of what was believed to be part of the human soul. Compare Chaucer's Wife of Bath's Prologue, where Alisoun brutalizes the hypothetical jealous husband with words, then reassures his spineless remnant of resistance: "Goode lief, taak keep / How mekely looketh Wilkyn, oure sheep! / Com neer, my spouse, lat me ba thy cheke!" (*CT* III[D]431–33). She adds insult to injury when she "uses the infantile *ba* for 'kiss,'" according to Larry D. Benson, ed. *Riverside Chaucer*, p. 869. In *Dame Sirith* the lover is young rather than old and jealous, but he has little more will power than the Wife's "husband" as he goes to *Femina* for advice (see head-note to Narrator). The diminutive form of the name may have found its way into English from the Middle Dutch of Flanders. B&S suggest that "[T]he native equivalent is represented in OE by *-cen* in *tyncen* 'small cask,' *thrynorcen*, 'a little thorn'" (p. 306). In the *Interludium de clerico et puella*, a comic play written decades later than *Sirith*, the clerk is unnamed.

45–49   In the margins of the MS adjacent to these lines are two caricatures, the first of a mature woman (probably Sirith), the second of a species either equine or canine. If equine, the image could represent the means by which Sirith would be publicly humiliated if found guilty of sorcery, if canine it may refer to the "weeping bitch" so integral to her trick.

88   *wold I.* MS: *woldi.* So also at lines 243, 249, and 309. Compare notes to lines 35 and 106.

        thing. MS: *thin.*

99   *To ben on hore.* The equation of adultery with prostitution may reflect a literary trope called the "calumniated wife" found in many Middle English romances and folk tales. In it, even the suggestion of adultery when made to a woman of integrity becomes an accusation of a much worse charge of prostitution though there is no financial arrangement mentioned. In the *Erle of Tolous*, Dame Beulybon, when her integrity is impugned, responds similarly: "Do you think me a whore?" In the Towneley play *Herod The Great* the first *miles* ("soldier") uses the term as an insult when one of the *mulieres* ("women") objects to his killing her baby: "What, hoore, art thou woode?" (line 390).

106   *shuld I.* MS: *shuldi.* See notes to lines 35 and 88.

108   *Ar his hom come.* This passage is vaguely reminiscent of the pressure placed on Penelope by her many suitors in Homer's *Odyssey*, though it is not likely that the author of *Sirith* knew Homer's work directly. But besieged women who hold out until their husband or betrothed returns are common in Middle English romance and Breton lays from *King Horn* on. Dorigen in Chaucer's The Franklin's Tale offers a pleasingly sentimental (albeit subsequent) parallel; perhaps the best example of the besieged yet faithful wife is found in *The Wright's Chaste Wife*, included in this volume.

114   The lover's assumption is that Margery, his beloved, will recognize his lovesickness and acquiesce out of pity for him. Again compare the situation in The Franklin's Tale, where Aurelius pleads his case in terms of the tears on his cheek (*CT* V[F]1078). Pity is often depicted by medieval writers as a feminine virtue modeled after the *Mater Dolorosa*.

116   *So ich ever mote biden Yol.* Ga translates this idiom "as sure as Christmas"; D&B translate it as "must await Yule"; T as "must wait for Christmas."

127   *lemmon.* MS: *lenmon.*

132   *finde.* MS: *fide.*

135   *leve brother.* This is not an acknowledgment of kinship, but rather a colloquial mode of address hinting at the beginning of sympathy and change of heart, if not mind.

136   *For ne wille ich thee love, ne non other.* MS: *For wille ich the love ne non other.* The missing negative *ne* is filled in for sense, though not for meter.

142   *maken menis.* To "make lament," B&S say, is an "idiom attested from 1400 onwards, in the sense 'get someone to intercede for one' (lit. 'employ as intermediary'), and is clearly what is required here" (p. 308). A go-between is a stock character of courtly love relations since communication between lovers must be discreet. Often this secretive mode of language requires a specialized reading of signs between the lovers. Such is the case in *Chevrefoil* by Marie de France, when Tristan must communicate with Isolde in ways indiscernible by others.

149–60 The action taken by Wilekin recalls the protagonist of the Latin fabliau, *Pamphilus de Amore.* In "*Pamphilus de Amore*: An Introduction and Translation," *Chaucer Review* 2 (1967), 108–34, Ga traces its use by several late medieval authors including Boccaccio, Chaucer, Gower, and Juan Ruiz in his *Libro de Buen Amor.* There are also strong allusions to the *Roman de la Rose*, particularly the Sirith character to the Old Woman or *La Vieille.* An important difference between *Pamphilus de Amore* and *Dame Sirith*, however, is that in the former the beloved "Galathea" is unmarried and assertive about protecting her maidenly reputation, while in the latter Margery is married and rather gullible. See also Priscilla Bawcutt, "*Pamphilus de Amore* 'in Inglish Toung,'" *Medium Aevum* 64 (1995), 264–72.

154   *Sirith.* MS: *siriz.* So also in lines 161 and 418. Ga suggests this spelling of Sirith's name to be the most prevalent, "but the rhyme shows the z to have been originally a thorn" (p. 446). John Hines clarifies: "The sporadic use of the graph <z> for sounds we should write <th> is a medieval English practice deriving from the unfamiliarity of Francophones with the <th> sounds. Sirith is an identifiable personal name while a Siriz pronounced with a z at the end is not; the pronunciation Sirith is confirmed by rhymes in the text" (*The Fabliau in English*, p. 43). According to B&S the spelling may be due to the "uncertainty of Anglo-Norman scribes regarding the use of the graph þ and its phonetic value" (p. 312).

157   *No . . . ni.* The double negative functions as an intensifier, thus "no man whatsoever."

162   *with.* MS: *wiz.* See note to line 154.

167   *leve sone.* Another colloquial term of familiarity rather than kinship.

173   *nelde.* Most editors agree that this should be read as *an elde* rather than *nelde.* Ga explains this as "an example of the wrong split between the indefinite article *an* and a noun with initial vowel" (p. 447), but the MED lists *nelde* as a noun, a "term of endearment" meaning "old woman," "grandmother," or "granny."

206   *On wicchecrafft nout I ne con.* Witchcraft is not officially codified as a heresy (from the Greek word for "free choice" or "alternative") until 1486 in a text entitled *Malleus Maleficarum* (*The Hammer of Witches*), although there was plenty of concern about it in the late thirteenth century when *Dame Sirith* was written. Rossell Hope Robbins, *The Encyclopedia of Witchcraft and Demonology* (New York: Bonanza Books, 1959), pp. 547–48, offers a brief and useful history of witchcraft:

> In the first thirteen centuries, witchcraft was punished by death only if some concrete injury resulted; divination or healing was considered about as bad as prostitution and was punished accordingly. In the fourteenth century, ecclesiastical law started to become more organized against sorcery. In 1310 the Church Council at Treves forbade divination, love potions, conjurations, and the like. In 1432 the Bishop of Beziers excommunicated sorcerers and their ilk. Legislation increased in the fifteenth century. These laws were not directed against the later witchcraft of pact and sabbat, although in the inquisitorial trials these crimes were being introduced, even as early as 1330 (at Toulouse).

B&S suggest that it is "on the score of 'bawdy' that Dame Sirith is so apprehensive" (p. 310).

209   *mi Pater Noster and mi Crede.* These prayers are important markers of medieval piety and occasionally served as tests for heresy, though most folks could recite them from memory whether or not they were heretics.

220   *that.* MS: *tha.*

225   The barter exchange, i.e., goods for service, suggests bawdry, placing Dame Sirith in the position of pander. Ga suggests that these kinds of gifts are typically extended to the go-between (p. 448).

247   *somer driven*. Being lashed backwards on a beast of burden was a particularly humiliating public punishment usually reserved for the worst criminals or traitors. Ga adds: "A bawdy woman was customarily driven on a sempter (a mule or an ass) facing its rump" (p. 247). The MED identifies the creature as a "packhorse."

274   *pones*. B&S follow the MS, as have I, while D&B emend to *penes*. The meaning is monetary either way.

276   *juperti*. MS: *aiuperti*.

279   *Pepir*. MS: *Pepis*.

279–84   Dame Sirith's address to her dog takes place in these lines. The frequent association of dogs with witches may be of importance to the trick about to be played in conjunction with the folk motif of the "weeping bitch," an *exemplum* found in the *Disciplina Clericalis* of Petrus Alphonsus, Jacques de Vitry's *Exempla*, the *Gesta Romanorum* (*Tales of the Romans*), as well as the *Historia Septem Sapientium* (*The History of the Seven Sages*). In late medieval England the story appears in the *Alphabetum Narrationem* (*An Alphabet of Tales*).

288   *boinard*. The word derives from OF *buisnart*, meaning buzzard. In the *Roman de Renart*, the famous medieval story of Reynard the Fox, the term is used as a proper name. According to B&S, the pejorative application of the word as it is used here "is rooted in the notion that the buzzard (which is a type of falcon) was sluggish and dull by nature" (p. 310).

306   *ansine*. MS: *ausine*. McK's emendation. B&S emend to *nausine*, despite the citation of the word *ansine* in the MED, 1 (a), where *fallen in ansene* is glossed as "decline or fail in appearance (?in the view of others)."

314   *God*. MS: *goed*. So also at lines 322 and 330. While B&S retain the name as written in MS, D&B emend, as have I.

324   *faste fourti daiis to non*. B&S (p. 311) point out a parallel in the Middle English version of *The Rule of St. Benedict*:

> In somer, fro Witsunday be past,
> Wedinsday and Friday sal þai fast,
> But if þai other swink or swete
> In hay or corn wiþ travel grete.
> And if þai non slike travel cone,
> On þos days sal thai *fast to none*. (Lines 1707–12)

The parallel is extended to include Christ's passion until the ninth hour. See *Three Middle English Versions of the Rule of St. Benet*, EETS o.s. 120 (London: Kegan Paul, 1902), p. 96. D&B read *daws* for *daiis*.

356   *breketh.* The thorn appears above the *k* in the MS.

390   *Godes houne belle.* B&S suggest that this phrase refers to the bell used at Mass when the Host is elevated (p. 311), while Ga suggests that the term may mean "belly," which refers to "an oath on part of Christ's body, like those on his bones and blood" but concludes that it more probably refers to the "chapel bell, as in bell, book and candle, or the bell in the Mass" (p. 453).

401   *mai I never.* MS: *mai never.* B&S add the personal pronoun, as do D&B.

433   *so ich evere bide noen.* B&S translate this as "As I hope to see the ninth hour" and suggest that this, along with the expression found at line 324, may be evidence that Wilekin is a "monastery-trained cleric," and that the author of *Dame Sirith* "may himself have been an inmate of a monastery" (p. 312). This could explain the hints of antifeminism in the text.

436   *Nelde, par ma fai.* Wilekin has more confidence than Troilus about what will follow and sends his pander away. In Chaucer Pandarus does, finally, leave the lovers alone, though not until after he has read much of the romance. See Chaucer, *Troilus and Criseyde*, Book 3.

445–50 This passage marks the moment that Dame Sirith turns to the audience and offers her services. Richard Axton's suggestion that this work could very well have been performed as an interlude by professional touring actors similar to jongleurs is interesting (see *European Drama of the Early Middle Ages*, pp. 19–23). This part would have been played by a male actor, which renders the moment all the more suggestive, perhaps offensive, if it is the case that interludes may have been performed for monastic communities as well as the public at large.

Interludium de clerico et puella

Clericus
"Damishel, reste wel!"   *Damsel*

Puella
"Sir, welcum, by Saynt Michel!"   *St. Michael*

Clericus
"Wer es ty sire, wer es ty dame?"   *Where is your father; mother*

Puella
"By Gode, es nother her at hame."   *neither is here at home*

Clericus
5   "Wel wor suilc a man to life   *Well-off would such a man [be in] life*
    That suilc a may mihte have to wyfe."   *such a maid might*

Puella
    "Do way, by Crist and Leonard,   *[St.] Leonard*
    No wil Y lufe na clerc fayllard,   *I will not love a good-for-nothing clerk*
    Ne kep I herbherg, clerc, in huse, no y flore,   *Nor; lodging; house; on floor*
10 Bot his hers ly wituten dore.   *Except that; arse; outside door*
    Go forth thi way, god sire,   *good sir*
    For her hastu losyd al thi wile."   *here you have lost all your desire*

Clericus
    "Nu, nu, by Crist and by Sant Jhon;   *St. John*
    In al this land ne wis hi none,   *know I none*
15 Mayden, that I luf mor than thee,   *love more*
    Hif me micht ever the bether be.
    For thee hy sory nicht and day,   *I sorrow [both] night*
    Y may say, hay waylevay!   *alas alas*
    Y luf thee mar than mi lif,   *I love you more; life*
20 Thu hates me mar than gayt dos chnief.   *more; goat; [the] knife*

53

	That es nouct for mysgilt,	*because of my having done amiss*
	Certhes, for thi luf ham hi spilt.	*Truly; I*
	A, suythe mayden, reu of me,	*Ah, wonderful; take pity on*
	That es ty luf hand ay sal be,	*your love and ever shall be*
25	For the luf of the moder of efne,	*love; mother of heaven*
	Thu mend thi mode and her my stevene!"	*change your mind; hear; plea (voice)*

Puella

	"By Crist of hevene and Sant Jone,	*St. John*
	Clerc of scole ne kep I non,	
	For many god wymman haf thai don scam —	*[to] many good; have they done shame*
30	By Crist, thu michtis haf ben at hame!"	*might [as well] have stayed home*

Clericus

	"Synt it nothir gat may be,	*Since*
	Jesu Christ bytech Y thee,	*commend*
	And send neulic bot tharinne,	*quickly (newly) remedy*
	That Yi be lesit of al my pyne."	*released; pain*

Puella

35	"Go nu, truan, go nu, go,	*now, beggar*
	For mikel canstu of sory and wo!"	*much do you know*

Clericus

	"God te blis, Mome Helwis!"	*bless you, Dame Eloise*

Mome Elwis

	"Son, welcum, by San Dinis!"	*St. Denis*

Clericus

	"Hic am comin to thee, mome,	*I*
40	Thu hel me noth, thu say me sone.	*[If] you cannot heal me, tell me at once*
	Hic am a clerc that hauntes scole,	
	Y lydy my life wyt mikel dole.	*I lead; much sorrow*
	Me wor lever to be dedh,	*I would rather be dead*
	Than led the lif that hyc ledh	*lead*
45	For ay mayden with and schen,	*white and shining*
	Fayrer ho lond haw Y non syen.	*Fairer in land have*
	Yo hat mayden Malkyn, Y wene.	*She was called; I think*

Interludium de clerico et puella

Nu thu wost quam Y mene.	*you know whom I mean*
Yo wonys at the tounes ende,	*She lives*
50 That suyt lif so fayr and hende.	*sweet*
Bot if yo wil hir mod amende,	*Unless she; mood (mind) change*
Neuly Crist my ded me send!	*Swiftly; death*
Men kend me hyder, uytuten fayle,	*sent; without fail*
To haf thi help an ty cunsalye;	*and your*
55 Tharfor am Y cummen here,	
That thu salt be my herand-bere,	*go-between (errand bearer)*
To mac me and that mayden sayct,	*make; reconciled*
And hi sal gef thee of my nayct,	*possessions*
So that hever al thi lyf	
60 Saltu be the better wyf.	*You shall be*
So help me Crist, and hy may spede,	*if I may prosper*
Riche saltu haf thi mede."	*Richly; reward*

Mome Elwis

"A, son, wat saystu? Benedicité!	*what did you say*
Lift hup thi hand and blis thee!	*up your; bless yourself*
65 For it es boyt syn and scam,	*is but; shame*
That thu on me hafs layt thys blam,	*blame (task)*
For hic am an ald quyne and a lam,	*an old woman; am lame*
Y led my lyf wit Godis love,	
Wit my roc Y me fede,	*distaff*
70 Can I do non othir dede,	*Know; occupation*
Bot my Pater Noster and my Crede,	*Except*
To say Crist for missedede,	*confess [to] Christ for [my] sins*
And myn Avy Mary —	*Ave Maria*
For my scynnes hic am sory —	*sins I; sorry*
75 And my *De profundis*	*"Out of the depths"*
For al that yn sin lys;	*lies*
For can I me non othir think —	
That wot Crist, of hevene kync.	
Jesu Crist of hevene hey,	*high*
80 Gef that thay may heng hey,	*hang high*
And gef that hy may se,	
That thay be henged on a tre,	
That this ley as leyit onne me.	*lie; laid on me*
For aly wyman am I on."	*holy woman; one*

Select Bibliography and Notes to Interludium de clerico et puella

Manuscript

British Library MS Additional 23986, vellum roll, verso side (early fourteenth century).

Editions

Bennett, J. A. W., and G. V. Smithers, eds. *Early Middle English Verse and Prose*. Second edition. Oxford: Oxford University Press, 1968. Pp. 196–200.

Chambers, E. K. *The Mediaeval Stage*. 2 vols. Oxford: The Clarendon Press, 1903. Pp. 324–26.

Cook, Albert Stanburrough, ed. *A Literary Middle English Reader*. Boston: Ginn and Company, 1915; rpt. 1943. Pp. 476–80. [Cook entitles the play "The Cleric and the Maiden" and adds scene divisions and stage directions.]

Dickins, B., and R. M. Wilson. *Early Middle English Texts*. London: Bowes & Bowes, 1956. Pp. 121–22.

Wright, Thomas, and James Orchard Halliwell, eds. *Reliquiae Antiquae. Scraps From Ancient Manuscripts, Illustrating Chiefly Early English Literature and the English Language*. 2 vols. London: John Russell Smith, 1845. Vol. 1, pp. 145–47.

Related Studies

Axton, Richard. "Popular Modes in the Earliest Plays." In *Medieval Drama*. Ed. Neville Denny. London: Edward Arnold, 1973. Pp. 13–39.

———. *European Drama of the Early Middle Ages*. Pittsburgh: University of Pittsburgh Press, 1975.

Notes to *Interludium de clerico et puella*

Busby, Keith. "*Dame Sirith* and *De Clerico et Puella*." In *Companion to Early Middle English Literature*. Ed. N. H. G. E. Veldhoen and H. Aertsen. Amsterdam: Free University Press, 1988. Pp. 69–81.

Gayley, Charles M. *Representative English Comedies*. London: Macmillan Co., 1903. Pp. xiii–xviii.

Heuser, W. "Das *Interludium de Clerico et Puella* und das Fabliau von *Dame Siriz*." *Anglia* 30 (1907), 306–19.

Miller, B. D. H. "Further Notes on *Interludium de Clerico et Puella*." *Notes and Queries* 208 [n.s. 10] (1963), 248–89.

Moore, Bruce. "The Narrator within the Performance: Problems with Two Medieval 'Plays.'" In *Drama in the Middle Ages: Comparative and Critical Essays: Second Series*. Ed. Clifford Davidson and John H. Stroupe. New York: AMS Press, 1991. Pp. 152–67.

Nicoll, Allardyce. *Masks, Mimes, and Miracles: Studies in the Popular Theatre*. London: Cooper Square, 1963. Pp. 171–75.

Richardson, Frances E. "Notes on the Text and Language of *Interludium de Clerico et Puella*." *Note and Queries* 207 [n.s. 9] (1962), 133–34.

Notes

Abbreviations: **B&S**: J. A. W. Bennett and G. V. Smithers; **Co**: Albert Cook; **MS**: British Library MS Additional 23986, vellum roll, verso side.

The incipit appears as follows: *Hic incipit Interludium de clerico et puella.*

2   *Saynt Michel*. B&S assert that "there seems to be no very specific point in this invocation" (p. 372), yet the invocation of this particular saint seems appropriate to the themes of the play and forms a rather suggestive subtext. The archangel Michael fights in a cosmic battle against Satan in the *Book of Revelation*. According to the *Oxford Dictionary of Saints*, ed. David Hugh Farmer (Oxford: Oxford University Press, 1982), in a second-century text called *The Testament of Abraham*, "Michael is the principal character whose intercession is so powerful that souls can be rescued from Hell. Perhaps this passage inspired the offertory

antiphon formerly used for the Roman liturgy for the dead" (pp. 300–01). Michael was also the patron saint of cemeteries; his cult was so powerful that by the end of the Middle Ages in England alone there were 686 churches dedicated to him.

4   *nother*. MS: *nouer*.

5   *Wel . . . to life*. B&S detect a "unique parallel to an idiom found in Shakespeare's *The Winter's Tale* III, iii, 124 and *The Merchant of Venice*, II, ii, 55 which is synonymous with well-to-do and well-to-pass and is constructed on the same syntactic pattern" (p. 372).

7   *Leonard*. St. Leonard was a sixth-century hermit who became the patron of pregnant women and prisoners of war and other such captives. As patron saint of captives and prisoners, he became particularly popular in England, where his cult inspired more than 177 churches and shrines. See the *Oxford Dictionary of Saints*, p. 264. N.b. Chaucer's reference to St. Leonard's nunnery in *House of Fame*: "On pilgrymage myles two / To the corseynt Leonard, / To make lythe of that was hard" (lines 116–18). See B. C. Koonce, *Chaucer and the Traditions of Fame: Symbolism in the House of Fame* (Princeton: Princeton University Press, 1966), pp. 70–71. *The Legenda Aurea* gives an etymology to his name: Leonardus means "the perfume of the people," from *leos*, people, and *nardus*, which is a sweet-smelling herb; and Leonard drew people to himself by the sweet odor of his good renown. See Jacobus de Voragine, *The Golden Legend: Reading on the Saints*, vol. 2, trans. William Granger Ryan (Princeton: Princeton University Press, 1993) p. 243. This applies well here, since Puella is concerned about her reputation in the eyes of God.

10   *hers*. MS: *s*.

12   *losyd*. MS: *losye*. Co has *losyt*.

           wile. Co emends to *hire*, based on his reading of line 1384 in the *Childhood of Jesus* (c. 1300); "Elles we leosez bothe ore ywile and huyre."

14   *this*. MS: *ys*.

           hi. In this poem's dialect the scribe frequently aspirates vowels — *hi/hy* for *I/Y* (see also lines 17, 22, 58, 61, and 81); *hic* for *ich* ("I") (lines 39, 41, 67, and 74); *hay* for *ay* (line 18, where the "hay weilaway" means "alas alas"); *ham* for *am* (line 22); *hand* for *and* (line 24); *hif* for *if* (line 16); *hers* for *arse* (line 10); *hever* for *ever* (line 59); and *hup* for *up* (line 64); or lisps on consonants such as *s > sh* in *Damishel* (line 1); *t > th* in *Certhes* (line 22); and *d > dh* in *dedh* (line 43) or *ledh* (line 44). In some instances he drops *h* as in *efne* for *hefne* (line 25) and *aly* for *haly* (line 84). See B&S's discussion of the dialect, pp. 370–72.

16   *micht*. MS: *miche*.

        the. MS: *ye*.

17   *sory*. B&S emend to *sorw*. Co retains *sory*, as have I. See also line 36.

25   *moder of efne*. MS: *y mod efne*.

32   *bytech*. MS: *by tethy*.

33   *neulic*. MS: *neulit*.

36   *canstu*. MS: *yu canstu*.

37   *Mome*. The MED defines the term as "an aunt, also affectionate term of address for [an] older woman." It can also mean "old woman." B&S suggest that it is an adaptation of the Old High German *muome* which means "maternal aunt" (p. 373). The name corresponds to "Dame" Sirith and partly explains why scholars insist on a softening of her character.

38   *San Dinis*. St. Denis was the first bishop of Paris, having been sent to convert France by Gregory of Tours. He built a center of Christianity on an island in the Seine where he was eventually martyred by decapitation, his body thrown into the Seine. Over his tomb was built the abbey of St. Denis.

41   *hauntes* MS: *haus*. Abbreviated, with hole in the MS between *u* and *s*.

42   *lydy*. Co emends to *led*.

47   *Malkyn*. According to the MED, this name has pejorative implications meaning "servant woman," "young woman of the lower classes," or "a woman of loose morals." See Chaucer's Introduction to The Man of Law's Tale, where lost time

is compared to "Malkynes maydenhede, / Whan she hath lost it in hir wantownesse" (*CT* II[B¹]30–31).

47   *Y wene*. MS: *or mene*.

62   *Riche*. MS: *Richc*. Co emends to *Riche*, as have I; B&S follow MS.

63   *wat*. MS: *vat*.

67–68   B&S (p. 373) detect either a corrupt rhyme word or a lacuna of two lines or more that rhyme with *lam* (line 67) and *love* (line 68).

75   *De profundis*. Derived from Psalm 130, this phrase is used in the Office of the Dead.

76   *yn*. MS: *y*. B&S's emendation.

79   B&S: "The rhyme words here show that a line has been omitted, and the contextual inadequacy of 80 that it was after this line" (p. 373).

80   *thay*. MS: *Hay*.

82   *henged*. MS: *heng'*.

83   *onne me*. B&S emend to *me on*. Co emends to *me onne*.

The Wright's Chaste Wife

	Allemyghty God, maker of all,	
	Save you my sovereyns in towre and hall,	
	And send you good grace!	
	If ye wylle a stounde blynne,	*[for] a while stop [talking]*
5	Of a story I wylle begynne,	
	And telle you alle the cas,	*predicaments*
	Meny farleyes that I have herde	*marvelous tales*
	Ye would have wondyr how yt ferde;	*turned out*
	Lystyn, and ye schalle here;	*Listen; hear*
10	Of a wryght I wylle you telle	*carpenter*
	That some tyme in thys land gan dwelle,	*dwelt*
	And lyved by hys myster.	*near; master*
	Whether that he were yn or oute,	*he (the wright)*
	Or erthely man hadde he no dowte,	*fear*
15	To werke hows, harowe, nor plowgh,	*pickaxes (hoes), harrow; plow*
	Or other werkes, what so they were	*no matter what*
	Thous wrought he hem farre and nere,	*them far*
	And dyd tham wele inough.	*enough*
	Thys wryght would wedde no wyfe,	
20	Butt yn yougeth to lede hys lyfe	*Except; youth*
	In myrthe and othre melody;	
	Over alle where he gan wende,	*Everywhere; went*
	Alle they seyd, "Welcome, frende,	
	Sytt downe, and do gladly."	
25	Tylle on a tyme he was wyllyng,	
	As tyme comyth of alle thyng,	
	So seyth the profesye,	*prophecy*
	A wyfe for to wedde and have	
	That myght hys goodes kepe and save,	
30	And for to leve alle foly.	
	Ther dwellyd a wydowe in that contré	
	That hadde a doughter feyre and fre;	*Who; lovely; noble*
	Of her, word sprang wyde,	

61

	For sche was bothe stabylle and trewe,	*constant*
35	Meke of maners, and feyre of hewe —	*complexion*
	So seyd men in that tyde.	
	The wryght seyde, "So God me save,	
	Such a wyfe would I have	
	To lye nyghtly by my syde."	
40	He thought to speke wyth that may,	*maiden*
	And rose erly on a daye	
	And thyder gan he to ryde.	
	The wryght was welcome to the wyfe,	
	And her saluyd alle so blyve,	*greeted; gladly*
45	And so he dyd her doughter fre:	
	For the erand that he for came	
	Tho he spake, that good yemane,	*yeoman*
	Than to hym seyd sche.	*When*
	The wydow seyd, "By heven kyng,	
50	I may geve wyth her nothing.	*have nothing to give*
	And that forthynketh me,	*I regret*
	Save a garlond I wylle thee geve,	*Except; give*
	Ye schalle never see, whyle ye lyve,	
	None such in thys contré.	
55	Have here thys garlond of roses ryche,	
	In alle thy lond ys non yt lyche,	*like it*
	For ytt wylle ever be newe;	
	Wete thou wele withowtyn fable,	*without lie*
	Alle the whyle thy wyfe ys stable	*faithful*
60	The chaplett wolle hold hewe;	*wreath; [its] color*
	And yf thy wyfe use putry,	*adultery*
	Or tolle eny man to lye her by,	*beguiles; go to bed with her*
	Than wolle yt change hewe,	*color*
	And by the garlond thou may see,	
65	Fekylle or fals yf that sche be,	*Fickle*
	Or ellys yf sche be trewe."	
	Of thys chaplett hym was fulle fayne,	*joyful*
	And of hys wyfe, was nott to layne,	*to tell the truth*
	He weddyd her fulle sone,	
70	And ladde her home wyth solempnité,	*led*
	And hyld her brydalle dayes thre.	*bridal*

Whan they home come,
Thys wryght in hys hart cast,
If that he walkyd est or west
75   As he was wonte to done,
"My wyfe that ys so bryght of ble
Men wolle desyre here fro me,
And that hastly and sone";
Butt sone he hym bythought
80   That a chambyr schuld be wrought
Bothe of lyme and stone,
Wyth wallys strong as eny stele,
And dorres sotylly made and wele,
He owte framyd yt sone;
85   The chambyr he lett make fast,
Wyth plaster of Parys that wylle last,
Such ous know I never none.
Ther ys kyng ne emperoure,
And he were lockyn in that towre,
90   That cowde gete owte of that wonne.
Nowe hathe he done as he thought,
And in the myddes of the flore wrought
A wondyr strange gyle,
A trapdoure rounde abowte
95   That no man myght come yn nor owte;
It was made wyth a wyle,
That whoso touchyd yt eny thyng,
Into the pytt he schuld flyng
Wythyn a lytylle whyle.
100   For hys wyfe he made that place,
That no man schuld beseke her of grace,
Nor her to begyle.

By that tyme the lord of the towne
Hadde ordeynyd tymbyr redy bowne
105   An halle to make of tre.
After the wryght the lord lett sende
For that he schuld wyth hym lende
Monythys two or thre.
The lord seyd, "Woult thou have thi wyfe?

63

110	I wylle send after her blyve	*quickly*
	That sche may com to thee."	
	The wryght hys garlond hadde take wyth hym,	
	That was bryght and nothing dymme,	
	Yt wes feyre on to see.	
115	The lord axyd hym as he satt,	*asked*
	"Felowe, where hadyst thou this hatte	*did you get*
	That ys so feyre and newe?"	
	The wryght answerd alle so blyve,	*gladly*
	And seyd, "Syr, I hadde yt wyth my wyfe,	*acquired it*
120	And that dare me nevere rewe;	*rue*
	Syr, by my garlond I may see	
	Fekylle or fals yf that sche be,	
	Or yf that sche be trewe;	
	And yf my wyfe love a paramoure,	
125	Than wylle my garlond vade coloure,	*fade*
	And change wylle yt the hewe."	
	The lord thought, "By Godys myght,	
	That wylle I wete thys same nyght	*learn*
	Whether thys tale be trewe."	
130	To the wryghtys howse anon he went,	*house soon*
	He fonde the wyfe therin presente,	
	That was so bryght and schene;	*beautiful*
	Sone he hayled her trewly,	*hailed*
	And so dyd sche the lord curtesly:	
135	Sche seyd, "Welcome ye be";	
	Thus seyd the wyfe of the hows,	
	"Syr, howe faryth my swete spowse	
	That hewyth uppon youre tre?"	*cuts*
	"Sertes, dame," he seyd, "wele,	
140	And I am come, so have I hele,	
	To wete the wylle of thee;	
	My love ys so uppon thee cast	*so [ardently]*
	That me thynketh my hert wolle brest,	*burst*
	It wolle none otherwyse be;	
145	Good dame, graunt me thy grace	*your permission*
	To pley with thee in some prevy place	*play [sexual games]; secret place*
	For gold and eke for fee."	*rich gifts (movable property)*
	"Good syr, lett be youre fare,	*stop; plan of action*

64

	And of such wordes speke no mare	*more*
150	For Hys love that dyed on Tre;	*(Christ's); Cross*
	Hadde we onys begonne that gle,	*once; fooling around*
	My husbond by his garlond myght see;	
	For sorowe he would wexe woode."	*grow angry*
	"Certes, dame," he seyd, "naye;	
155	Love me, I pray you, in that ye maye:	
	For Godys love change thy mode,	*mind*
	Forty marke schalle be youre mede	*payment*
	Of sylver and of gold so rede,	*red*
	And that schalle do thee good."	*you*
160	"Syr, that deed schalle be done;	
	Take me that mony here anone."	*Give; money; at once*
	"I swere by the holy Rode	*Cross*
	I thought when I cam hyddere	*here*
	For to bryng yt alle togyddere,	
165	As I mott breke my heele."	
	Ther sche toke forty marke	*forty marks*
	Of sylver and gold styff and sterke:	
	Sche toke yt feyre and welle;	
	Sche seyd, "Into the chambyr wylle we,	*will we [go]*
170	Ther no man schalle us see;	
	No lenger wylle we spare."	*hold back*
	Up the steyer they gan hye:	*stair; climb*
	The stepes were made so queyntly	*cleverly*
	That farther myght he nott fare.	
175	The lord stumbyllyd as he went in hast,	
	He felle donne into that chaste	*down; chest (compartment)*
	Forty fote and somedele more.	*feet; somewhat*
	The lord began to crye;	
	The wyfe seyd to hym in hye,	
180	"Syr, what do ye there?"	
	"Dame, I can nott seye howe	
	That I am come hydder nowe	
	To thys hows that ys so newe;	
	I am so depe in thys sure flore	*sturdy floor*
185	That I ne can come owte att no dore;	
	Good dame, on me thou rewe!"	*have pity*
	"Nay," sche seyd, "so mut y the,	*as I might thrive*

65

Tylle myne husbond come and se,
I schrewe hym that yt thought."   *curse*
190   The lord arose and lokyd abowte
If he myght eny where get owte,
But yt holpe hym ryght noght,
The wallys were so thycke wythyn,   *walls; within*
That he nowhere myght owte wynne   *go*
195   But helpe to hym were brought;   *Unless*
And ever the lord made evylle chere,
And seyd, "Dame, thou schalt by thys dere."   *for this [pay] dearly*
Sche seyd tat sche ne rought;   *did not care*
Sche seyd, "I recke nere
200   Whyle I am here and thou art there,
I schrewe herre that thee doth drede."   *curse her who fears you*
The lord was sone owte of her thought,
The wyfe went into her lofte,
Sche satte and dyd here dede.   *her work*
205   Than yt fell on that other daye   *second day*
Of mete and drynke he gan her pray,   *food*
Thereof he hadde gret nede.
He seyd, "Dame, for seynt charyté,   *holy charity*
Wyth some mete thou comfort me."   *food*
210   Sche seyd, "Nay, so God me spede,
For I swere by swete seynt Johne,   *St. John*
Mete ne drynke ne getyst thou none
Butt thou wylt swete or swynke;   *sweat and labor*
For I have both hempe and lyne,   *flax*
215   And a betyngstocke fulle fyne,   *beating block*
And a swyngylle good and grete;   *board*
If thou wylt worke, tell me sone."
"Dame, bryng yt forthe, yt schalle be done,
Fulle gladly would I ete."
220   Sche toke the stocke in her honde,
And into the pytt sche yt schlang   *threw*
Wyth a grete hete: *passion (gusto)*
Sche brought the lyne and hempe on her backe,   *flax*
"Syr lord," sche seyd, "have thou that,   *take that*
225   And lerne for to swete."   *sweat*
Ther sche toke hym a bonde

For to occupy hys honde,
And bade hym fast on to bete.   *quickly begin*
He leyd yt downe on the stone,
230   And leyd on strockes welle good wone,
And sparyd nott on to leyne.   *beat*
Whan that he hadde wrought a thrave,   *measure*
Mete and drynke he gan to crave,
And would have hadde yt fayne;   *gladly*
235   "That I hadde somewhat for to ete
Now after my gret swete;
Me thynketh yt were ryght,
For I have labouryd nyght and daye
Thee for to plese, dame I saye,
240   And therto putt my myght."
The wyfe seyd, "So mutt I have hele,   *good fortune*
And yf thi worke be wrought wele
Thou schalt have to dyne."
Mete and drynke sche hym bare,
245   Wyth a thrafe of flex mare   *measure; flax more*
Of fulle long boundyn lyne.   *flax*
So feyre the wyfe the lord gan praye
That he schuld be werkyng aye,   *ever*
And nought that he schuld blynne;   *cease*
250   The lord was fayne to werke tho,
Butt hys men knewe nott of hys woo   *suffering*
Nor of ther lordes pyne.   *their lord's suffering*

The stuard to the wryght gan saye,   *steward*
"Sawe thou owte of my lord todaye,   *Saw you*
255   Whether that he ys wende?"
The wryght answerde and seyd, "Naye,
I sawe hym nott syth yesterdaye;   *since*
I trowe that he be schente."   *believe; may be in trouble (injured)*
The stuard stode the wryght by,
260   And of hys garlond hadde ferly   *marveled*
What that yt bemente.   *might mean*
The stuard seyd, "So God me save,
Of thy garlond wondyr I have,
And who yt hath thee sent."

67

265	"Syr," he seyd, "be the same hatte	*headpiece*
	I can knowe yf my wyfe be badde	*unfaithful (bad)*
	To me by eny other man;	
	If my floures outher fade or falle,	*flowers either*
	Then doth my wyfe me wrong wythalle,	
270	As many a woman can."	
	The stuard thought, "By Godes myght,	
	That schalle I preve thys same nyght	*prove*
	Whether thou blys or banne."	*bless or curse*
	And into hys chambyr he gan gone,	
275	And toke tresure fulle good wone,	*a great quantity*
	And forth he spedde hem than.	
	Butt he ne stynt att no stone	*stop*
	Tylle he unto the wryghtes hows come	*house*
	That ylke same nyght.	*very*
280	He mett the wyfe amydde the gate,	*in the middle of*
	Abowte the necke he gan her take,	
	And seyd, "My dere wyght,	*lady*
	Alle the good that ys myne	
	I wylle thee geve to be thyne	*give*
285	To lye by thee alle nyght."	
	Sche seyd, "Syr, lett be thy fare	*stop; behavior*
	My husbond wolle wete wythowtyn mare	*know*
	And I hym dyd that unryght;	*If; injustice*
	I would nott he myght yt wete	*know*
290	For alle the good that I myght gete,	*Despite*
	So Jhesus mutt me spede;	*might; deliver*
	For, and eny man lay me by,	*if any*
	My husbond would yt wete truly,	
	It ys wythowtyn eny drede."	*doubt*
295	The stuard seyd, "For hym that ys wrought,	
	Thereof, dame, dred thee noght	*fear you not*
	Wyth me to do that dede;	
	Have here of me twenty marke	*marks*
	Of gold and sylver styf and starke,	
300	Thys tresoure schalle be thy mede."	*reward*
	"Syr, and I graunt that to you,	*if I*
	Lett no man wete butt we two nowe."	*know*
	He seyd, "Nay, wythowtyn drede."	*never fear*

	The stuard thought, "Sykerly	*Certainly*
305	Women beth both queynte and slye."	*cunning*
	The mony he gan her bede;	
	He thought wele to have be spedde,	
	And of her erand he was onredde	*reluctant*
	Or he were fro hem i-gone.	
310	Up the sterys sche hym leyde	*stairs*
	Tylle he saw the wryghtes bedde:	
	Of tresoure thought he none;	*nothing*
	He went and stumblyd att a stone,	
	Into the sellere he fylle sone	*cellar*
315	Downe to the bare flore.	
	The lord seyd, "What devylle art thou?	
	And thou hadest falle on me nowe,	
	Thowe hadest hurt me fulle sore."	
	The stuard stert and staryd abowte	*looked around*
320	If he myght ower gete owte	*anywhere*
	Att hold lesse or mare.	
	The lord seyd, "Welcome, and sytt betyme,	
	For thou schalt helpe to dyght thys lyne	*prepare; flax*
	For alle thy fers fare."	*fierce behavior*
325	The stuard lokyd on the knyght,	
	He seyd, "Syr, for Godes myght,	
	My lord, what do you here?"	
	He seyd, "Felowe, wythowtyn oth,	*lie*
	For o erand we come bothe,	
330	The sothe wolle I nott lete."	*conceal*
	Tho cam the wyfe them unto,	*Then*
	And seyd, "Syrres, what do you to,	*two*
	Wylle ye nott lerne to swete?"	*i.e., work*
	Than seyd the lord her unto,	
335	"Dame, youre lyne ys i-doo,	*flax; done*
	Nowe would I fayne ete:	
	And I have made yt alle ilyke,	*the same*
	Fulle clere, and nothing thycke,	
	Me thynketh yt gret payne."	
340	The stuard seyd, "Wythowtyn dowte,	
	And ever I may wynne owte,	*If*
	I wyll breke her brayne."	*break; brain (head)*

"Felowe, lett be, and sey nott so,   *shut up*
For thou schalt worke or ever thou goo,   *before*
345   Thy wordes thou torne agayne,
Fayne thou schalt be so to doo,   *willing*
And thy good wylle put therto;
As a man buxome and bayne   *obedient; compliant*
Thowe schalt rubbe, rele, and spynne,   *wind; spin*
350   And thou wolt eny mete wynne,   *If; food*
That I geve to God a gyfte."
The stuard seyd, "Then have I wondyr;
Rather would I dy for hungyr
Wythowte hosylle or shryfte."   *confession; absolution*
355   The lord seyd, "So have I hele,
Thowe wylt worke, yf thou hungyr well,
What worke that thee be brought."
The lord satt and dyd hys werke,
The stuard drewe into the derke.
360   Gret sorowe was in hys thought.
The lord seyd, "Dame, here ys youre lyne,   *flax*
Have yt in Godes blessyng and myne,
I hold yt well i-wrought."
Mete and drynke sche gave hymn yn,
365   "The stuard," sche seyd, "wolle he nott spynne,
Wylle he do ryght noght?"
The lord seyd, "By swete sen Jone,   *St. John*
Of thy mete schalle he have none
That ye have me hydder brought."
370   The lord ete and dranke fast,
The stuard hungeryd att the last,
For he gave hym nought.   *nothing*
The stuard satt alle in a stody,   *stupor*
Hys lord hadde forgote curtesy:
375   Tho seyd the stuard, "Geve me some."   *Then*
The lord seyd, "Sorow have the morselle or sope   *sop*
That schalle come in thy throte;
Nott so much as a crome!   *crumb*
Butt thou wylt helpe to dyght this lyne,   *Unless; prepare; flax*
380   Much hungyr yt schalle be thyne
Though thou make much mone."   *complaint*

Up he rose, and went therto,
"Better ys me thus to doo
Whyle yt must nedys be do."
385 The stuard began fast to knocke,
The wyfe threw hym a syngelyng stocke,　*beating board*
Hys mete therwyth to wyn;　*food*
Sche brought a swyngylle at the last,
"Good syres," sche seyd, "swyngylle on fast;
390 For nothing that ye blynne."　*nothing; cease*
Sche gave hym a stocke to sytt uppon,　*bench*
And seyd, "Syres, this werke must nedys be done,
Alle that that ys here yn."
The stuard toke up a stycke to saye,
395 "Sey, seye, swyngylle better yf ye may,
Hytt wylle be the better to spynne."
Were the lord never so gret,
Yet was he fayne to werke for hys mete　*eager*
Though he were never so sadde;
400 Butt the stuard that was so stowde,　*Unless*
Was fayne to swyngelle the scales owte,
Therof he was nott glad.
The lordys meyné that were att home　*company*
Wyst nott where he was bycome,　*i.e., knew what had become of him*
405 They were fulle sore adrad.　*worried*

The proctoure of the parysche chyrche ryght　*pastor*
Came and lokyd on the wryght,
He lokyd as he were madde;　*crazy*
Fast the proctoure gan hym frayne,　*to ask*
410 "Where hadest thou this garlond gayne?　*did you get*
It ys ever lyke newe."
The wryght gan say, "Felowe,
Wyth my wyfe, yf thou wylt knowe;
That dare me nott rewe;　*cause sadness*
415 For alle the whyle my wyfe trew ys,
My garlond wolle hold hewe iwys,
And never falle nor fade;　*diminish*
And yf my wyfe take a paramoure,
Than wolle my garlond vade the floure,　*fade*

420	That dare I ley myne hede."	
	The proctoure thought, "In good faye	*faith*
	That schalle I wete thy same daye	*learn*
	Whether yt may so be."	
	To the wryghtes hows he went;	*house*
425	He grete the wyfe wyth feyre entente.	*greeted*
	Sche seyd, "Syr, welcome be ye."	
	"A! dame, my love ys on you fast	
	Syth the tyme I sawe you last;	
	I pray you yt may so be	
430	That ye would graunt me of youre grace	
	To play wyth you in some privy place,	
	Or ellys to deth mutt me."	*must [I go]*
	Fast the proctoure gan to pray,	
	And ever to hym sche seyd, "Naye,	
435	That wolle I nott doo.	
	Hadest thou done that ded wyth me,	*deed*
	My spouse by hys garlond myght see:	
	That schuld torne me to woo."	*turn*
	The proctoure seyd, "By heven kyng,	
440	If he sey to thee anything	
	He schalle have sorowe unsowte;	
	Twenty marke I wolle thee geve,	
	It wolle thee helpe welle to lyve,	
	The mony here have I brought."	
445	Nowe hath sche the tresure tane,	*taken*
	And up the steyre be they gane,	*gone*
	(What helpyth yt to lye?)	
	The wyfe went the steyre besyde,	
	The proctoure went a lytylle to wyde	*too*
450	He felle downe by and by.	
	Whan he in the seller felle,	*cellar*
	He wente to have sonke into hell,	*thought; sunk*
	He was in hart fulle sory.	
	The stuard lokyd on the knyght,	
455	And seyd, "Proctoure, for Godes myght,	
	Come and sytt us by."	
	The proctoure began to stare,	
	For he was he wyst never whare,	*he was he did not know where*

72

Butt wele he knewe the knyght

460 And the stuard that swyngelyd the lyne.   *pounded; flax*

He seyd, "Syres, for Godes pyne,   *suffering*

What do ye here thys nyght?"   *are you doing*

The stuard seyd, "God geve thee care,

Thowe camyst to loke howe we fare,

465 Nowe helpe this lyne were dyght."   *prepare*

He stode stylle in a gret thought,   *[The pastor]*

What to answer he wyst noght: *knew*

"By Mary fulle of myght,"

The proctoure seyd, "What do ye in this yn   *dwelling*

470 For to bete thys wyfees lyne?   *beat; flax*

For Jhesus love, fulle of myght,"

The proctoure seyd ryght as he thought,

"For me yt schalle by evylle wrought

And I may see aryght,

475 For I lernyd never in londe

For to have a swyngelle in hond

By day nor by nyght."

The stuard seyd, "As good as thou

We hold us that be here nowe,   *know ourselves who*

480 And lett preve yt be syght;

Yet must us worke for owre mete,   *our food*

Or ellys schalle we none gete,

Mete nor drynke to owre honde."

The lord seyd, "Why flyte ye two?   *debate*

485 I trowe ye wylle werke or ye goo   *trust; before*

If yt be as I undeyrstond."

   Abowte he goys twyes or thryes;

They ete and drunke in such wyse

That they geve hym ryght noght.   *nothing*

490 The proctoure seyd, "Thynke ye no schame,

Geve me some mete, ye be to blame,

Of that the wyfe ye brought."

The stuard seyd, "Evylle spede the soppe

If eny morcelle come in thy throte

495 Butt thou wyth us hadest wrought."   *Until; worked*

The proctoure stode in a stody   *quandary*

Whether he myght worke hem by;

73

And so to torne hys thought,
To the lord he drewe nere,
500 And to hym seyd wyth myld chere,
"That Mary mott thee spede."
The proctour began to knocke.
The good wyfe rawte hym a rocke,   *gave; distaff*
For therto hadde sche nede.
505 Sche seyd, "Whan I was mayde att home,   *a young woman*
Other werke dowde I do none   *did*
My lyf therwyth to lede."
Sche gave hym in hande a rocke hynde,   *well-made (nearby?) distaff*
And bade hem fast for to wynde
510 Or ellys to lett be hys dede.   *death*
"Yes, dame," he seyd, "so have I hele,   *health*
I schalle yt worke both feyre and welle
As ye have taute me."   *directed*
He wavyd up a strycke of lyne,   *handful of linen fibers*
515 And he span wele and fyne
Byfore the swyngelle tre.
The lord seyd, "Thou spynnest to grete,   *too fast*
Therfore thou schalt have no mete,   *food*
That thou schalt well see."
520 Thus they satt and wrought fast   *worked*
Tylle the weke dayes were past.

    Then the wryght, home came he,
And as he cam by hus hows syde   *his*
He herd noyse that was not ryde   *usual*
525 Of persons two or thre;
One of hem knockyd lyne,   *bundled the heckled flax*
Anothyr swyngelyd good and fyne[1]
Byfore the swyngylle tre,   *flail*
The thyrde did rele and spynne,
530 Mete and drynke therwyth to wynne,
Gret nede therof hadde he.
Thus the wryght stode herkenyng;   *listening*

_____

[1] *Another beat it with swingles (wooden flails) to separate the fine fibers from the pulp*

	Hys wyfe was ware of hys comyng,	*aware*
	And ageynst hym went sche.	*towards*
535	"Dame," he seyd, "what ys this dynne?	*din*
	I here gret noyse here wythynne;	
	Telle me, so God thee spede."	
	"Syr," sche seyd, "workemen thre	
	Be come to helpe you and me,	
540	Therof we have gret nede;	
	Fayne would I wete what they were."	*Joyfully*
	But when he sawe hys lord there,	
	Hys hert bygan to drede	*fear*
	To see hys lord in that place,	
545	He thought yt was a strange cas,	
	And seyd, "So God hym spede,	
	What do ye here, my lord and knyght?	
	Telle me nowe for Godes myght	
	Howe cam thys unto?"	
550	The knyght seyd, "What ys best rede?	*explanation*
	Mercy I aske for my mysdede,	*misdeed*
	My hert ys wondyr wo."	*very sorrowful*
	"So ys myne, verament,	*truly*
	To se you among thys flex and hempe,	
555	Fulle sore yt ruyth me,	*grieves*
	To se you in such hevynes;	
	Fulle sore myne hert yt doth oppresse,	
	By God in Trinité."	
	The wryght bade hys wyfe lett hym owte,	*Then*
560	"Nay, then sorowe come on my snowte	*countenance*
	If they passe hens todaye	*hence*
	Tylle that my lady come and see	*Until; (the lord's wife)*
	Howe they would have done wyth me,	
	Butt nowe late me saye."	
565	Anon sche sent after the lady bryght	
	For to fett home her lord and knyght,	*fetch*
	Therto sche seyd noght;	
	Sche told her what they hadde ment,	*She (the wright's wife)*
	And of ther purpos and ther intente	
570	That they would have wrought.	
	Glad was that lady of that tydyng;	*message*

75

When sche wyst her lord was lyvyng,   *learned; living*
Therof sche was fulle fayne: *happy*
Whan sche came unto the steyre aboven,
575   Sche lokyd unto the seller downe,
And seyd, (this ys nott to leyne),   *(I am not lying)*
"Good syres, what doo you here?"
"Dame, we by owre mete fulle dere,   *buy*
Wyth gret travayle and peyne;
580   I pray you help that we were owte,
And I wylle swere wythowtyn dowte   *fail*
Never to come here agayne."
The lady spake the wyfe untylle,
And seyd, "Dame, yf yt be youre wylle,
585   What doo thes meyny here?"   *group*
The carpentarys wyfe her answerd sykerly,   *assuredly*
"Alle they would have leyne me by,   *bedded*
Everych in ther manere,   *Each one; own way*
Gold and sylver they me brought,
590   And forsoke yt, and would yt noght,   *[I] rejected; not [take]*
The ryche gyftes so clere.   *precious (glittering)*
Wyllyng they were to do me schame,
I toke ther gyftes wythowtyn blame,
And ther they be alle thre."
595   The lady answerd her anon,
"I have thynges to do att home
Mo than two or thre;
I wyst my lord never do ryght noght
Of nothing that schuld be wrought,
600   Such as fallyth to me."
The lady lawghed and made good game
Whan they came owte alle in-same   *together*
From the swyngylle tre.
The knyght seyd, "Felowys in fere,   *together*
605   I am glad that we be here,
By Godes dere pyté;   *dear pity*
Dame, and ye hadde bene wyth us,   *if you*
Ye would have wrought, by swete Jhesus,   *worked*
As welle as dyd we."
610   And when they cam up aboven

76

They turnyd abowte and lokyd downe,
The lord seyd, "So God save me,
Yet hadde I never such a fytte   *an experience*
As I have hadde in that lowe pytte;
615   So Mary so mutt me spede."
        The knyght and thys lady bryght,
Howe they would home that nyght,
For nothyng they would abyde;
And so they went home;
620   Thys seyd Adam of Cobsam
By the weye as they rode
Throwe a wode in ther playeng,   *forest*
For to here the fowlys syng   *hear; birds*
They hovyd stylle and bode.   *halted; waited*
625   The stuard sware by Godes ore,
And so dyd the proctoure much more,
That never in ther lyfe
Would they no more come in that wonne   *place*
Whan they were onys thens come,   *once had been*
630   Thys forty yere and fyve.
        Of the tresure that they brought
The lady would geve hem ryght noght,   *return nothing*
Butt gave yt to the wryghtes wyfe.
Thus the wryghtes garlond was feyre of hewe,
635   And hys wyfe bothe good and trewe:
Thereof was he fulle blythe;   *happy*
I take wytnes att gret and smalle,   *witness*
Thus trewe bene good women alle
That nowe bene on lyve,   *live now*
640   So come thryste on ther hedys   *[may] spiritual desire (thirst) come upon*
Whan they mombylle on ther bedys   *mumble*
Ther Pater Noster ryve.   *Their Our Father many times (rife)*

        Here ys wretyn a geste of the wryght   *adventure*
That hadde a garlond well i-dyght,
645   The coloure wylle never fade.
Now God that ys hevyn kyng
Graunt us alle hys dere blessyng
Owre hertes for to glade;   *to gladden*

	And alle tho that doo her husbondys ryght,	*those; justice*
650	Pray we to Jhesu fulle of myght,	
	That feyre mott hem byfalle,	*good things must them*
	And that they may come to heven blys,	
	For they dere moderys love therof nott to mys,	*mother's*
	Alle good wyves alle.	
655	Now alle tho that thy tretys hath hard,	*treatise; heard*
	Jhesu graunt hem for her reward	*them; their*
	As trew lovers to be	
	As was the wryght unto hys wyfe	
	And sche to hym duryng her lyfe.	
660	Amen, for charyté.	

	Here endyth the wryghtes processe trewe	*orderly story (pageant)*
	Wyth hys garlond feyre of hewe	
	That never dyd fade the coloure.	
	It was made by the avyse	
665	Of hys wywes moder wytty and wyse	*By; wife's mother*
	Of flourys most of honoure,	
	Of roses whyte that wylle nott fade,	
	Whych flour all Ynglond doth glad	

	Wyth trewloves medelyd in syght;	*trueloves (flower of chastity) mingled*
670	Unto the whych flour iwys	
	The love of God and of the comenys	*commons*
	Subdued bene of ryght.	

Explicit

Select Bibliography and Notes to The Wright's Chaste Wife

Manuscript

Lambeth Palace Library MS 306, fols. 178a–187a (1460s).

Edition

Adam of Cobsam. *The Wright's Chaste Wife*. Ed. Frederick J. Furnivall. EETS o.s. 12. Oxford: Oxford University Press, 1865; rpt 1891, 1905, 1965.

Related Studies

DuVal, John. "*The Wright's Chaste Wife*: A Satiric Fabliau." *Publication of the Missouri Philological Association* 2 (1977), 8–14.

Goodall, Peter. "An Outline History of the English Fabliau after Chaucer." *AUMLA: Journal of the Australasian Universities Language and Literature Association* 57 (May 1982), 5–23.

Hanawalt, Barbara A. "Separation Anxieties in Late Medieval London: Gender in *The Wright's Chaste Wife*." *Medieval Perspectives* 11 (1996), 23–41.

———. *'Of Good and Ill Repute': Gender and Social Control in Medieval England*. Oxford: Oxford University Press, 1998. Pp. 88–103.

Llewellyn, R. H. "*The Wright's Chaste Wife* Disinterred." *Southern Folklore Quarterly* 16 (1952), 251–54.

Notes

Abbreviations: **F**: Frederick J. Furnivall, ed., *The Wright's Chaste Wife*; **MS**: Lambeth Palace Library MS 306, fols. 178a–187a.

Satire and Fabliaux in Verse and Prose

Incipit   *A fable of a wryght that was maryde to a pore wydows dowtre / the whiche wydow*
havyng noo good to geve with her / gave as for a precyous Johelle to hym a Rose
garlond / the whyche she affermyd wold never fade while she kept her wedlok.

1–9   Conventional exhortation to listen also found in Middle English romances and
Breton lays. Such requests remind an audience of the inherent orality of medieval
literary genres as well as the patronage of *my sovereyns* (line 2).

10   *wryght.* This term is usually taken to mean carpenter such as John in Chaucer's
The Miller's Tale or others of more divine ranking including Joseph, elderly
husband of the Virgin Mary, and Jesus himself. However, as John DuVal points
out, "wright" can also signify a working man in the generic sense. "This is the
only name given him in the poem. He is a worker at anything. Although the work
he does in this poem is skilled carpentry and masonry, he does not scorn
peasantry work either" (p. 9):

Or erthely man hadde he no dowte,	*fear*
To werke hows, harowe, nor plowgh,	*pickaxes (hoes), harrow; plow*
Or other werkes, what so they were	*no matter what*
Thous wrought he hem farre and nere.	*them far*
(Lines 14–17)	

Note, however, that in line 586 his wife is referred to as the "carpentarys wyfe."

15   *werke hows.* I have glossed *hows* as pickaxes (hoes), to go with harrowing and
plowing. But the sense of the phrase might also be "build a house," which suits
a wright's skills well, but is less congruent with his other skills.

20   Like Chaucer's carpenter in The Miller's Tale, the wright prefers to wed late in life.

26–27   *As tyme comyth of alle thyng, / So seyth the profesye.* A proverbial expression,
"there is a time for everything," cited also in William Caxton's *Ovyde* in 1480 and
probably comes ultimately from Ecclesiastes 3:1. See Bartlett Jere Whiting, with
the collaboration of Helen Wescott Whiting, *Proverbs, Sentences, and Proverbial
Phrases from English Writings Mainly Before 1500* (Cambridge, MA: The
Belknap Press of Harvard University Press, 1968), T320.

43   *wyfe.* There may be a link between the word "wife" (wife or woman) and weaving
since "to wifeth" or "to weave" in Old English becomes "to wife"; also spinning
was considered a female occupation. The OED defines *wife* as a woman
"formerly in general sense; in later use restricted to a woman of humble rank or

'of low employment,' especially one engaged in the sale of some commodity."
Examples given are "ale-wife," "apple-wife," " fishwife," and "oyster-wife."

52   *garlond*. The garland of roses as a chastity test is rather unusual compared with the extent of the tradition belonging to drinking horns and mantles. See the *New Arthurian Encyclopedia*, ed. Norris J. Lacy (New York: Garland, 1996), pp. 81–83. Nuptial garlands minus the chastity test, however, were an ancient custom carried on in England in the late Middle Ages. In Chaucer's The Second Nun's Tale, both husband and wife receive garlands to signify their spiritual marriage.

55   *roses ryche*. According to George Ferguson's *Signs & Symbols in Christian Art* (New York: Oxford University Press, 1954), the red rose is a symbol of martyrdom while the white rose is a symbol of purity. "St. Ambrose relates how the rose came to have thorns: Before it became one of the flowers of the earth, the rose grew in Paradise without thorns. Only after the fall of man did the rose take on its thorns to remind man of the sins he had committed and his fall from grace; whereas its fragrance and beauty continued to remind him of the splendor of Paradise. It is probably in reference to this legend that the Virgin Mary is called a 'rose without thorns,' because of the tradition that she was exempt from the consequences of original sin. . . . Wreaths of roses worn by angels, saints, or by human souls who have entered into heavenly bliss are indications of heavenly joy" (p. 48).

61   *putry*. The MED defines *putry* as prostitution, lechery, adultery. Chaucer's Parson adds "bawdry":

> What seye we eek of putours that lyven by the horrible synne of putrie, and constreyne wommen to yelden hem a certeyn rente of hire bodily puterie, ye, somtyme of his owene wyf or his child, as doon thise bawdes? (X[I]886)

Putours are pimps, procurers, fornicators (MED).

68   *to layne*. F glosses *layne* as "hide, conceal" (p. 21), the sense being "there's no hiding the fact." The phrase is commonly used as an interjection, comparable to "indeed," "truly." See MED *leinen* v. (c).

71   *And hyld her brydalle dayes thre*. Since marriage was a public event, it would not be unusual to celebrate it over a three-day period.

86   *plaster of Parys*. Sulphate of lime or gypsum which has undergone calcination. The early association of plaster with the city of Paris is described by John Trevisa in his

translation of Ranulph Higden's *Polychronicon*, ed. Churchill Babington, vol. 1, Rolls Series (London, Longman, Green, 1865), p. 271: "Bysides Parys is greet plente of a maner stoon that hatte gypsus and is i-cleped white plaister." Trevisa defines plaster under *De cemento*:

> Cement is lyme, sond, and water ytempred togidre and ymedlid. And such medlyng is most nedeful to ioyne stones togidre and to pergette and to whitelyme walles. In peyntures and colours of walles þe ferste ground and chief to fonge colours is cement, and cleueþ to wete walls, and nameliche if it is plastre [or s]perstone. For as Isider seiþ, þe beste cement ymade of alle stoones is of þe flynt stoone oþer of plastre þat is icalled *gypsum*, þe which stoon schyneþ as it were glas.

See *On the Properties of Things: John Trevisa's Translation of De Propriatatibus Rerum*, vol. II (Oxford: Clarendon Press, 1975), p. 839.

106   *lord lett sende*. The lord is the first of the three — a lord, a steward, and a proctor — to be involved in the test. See F on the numerous analogues to the tale, especially a *Gesta Romanorum* version, where the three knights are equated with "the pride of life, the lust of the eyes, and the lust of the flesh" (p. vii). See also W. A. Clauston's essay on "additional analogues" to the tale that F prints at the end of his edition (pp. 25–39).

109   *Woult thou have thi wyfe*. This brilliantly ambiguous line, to which the wright makes no reply, suggests: 1) the lord's desire (largess?) to accommodate the carpenter; 2) the lord's interest in the carpenter's wife, so characteristic of fabliau settings; 3) an implicit challenge to the wright's dominion, especially after the lord learns the meaning of the "garlond" (line 121). *Have* can mean "be with," "possess," "enjoy"; but it can also mean to cuckold rather than to invite her to be with her husband. The court challenge among men to dominate women by testing their obedience is a common literary trope. Compare the contest between Collatin and Arrons that costs Lucrece her life (in Gower's *Confessio Amatis* 7.4754–5123) or the more benign obedience tests in Shakespeare's *Taming of the Shrew*. It is perhaps this context that allows the lord's wife to be so understanding of the wright's wife when she finds her husband trapped in the wife's cellar. Likewise, she is non-judgmental of her husband, as if to say, "That's just the way men are."

148   *fare*. "A plan of action or demeanor"; but it might also be glossed as "gifts," material goods he has hoped to beguile her with, which she tells him to put aside.

157   *Forty marke*. The symbolic value of "forty" is hinted at here. Symbolic of a period of protection or trial, it recalls the Israelites' ordeal in the wilderness for

forty years, bondage to the Philistines, Moses' sojourn on Mt. Sinai, the duration of the rain at the time of the Flood, and Christ's trial in the desert. The drop into the pit, a rather symbolic fall in itself, measures forty feet.

158   *gold so rede.* MS: *gold rede.* I have added *so* for meter and because of the commonness of the phrase. Red gold is more valuable than yellow gold.

208   *seynt charyté.* Since there is no saint of this name, what is probably being invoked is charity as a theological virtue. Together with faith and hope it forms a triumvirate of virtues to which all Christians were expected to aspire. Spenser makes an allegorical figure of Charity in *The Faerie Queene.*

245   *thrafe.* A bundle of wheat, straw, or, in this case, flax, containing twelve or twenty-four sheaves.

324   *fers.* F adds a final *-e.*

338   *Fulle clere, and nothing thycke.* The lord is proud of how he has done the jobs assigned to him. The thread is clear of particles of hemp and of a consistent thickness, ready for spinning.

373   *The stuard satt alle in a stody.* The steward is amazed that his social superior should not demonstrate courtesy, a means by which social class was imagined to be defined in part, and share his hard-won meal.

469–77 The proctor is more surprised by the chores in which his fellow inmates are engaged than by the fact that he has just been duped into a humiliating position.

503   *rocke.* A distaff "held in the hand from which thread was spun by twirling a ball below" (F, p. 21).

508   *hynde.* F glosses as "natty." The word is apparently a form of *hende*, which has a wide variety of meanings (see MED) from courtly terms such as "noble, gentle, courteous, refined" to more practical senses, such as "valuable, helpful, clever, crafty, well-made, and handy (i.e., available, near at hand)." The latter usages seem more plausible here.

515   The proctor is assigned the spinning, a job done exclusively by women. The beating of the flax or hemp was occasionally done by men.

527   *swyngelyd*. The first of three parts of the preparation of flax for spinning. To swingle is to beat the flax in order to remove the coarse particles still clinging to the fibers. The fibers are then heckled (combed) or scutched and "knocked" (bundled) in preparation for spinning fine linen. The poet places the knocking before the swingling. Perhaps he imagines that the flax is first bundled (knocked) and then beaten (swingled), though that would go against the flailing process which is normally done on a threshing floor.

528   *swyngylle tre*. Made of wood, these implements resemble swords and are used for beating and scraping raw flax or hemp.

560   *snowte*. According to the MED when referring to a human nose, the term is often used derisively. See Chaucer's The Shipman's Tale: "What! Yvel thedam on his monkes snowte" (VII[B²]1595). In *The Wright's Chaste Wife* it is used to describe a facial expression.

593   The wife is not guilty of prostitution because she had no intention of entering into the arrangement. She is not complicit in their intent to commit adultery.

596   *I have thynges to do att home*. The lady is industrious, too; like the chaste wife, she objects to having her work interrupted by her wayward husband.

620   *Thys seyd Adam of Cobsam*. The name is commonly taken to be that of the author.

623–24   The lord and lady's stopping in the woods to listen to the birds suggests a return to natural harmony after the lord's aberrant and humiliating behavior.

631 ff.   Chastity in the sense of fidelity apparently pays. The lady gives all the money to the wright's chaste wife. The definition of chastity in the Middle Ages was ambiguous: it could mean purity from unlawful sexual intercourse, abstinence from all sexual intercourse or ceremonial purity. Here it is used in the sense of unlawful sexual intercourse, though it is not clear whether the marriage between the wright and his wife has been consummated. Conceivably theirs is a "chaste" or "spiritual" marriage which was used by late medieval authorities, according to Dyan Elliott "to designate a union in which the individuals were true to their marriage vows"; they agreed to abstain from sexual relations. See Dyan Elliott, *Spiritual Marriage: Sexual Abstinence in Medieval Wedlock*, p. 4. Chaucer's Cecilia and her husband in The Second Nun's Tale agree to such living arrangements in fiction; Margery Kempe and her husband also negotiate the issue.

84

Ballad of a Tyrannical Husband

Jhesu that arte jentylle, for joye of Thy dame,   *who; gentle; (i.e., Mary)*
As Thu wrought thys wyde worlde, in hevyn is Thi home,   *made*
Save alle thys compeny and sheld them from schame,   *shield*
That wylle lystyn to me and tende to thys game.   *give themselves over*

5   God kepe alle women that to thys towne longe,   *belong*
Maydens, wedows, and wyvys amonge;   *widows; wives*
For moche they ar blamyd and sometyme with wronge,
I take wyttenes of alle folke that herythe thys songe.   *who hear*

Lystyn good serrys, bothe yong and olde,   *Listen [attentively] good sirs*
10   By a good howsbande thys tale shal be tolde;   *husband*
He weddyd a womane that was fayre and bolde,
And hade good inow to wende as they wolde.   *had sufficient [wealth] to go*

She was a good huswyfe, curteys and heynd,   *housewife; clever*
And he was an angry man, and sone wold be tenyd,   *enraged*
15   Chydyn and brawlynge, and farde leyke a feynd,   *Chiding; [he] behaved like*
As they that oftyn wyl be wrothe with ther best frend.   *angry*

Tylle itt befelle uppon a day, shortt talle to make,   *tale*
The goodman wold to the plow, his horse gan he take;
He calyd forthe hys oxsyn, the whyt and the blake,   *oxen*
20   And he seyd, "Dame, dyght our denner betyme, for Godes sake."[1]

The goodman an hys lade to the plow be gone,   *and his young male servant*
The goodwyfe had meche to doo, and servant had she none,   *much*
Many smale chyldern to kepe besyd hyrselfe alone,   *besides*
She dyde mor then sho myght withyn her owne wone.   *than she; dwelling*

---

[1] *"Dame, be sure our dinner is ready on time, for God's sake"*

25	Home com the goodman betyme of the day,	*i.e., when dinner time came*
	To loke that al thing wer acordyng to hes pay,	*his pleasure*
	"Dame," he sed, "is owr dyner dyght?" "Syr," sche sayd, "naye;	*ready*
	How wold yow have me doo mor then I cane?"	

	Than he began to chide and seyd, "Evelle mott thou the!	*may you suffer*
30	I wolde thou shuldes alle day go to plowe with me,	*wish*
	To walke in the clottes that be wette and mere,	*clumps of earth; swampy*
	Than sholdes thou wytt what it were a plowman to bee."	*know*

	Than sware the goodwyff, and thus gane she say,	
	"I have mor to doo then I doo may;	
35	And ye shuld folowe me foly on day,	*If; one full*
	Ye wold be wery of your part, my hede dar I lay."	*weary; head; wager*

	"Wery! yn the devylles nam!" seyd the goodman,	*name*
	"What hast thou to doo, but syttes her at hame?	*sit here at home*
	Thou goyst to thi neybores howse, be on and be one,	*neighbor's house, repeatedly*
40	And syttes ther janglynge with Jake an with John."	*gossiping*

	Than sayd the goodwyffe, "Feyr mot yow faylle!	*fail*
	I have mor to do, who so wyst alle;	*knew*
	Whyn I lye in my bede, my slepe is butt smalle,	*short*
	Yett eyrly in the morneng ye wylle me up calle.	*early*

45	"Whan I lye al nyght wakyng with our cheylde,	*child*
	I ryse up at morow and fynde owr howse wylde;[1]	*in disarray*
	Then I melk owre kene and torne them on the felde.[1]	
	Whyll yow slepe fulle stylle, also Cryst me schelde!	*soundly; protect*

	"Than make I buter ferther on the day;	*later*
50	After make I chese, — thes holde yow a play;	*Next; cheese; sport*
	Then wyll owre cheldren wepe and upemost they,	*weep at the top of their lungs*
	Yett wyll yow blame me for owr good, and any be awey.	*if; misplaced (missing)*

---

[1] *Then I milk our kine (lactating livestock, such as cows, sheep, goats) and turn them out into the field*

Ballad of a Tyrannical Husband

"Whan I have so done, yet ther comys more eene,   *remains more to do*
I geve our chekyns met, or elles they wyl be leyne: *chickens food; scrawny (lean)*
55   Our hennes, our capons, and owr dokkes be-dene.   *all together*
Yet tend I to owr goslyngs that gothe on the grene.   *geese*

"I bake, I brew, yt wyll not elles be welle:
I bete and swyngylle flex, as ever have I heylle: *pound flax; health*
I hekylle the towe, I kave, and I keylle,
60   I toose owlle and card het and spyn het on the wheylle."[1]

"Dame," sed the goodman, "the develle have thy bones!
Thou nedyst not bake nor brew in fortynght past onys;[2]
I sey no good that thou dost within thes wyd wonys,   *spacious dwellings*
But ever thow excusyst thee with grontes and gronys."   *yourself; grunts; groans*

65   "Yefe a pece of lenyn and wolen I make onys a yere,   *If; linen; wool*
For to clothe owreself and owr cheldren in fere;   *together*
Elles we shold go to the market, and by het ful deer, *buy it full dear (pay full price)*
I ame as bessy as I may in every yere.

"Whan I have so donne, I loke on the sonne,   *see the dawn*
70   I ordene met for owr bestes agen that yow come home,   *provide food; before*
And met for owrselfe agen het be none,   *before it is noon*
Yet I have not a feyr word whan that I have done.   *kind*

"Soo I loke to owr good withowt and withyn,   *outside; inside*
That ther be none awey noder mor nor myn,   *nothing missing neither more or less*
75   Glade to ples yow to pay, lest any bate begyn,   *debate (argument)*
And fort to chid thus with me, I feyght yow be in synne."   *think*

Then sed the goodman in a sory tyme,
"Alle thys wold a good howsewyfe do long ar het were prime;   *before; six a.m.*
And sene the good that we have is halfe dele thyn,   *since; your part*
80   Thow shalt laber for thy part as I doo for myne.

---

[1] Lines 59–60: *I comb the pounded but unworked flax, I separate the chaff from the grain, and I stir the pot, / I pull apart wool and card it and spin it on the wheel*

[2] *You need not bake nor brew more than once every fourteen days*

"Therffor, dame, make thee redy, I warne thee, anone,   *soon*
Tomorow with my lade to the plowe thou shalt gone;   *lad*
And I wyl be howsewyfe and kype owr howse at home,
And take my ese as thou hast done, by God and Seint John!"

85   "I graunt," quod the goodwyfe, "as I understonde,
     Tomorowe in the mornyng I wyl be walkande:
     Yet wyll I ryse whyll ye be slepande,   *rise while you are still sleeping*
     And see that alle theng be redy led to your hand."   *laid*

     Soo it past alle fo the morow that het was dayleyght;   *until it*
90   The goodwyffe thoght on her ded and upe she rose ryght: *task*
     "Dame," seid the goodmane, "I swere be Godes myght!
     I wyll fette hom owr bestes, and helpe that the wer deght."   *fetch*

     The goodman to the feeld hyed hym fulle yarne;   *quickly*
     The godwyfe made butter, her dedes war fulle derne,   *secret*
95   She toke agen the butter-melke and put het in the cheryne,   *churn*
     And seid yet of on pynt owr syer shal be to lerne.   *one pint; sire*

     Home come the goodman and toke good kype,   *made an observation*
     How the wyfe had layd her flesche for to stepe: *meat to marinate*
     She sayd, "Sir, al thes day ye ned not to slepe,   *this*
100 Kype wylle owr chelderne and let them not wepe.   *Keep well*

     "Yff yow goo to the kelme malt for to make,   *oven*
     Put smal feyre ondernethe, sir, for Godes sake;   *Make; fire*
     The kelme is lowe and dry, good tend that ye take,   *watch it carefully*
     For and het fastyn on a feyr it wyl be eville to blake.   *if it catch on fire; too burnt*

105 "Her sitt two gese abrode, kype them wylle from woo,   *There*
     And thei may com to good, that wylle weks sorow inow."   *enough*
     "Dame," seid the goodmane, "hy thee to the plowe,
     Teche me no more howsewyfre, for I can inowe."   *know enough*

     Forthe went the goodwyff, curtes and hende,
110 Sche callyd to her lade, and to the plow they wend;   *went*

Ballad of a Tyrannical Husband

They wer bese al day, a fytte here I fynde,   *busy*
And I had dronke ones, ye shalle heyre the best behund.   *And [if]; hear; that follows*

A fytte

Here begenethe a noder fytte, the sothe for to sey. . . .   *another fit (section)*

Select Bibliography and Notes to Ballad of a Tyrannical Husband

Manuscript

Chetham Library MS 8009, fols. 370–372 (c. 1500).

Edition

Wright, Thomas, and James Orchard Halliwell, eds. *Reliquiae Antiquae. Scraps From Ancient Manuscripts, Illustrating Chiefly Early English Literature and the English Language.* 2 vols. London: John Russell Smith, 1845. Vol. 2, pp. 196–99.

Related Studies

Purdie, Rhiannon. "Sexing the Manuscript: The Case for Female Ownership of MS Chetham 8009." *Neophilologus* 82 (1998), 139–48.

Notes

Abbreviations: **MS**: Chetham Library MS 8009, fols. 370–372; **W&H**: Thomas Wright and James Orchard Halliwell.

1–8   The first two stanzas serve as a prologue in defense of women. The exhortation to Christ as the "joy" of his mother is a conventional invocation with a particularly appropriate emphasis on the Virgin Mary. It would certainly appeal to an audience of women as has been suggested for the manuscript in which this narrative is found. See Rhiannon Purdie, "Sexing the Manuscript." Other items found in the manuscript include six of Osbern Bokenham's *Legendys of Hooly Wommen*, lives of saints Katherine, Juliana, and Margaret, Lydgate's "Invocation to St. Anne," "Legend of St. Margaret," and "Fifteen Joys of Our Lady," two Marian lyrics — "A Lamentation of Our Lady," and "A Prayer of Oure Lady" —

both of which feature female speakers, and the romances of *Bevis of Hamptoun*, *Torrent of Portyngale*, and *Ipomadon*.

8   *songe.* MS: *song.*

9   *Lystyn good serrys.* After having made concessions to the much maligned women and those who would find fault and blame, the poet constructs a male audience.

10   *By.* Or about? There seems to be an omniscient speaker here.

17   *befelle.* MS: *befell.* W&H have added final *-e,* no doubt for consistency.

20   *denner.* The noontime meal, when the farm hands come in to eat, as opposed to supper at the end of the day.

21   *The goodman an hys lade.* That the husband has an apprentice/helper while the wife must do all the housework herself is not unusual, since according to Judith M. Bennett, "the husband's work took on primary importance; the wife's work both supplemented and conformed to the demands of the husband's tasks" (*Women in the Medieval English Countryside: Gender & Household in Brigstock Before the Plague* [New York: Oxford University Press, 1987], p. 119). A plowman's job resembled that of a farmer: plowing the fields, sowing seeds, harvesting crops, though the plowman worked for the lord of the manor and rented out his land. Because a plowman did humble work, his occupation was used as a metaphor for the good Christian, the most famous example in Middle English being William Langland's *Piers Plowman.*

       goodman. A synonym for "the head of the household," which does not necessarily define his moral standing. Nathaniel Hawthorne's "Young Goodman Brown" reflects the term's traditional meaning.

22   *goodwyfe.* MS: *goodwyf. Goodwyfe* is a common generic term for a married woman. See *How the Goode Wife Taught Hyr Doughter,* included in this volume.

       she. MS: *se.*

38–40 The husband's assumptions about women's work are part of a masculine ideology that presumed the inferiority of domestic work not necessarily because it was gendered feminine but because it was less strenuous and demanding of physical strength than agricultural chores could be.

43   *smalle*. MS: *small*. W&H have added final *-e*.

45   *cheylde*. Since there are other children mentioned in line 51, this child is probably a nursing infant. It was not uncommon for unweaned children to be taken into the conjugal bed.

50   *play*. Further evidence that the husband does not consider domestic chores "real" work but rather something done for sport.

56   *goslyngs that gothe on the grene*. The green is a common area which all can use. Some might have a goose girl to look after the flock to make sure all get home, but the goodwife, having no servant, has to be in two places at once.

57–60 *I brew . . . spyn het on the wheylle*. It was common for women to brew beer as well as be in charge of the baking. Witness Margery Kempe's failed attempt in her autobiography. Preparation of flax and wool was time-consuming and arduous work done in stages during which time the raw material was progressively refined until the threads could be spun on a wheel by hand. See the dame in *The Wright's Chaste Wife*, who gets help for the multiple tasks through her clever entrapment of men to do her bidding.

58   *heylle*. MS: *heyll*. W&H have added final *-e*.

59   *keylle*. MS: *keyll*. A final *-e* in the preceding line and in lines 57 and 60 determines the need for consistency here.

68   *yere*. W&H have conjectured and added the word.

69   *Whan I have so donne, I loke on the sonne*. The goodwife does all this *before* the sun comes up.

72   *that*. W&H have omitted this word in the line.

81   The husband proposes a role reversal to which the wife acquiesces without hesitation. Perhaps she relishes the change despite the hard labor.

88   *alle*. MS: *all*. W&H have added final -*e* in this line and the next.

That she needs to prepare everything for him before she goes off to plow suggests his unfamiliarity with the tasks at hand.

93   *fulle*. MS: *full*. The word appears with a final -*e* in the next line in the manuscript. W&H have imposed consistency.

112   The balladeer calls for ale before proceeding further — a common and practical convention.

The poem is unfortunately unfinished but leaves an enticing gap for an audience to fill.

A Talk of Ten Wives on Their Husbands' Ware

Leve, lystynes to me   *Friends, listen*
Two wordys or thre,
And herkenes to my songe;   *be attentive*
And I schall tell yow a tale,

5   Howe ten wyffys satt at the nale,   *tavern*
And no man hem amonge.   *no man among them*

"Sen we have no othere songe   *Since*
For to singen us amonge,
Talys lett us tell

10   Of owre hosbondes ware,   *Of our; merchandise*
Wych of hem most worthy are
Today to bere the bell.   *take the prize*

And I schall nowe begyn att myne: *with mine*
I knowe the mett well and fyne,   *measurement*

15   The lenghte of a snayle,   *snail*
And ever he warse is from day to day.   *worse*
To grete God ever I pray
To gyve hym evyle hayle."   *bad fortune*

The secund wyffe sett her nere,   *sat near her*

20   And seyd, "By the Rode, I have a ware   *Cross; member*
That is two so mene: *also; inferior*
I mete hym in the morowe tyde,   *measure (meet with); in the morning*
When he was in his moste pryde,   *greatest glory*
The lenghte of thre bene.   *three beans*

25   "Howe schuld I be served with that?
I wold Gybbe, owre gray catt,
Were cord there on!   *accorded (in union with) him*
By Sayne Peter owte of Rome,

30	I se never a wars lome	*worse instrument*
	Stondyng opon mone."	*Standing ready*
	The third wyff was full woo,	*emphatically upset*
	And seyd that, "I have one of thoo	*those*
	That noghte is at nede;	*worthless is [in time of] need*
	Owre syre breche, when hit is torn,	*sire's breeches*
35	Hys pentyll pepythe owte beforn	*member peeps out*
	Lyke a warbrede:	*parasitic worm (maggot)*
	"Hit growethe all within the here:	*hair*
	Sychon se I never ere,	*Such a one saw; before*
	Stondyng opon schare.	*pubic region*
40	Yett the schrewe is hodles,	*rascal; hoodless*
	And of all thynge goodles!	*useless*
	There Cryste gyve hym care!"	
	The fourth wyfe of the floke	*flock*
	Seyd, "Owre syre fydecoke	*sire's penis*
45	Fayn wold I skyfte:	*Happily; change*
	He is longe, and he is smalle,	
	And yett hathe the fydefalle;	*drooping ailment*
	God gyve hym sory thryfte!	*pitiful vitality (power to grow)*
	"The leste fyngere on my honde	*smallest (least)*
50	Is more than he, whan he dothe stonde:	
	Alasse that I am lorn!	*undone (deprived)*
	Sory mowntyng com thereon!	*mounting*
	He schold a be a womon	*should have been; woman*
	Had he be eere born."	*ever*
55	The fifth wyffe was full fayn	*blithe*
	When sche hard her felowys playn,	*complain*
	And up sche gan stone:	*to rise*
	"Now ye speke of a tarse!	*penis*
	In all the warld is not a warse	*worse*
60	Than hathe my hosbond.	

"Owre syre bradys lyke a dere,   *jerks off (breeds); deer*
He pysses his tarse every yere,   *discharges his semen once a year*
Ryghte as dothe a boke: *buck*
When men speke of archery,   *[As]*
65   He mon stond faste thereby,   *very close*
Or ellys hys schote woll troke."   *shot fall short*

The sixth wyffe hyghte sare;
Sche seyd: "My hosbondys ware
Is of good asyse;   *size*
He is whyte as ony mylke,   *milk*
70   He is softe as ony sylke,   *silk*
Yett sertis he may not ryse.   *surely*

"I lyrke hym up with my hond,   *squeeze*
And pray hum that he woll stond,
And yett he lythe styll.   *lies still*
75   When I se that all is noghte,   *useless*
I thynke mony a thro thoughte;   *angry (courageous/desirous)*
Bot Cryste wote my wyll."

The seventh wyffe sat on the bynch,   *bench*
And sche caste her legge on wrynch,   *crosswise*
80   And bad fyll the wyne: *bade replenish; wine*
"By Seynt Jame of Galys,
In Englond ne in Walys   *Wales*
Is not a wars than myne!   *worse [husband]*

"Whon owre syre comys in,   *When*
85   And lokes after that sory pyne   *pin*
That schuld hengge bytwen his leggis,   *hang; legs*
He is lyke, by the Rode,   *Cross*
A sory laveroke satt on brode   *lark; nest*
Opon two adyll eggis."   *addled eggs*

90   The eighth wyffe was well i-taghte,   *experienced*
And seyd, "Seldom am I saghte,
And so I well may:
When the froste fresys,   *freezes*

97

Owre syris tarse lesys,	*member grows small*
95 And allway gose away.	*i.e., disappears*
When the yeke gynnys to synge,	*cuckoo begins*
Then the schrewe begynnys to sprynge,	*rascal*
Lyke a humbulbe;	*bumblebee*
He cowres upon othere two, —	*cowers; other two (i.e., testicles)*
100 I know not the warse of tho,	*those*
I schrew hem all three!"	*curse them*
The ninth wyffe sett hem nyghe,	*sat near them*
And held a mett up on hyghe	*measure (piece of meat/sausage)*
The lenghte of a fote:	*foot long*
105 "Here is a pyntell of a fayre lenghte,	*penis*
But he berys a sory strenghte, —	*bears*
God may do boote; —	*remedy*
"I bow hym, I bend hym,	
I stroke hym, I wend hym;	*twist*
110 The devell mot hym sterve!	*kill*
Be he hote, be he cold,	
Tho I torn hym twofold,	
Yett he may not serve."	
The tenth wyffe began her tale,	
115 And seyd, "I have on of the smale,	*one*
Was wynnowed away.	
Of all noghtes it is noghte:	*nothings; nothingest*
Sertis, and hit schuld be boghte,	*Clearly; should it be for sale*
He is not worth a nay."	*would not be worth anything*

AMEN

Select Bibliography and Notes to
A Talk of Ten Wives on Their Husbands' Ware

Manuscript

Porkington MS, no. 10 (National Library of Wales at Aberystwyth; now called Brogynton MS II.1), fols. 56v–59v (1453–1500).

Edition

Furnivall, Frederick J., ed. *Jyl of Breyntford's Testament, by Robert Copland, Bokeprynter, The Wyll of the Deuyll and His Last Testament, A Talk of Ten Wives on Their Husband's Ware, A Balade or Two by Chaucer, and Other Short Pieces*. London: Printed for private circulation by Taylor & Co., 1871. Pp. 29–33. [Also contains *The Meaning of Marriage*.]

Notes

Abbreviations: **F**: Frederick J. Furnivall; **MS**: Porkington MS, no. 10, fols. 56v–59v.

The alternate title of the work is "Gossips' Meeting," under which it is listed in the *Manual of the Writings in Middle English 1050–1500*, vol. 5, ed. Albert E. Hartung and J. Burke Severs (New Haven: The Connecticut Academy of Arts and Sciences, 1993), p. 1464.

1   *Leve, lystynes to me.* The exhortation is similar to those found in Middle English romances, though here *leve* signals a deferential mode of address. F takes the flourish or "curl" at the end of certain letters, i.e., *d, g, m, n*, to indicate a final *e*. Indeed, the meter requires the extra stress at the end of many couplets.

8   *For to singen us amonge.* This line is added presumably by F to maintain the six-line stanza.

10   *ware.* Translated to "merchandise," *ware* is a euphemism for male genitalia which effectively imposes a sexual economy on the women's discussion of private matters.

14   *mett.* The poet has fun here and elsewhere with puns on *mett* — here meaning "measurement" but also suggesting "meat." Similarly, in line 22 the sense is "measure" as she "meets" him (i.e., has sex with him).

16   *ever.* MS: *ev.* The scribal flourish that F reads as a final *e*, is also sometimes used as an abbreviation for *er*.

17   *ever.* MS: *ev.*

22   *in the morowe tyde.* Apparently this husband rests up before rising to his glory. See also note to line 14.

25   *Howe schuld I be served with that.* MS: *Howe schule I be sved wt t.* F has effectively filled in abbreviated syllables.

28   *By Sayne Peter owte of Rome.* A common expletive referring to the apostle and first vicar of Christ who was enormously popular in late medieval England.

26   *gray.* MS: *gy.*

       Gybbe. Gybbe is a popular name at the time for cats.

29   *lome.* Usually a club or weapon, as in *Sir Gawain and the Green Knight* (line 2309), where the Green Knight lifts his great weapon; but also a euphemism for penis.

30   *mone.* Of the range of meanings listed in the MED for this word, the most likely possibilities suggest sexual intercourse or preparation for participation in sexual activities. The female critique is all the more scathing when addressed to a fully aroused male.

34   *Owre.* The plural reference to individual husbands has the effect of stereotyping all married men. Like the so-called "royal" we, it unites the group in a collective mentality. It is used again in lines 44, 61, 84, and 94.

39   *schare*. This term derives from the Anglo-Saxon word *scearu* meaning cutting implements such as scissors or plow share but is also understood as the juncture between a man's legs. The verbal form is sometimes used for circumcision. Given the "hodles schrewe" of line 40 perhaps there is some sense of a truncated pin here.

44   *fydecoke*. F glosses this term as "fiddle de-dee," "nonsense," "fiddle-head," and "stupid." But the MED reads the term as a compound: *fid* (peg or plug) and *cock* (penis). See fide-cok (n).

45   *skyfte*. From *sciftan*, the Anglo-Saxon word for "shift" or "change."

58   *tarse*. James Orchard Halliwell, in his *Dictionary of Archaic and Provincial Words, Obsolete Phrases, Proverbs, and Ancient Customs, From the XIV Century* (London: John Russell Smith, 1847; rpt. 1860, 1872, 1924), defines this word in Latin, i.e., *mentula virga*, meaning "virile member" or "rod." The MED simply says "penis."

61   *bradys*. "Jerks off" is perhaps more colloquial than some would prefer, but it gets well at the tone of the wife's derogatory insult. The OED sheds light on the action being performed under a set of definitions for *braid*: 1) to make a sudden jerky movement as to brandish a spear; 2) to draw a sword or a knife; 3) to jerk, snatch, wrench, fling, etc., with a sudden effort; frequently with up, down, out. It could also be a form of *breden*. See MED *breden* v. (3).

66   *troke*. From the Anglo-Saxon *trucian*, meaning "to fail."

96   *yeke*. From the Anglo-Saxon *geac* which refers to a cuckoo, gawk, or simpleton, all of which are referents to humans. F prefers to gloss this as "cuckoo," which, when applied to a person becomes a synonym for cuckoldry, since the cuckoo lays its eggs in other birds' nests. Thus there is a veiled threat in the eighth wife's reflections. The OED cites another meaning which has particular resonance in this poem: "to push out from the nest like a cuckoo." Chaucer uses the lore of the cuckoo bird to fill out his avian hierarchy in *The Parliament of Fowles*. Toward the bottom of the list is "the cukkow ever unkynde" (line 358). In his use of the term "unkynde" Chaucer means "unnatural" in the sense that the cuckoo lays its eggs in the nests of other birds. Later in the same poem, the cuckoo's reputation is impugned by the merlin, a bird higher in status:

"Ye, have the glotoun fild inow his paunche,
Thanne are we wel!" seyde the merlioun;
"Thow mortherere of the heysoge on the braunche
That broughte the forth, thow reufullest glotoun!
Lyve thow soleyn, wormes corupcioun,
For no fors is of lak of thy nature!
Go, lewed be thow whil the world may dure!" (lines 610–16)

The merlin, being a noble bird (raptor), is concerned with lineage and thus feels threatened by the cuckold bird. The popular "Cuckoo Song" of the thirteenth century renders the bird an unstoppable harbinger of the summer solstice, when no one follows ordinary rules: "Sumer is icumen in / . . . murie sing cuccu! / Cuccu! Cuccu! / Wel singes thu cuccu; / Ne swik thu naver nu" (Lines 1–14).

John Lydgate (?), *Prohemy of a Mariage Betwixt an Olde Man and a Yonge Wife, and the Counsail*

Edited by Mary Elizabeth Ellzey and Douglas Moffatt
With revisions by Eve Salisbury

	A philosophre, a good clerk seculer,	*scholar (priest)*
	Had a frend that sumwhat was aged,	
	In such tymes as wyttes wex uncler,	
	Which frend of his was at last encoraged,	
5	By flateres that by plesaunce hym faged,	*flatterers; flattered*
	To have a wif, as happeth oftyn tyme,	
	Where that regneth this fage, this sory cryme.[1]	
	And yet the man wolde his counsel take,	
	Of his trewe frende, the clerk that I of tolde,	
10	Which was ful fayne feithful counsel to make,	*pleased*
	For he was scient, expert, and ful bolde;	*wise*
	And spared nat the man thouh he were olde,	
	For he set not by his wreth a whistel,	*wrath*
	But wrot to hym this esuyng epistel:	*following*
15	Myn olde dere frend, whi aske ye me counsaile	
	If ye shal wedde to plesaunce of your lif?	
	Fayn wolde ye wyte, if it were for availe	
	For you to have a goodly one to wyf, —[2]	
	Yong, fressh, and fair, to stynt al maner strif,	*end*
20	To your semyng, and ye be ronne in age,	*In your judgment, if; getting on*
	Which other men calle bondage and dotage.	

---

[1] *Wherever this flattery rules, this wicked offense*

[2] Lines 15–18: *My old dear friend, why do you ask advice of me / Whether you shall wed in order to have joy in your life? / Eagerly would you learn, if it were an advantage / For you to have a goodly one to wife*

	Take good leyser or thou have mariage.	*before*
	Be avised on Justynes counsail,	
	The long cart offte hath hevy cariage.	*The big wagon often has [the] heavy load*
25	War Placebo, leave hym for thine avail.	*Beware*
	After the knot it helpeth nat to bewail,	
	Thanne is to late to sey, "If I had wiste";	*known*
	Thynk on the end thouh never so much thee liste.	*though it pleases you little*

	Remembre wele on olde January,	
30	Which mayster Chauuceres ful seriously descryveth,	*Chaucer*
	And on fressh May, and how Justyne did vary	
	Fro Placebo, but yet the olde man wyveth:	
	Thus sone he wexeth blynde, and than outhryveth	*departed*
	Fro wordly joye, for he sued bad doctryne;	*worldly; followed*
35	Thenk on Damyan, Pluto, and Proserpyne.	

	Thenk wisely thus, "I have but yeres fewe,	
	And feble I am, and febler shal bee.	
	If it me happe be coupled to a shrewe,	
	My dayes are done; I may not flyt ne flee.	*escape*
40	To shorte my lif and make bonde that was free,	*enslave*
	Become prentise and newe to go to scole,	*apprentice*
	Why shulde I so than were I but a fole?"	*unless I were; fool*

	Thou seist to me that she is ful demure,	
	And for thi luf dothe moorne, weep, and sihe;	*sigh*
45	I say an hauke cometh oftyn unto lure,	
	Whan that a kyte at al wol not come nyghe;	
	A curre berketh and fleeth for he is slighe,	*cur barks; sly*
	The tauht grehound may sone be ledde away,	*tightly bound*
	Weping is wayt vengeable, this no nay.[1]	

50	Thou answerist me, thou maist none other do;	*do nothing else*
	I sey to thee, thou myhtest if thou wolde;	
	Thou seist ageyn, constreyned I am therto;	
	And I sey efte, that many a coke is colde	*cock*

---

[1] *[Her] weeping is a wicked trap, no doubt about it*

Which is aged; and many a cok is olde
55   On the dungehil, and maynteneth al his flokke,
But alle oure eyren comen of the yong cokke.   *eggs*

Thou seist me thus, "Now in my tyme of age,
I am feble, and need good help to have,
To keep my good." I sey, "Thou seist dotage."   *possessions; a foolish word*
60   Seest thou not ofte a wedowe wed a knave;   *young servant*
And that the good man hadde, that shal he have
At least, the yong that can hym well bestere;[1]
Thus may thi man at thi pelouh appere.   *servant; pillow appear*

Is ther no man that thou may on truste
65   To keep thi good? Is no man trewe at al?
Ful ofte a wif is a broken poste,
And he that leneth may lihtly cache a fal: *easily*
One prively she loveth in especial;
Whan the man deieth, ful often tyme is seen,
70   Riht sone aftyr, ho before loved hath been.   *who*

Bethenk on this, the fal of thi colour;   *fading*
Thy skyn sumtyme was ful, now is it slakke;   *flaccid*
For eyen and nose thee nedeth a mokadour   *a type of handkerchief*
Or sudary; now coorbed is thi bakke,   *face towel; stooped*
75   Or sone shal bene, as pedeler to his pakke;
Thi chekes hangen, thyn eyen wax read as wyne,
And wel belyned with good read tartaryne.[2]

Thy mone-pynnes bene lyche old yvory: *teeth*
Here are stumpes feble and her are none,
80   Holes and gappes ther are inowe; for why   *enough; therefore*
The harpe discordeth, for the pynnes are gone;   *tuning pegs*
Two and thretty made of ful myhti bone,

---

[1] Lines 61–62: *And that which the good man (the old husband) had, he (the knave) shall have it / At last, the young [one] who can well bestir himself (is energetic)*

[2] *And well lined with good red silk (thread), i.e., bloodshot*

105

Which thou had erst, telle weel and see what faileth,   *before, count; is missing*
And loke aboute to wive if it availleth.   *affords help*

85   Loke sone after a potent and spectacle;   *crutch; eye glass*
Be not ashamed to take hem to thyn ease,
And than to wyving be thou nat racle.   *not hasty*
Bewar of hast thouh she behest to please,   *haste though; promise*
For whil she leveth thou lyvest but in disease,   *remains; discomfort*
90   And casteth one to chese to hir delite,   *[she] plots*
That may better astaunche hir appetite.   *satisfy*

And where thou seist thou hast a stomak colde,
Therfore thou must have one to lig thertoo,   *lay*
For to be sekyr, not to be cokolde,   *certain*
95   Hete thi pelow, this counsel I thee to doo,   *Heat*
And no juvencle; for if thou say thus, "Loo,   *young woman; whereas*
Yong womman may do more than fyere heet,"   *fiery*
She thynketh thi colde for hir is nothing meet.   *fitting*

Thou tellest me ofte that thouh thou aged be,
100   Thou hast gret lust and that thou felest wele.   *capable*
Abated sone may it be, telle I thee,
Sone hast thou done, it is not worth a dele: *much*
Ful esily thou may thi corage kele.   *desire cool*
Be nat to hasty to venge thee on thi foo,
105   Rise up, go walk, and than is al agoo.   *gone (dispersed)*

Thou seist thou haddyst in yong age wantounesse,
Therfore in olde age thee nedith have trewe spousaill.   *wedlock*
Canst thou no better come to holynesse,
Than lese thiself al for a tikeltayll?   *lose; loose woman*
110   Ful wery wil she be for hir avayll,   *attentive; advantage*
For lust and good, if summe better can pay,   *possessions*
Whereby she bideth thi passage every day.   *awaits; death*

War the siknesse that called is the pank,
A terme of court for the tide bitte no man,[1]
115   A maladie called "male de flank,"   *a pain in the groin or abdomen*
A bocche that nedeth a good cirurgian;   *swelling; surgeon*
And but he be, she wol have men that can,[2]
That hath the crafte and the kunnyng pure,   *Who*
To make a parfytt and a redy cure.

120   Thou tolde me, frende, I herd it of thiself,
That thou kneuhest one, nameles of me as nowh,   *knew; now*
Unsatisfied a day in tymes twelf,   *months*
Whan twelve plowmen ered at the plowh.   *plowed*
She had sikenesse, I wot not where nen houh,   *know; nor*
125   But thou calledest it the fevere of the crevil,   *itch*
Nyne tyme a nyhte she had the wicked evyl.

Put nat the wyte of this tale upon me,   *blame*
That I forged it upon my hed,   *imagined it in*
For I herd it first of al of thee,
130   And than of othere ful ofte in many a steed.   *place*
Many an *Ave*, and many an hooly beed,   *Ave Maria; prayer*
Myht thou say, and praye for them may,   *pray by means of*
If thou myht wynne so fair a weddyng day.

Thi lusty leapes of thi coragious age,   *desirous*
135   Thei are agoo, thi rennyng and thi trippes,   *capers (skips)*
In thi forehed fele Fridayes, this no fage,[3]
Farwele the rudde that was upon thi lippes;   *ruddiness*
Unweldy wol thei be, both knees and hippes,
Fele wel thyself, and parceyve every dele,   *part*
140   For wommans eye al this parceyveth well.

---

[1] Lines 113–14: *Beware the illness called the pank [? a fabricated ailment to cover sexual desire]. / [Beware] a term of court (i.e., when you are away attending to your legal affairs), for the tide (i.e., time) waits for no man*

[2] *Unless he (i.e., the husband) is [a good "surgeon"], the wife will find a man who is able [?knows]*

[3] *On your forehead [the marks (i.e., wrinkles)] of many Fridays (i.e., days of fasting and penance) [appear], this is no lie*

Thei can ful wele aspye in every syde,
He bereth a name of godes and richesse;   *He [who]*
Thouh she be yong, yet wol she wele abide
Uncoupled to a fressh man of junesse   *Unattached; youth*
145   And take a buffard riche of gret vilesse,   *stupid buffoon; old age*
In hope that he shal sterve withynne a while,   *die*
After to have a yong one al by gyle.   *through [her] cleverness*

Than is ther crafte, whan she begynne to feyne
As thowh she loved the olde man al of herte.
150   Halseth and kisseth and wol him not with-seyne,   *Hugs; contradict*
But flatereth fast that goode now nat asterte   *possessions; escape*
But she have al; than thouh he be nat querte,   *Until; then; healthy*
But turn up too and caste his clook away: *turn up [his] toes*
That is to sey, she careth nat thouh he dey.   *die*

155   She wol thee chastise, if thou love honesté,
Voydyng slaundre, wyte thee of gelousye;[1]
Doute nat than but rebuked shalt thou be,
She wol make men wonder on thi bodye;
Liche confessoures thei wil rown pryvelye[2]
160   With other men, as it were gret counsail,
Long and often; war than the countertaile.[3]

Wenest thou nat ther wol be mekil stryve   *Do you not expect; great*
Who shal have maistrie and the sovereynté?
By trewe conquest, betwix thee and thi wife,
165   Who shal prevail? Forsothe it wol be she!
Elles pease and rest out of thine hous shal fle,
And mydnythe, matynes, evensong, prime, and houres,
She wol thee syng and weep, sharp are thoo shoures!   *those showers*

---

[1] Lines 155–56: *She will chastise you, if you love honesty / Avoiding slander [thereby], [and] accuse you of jealousy*

[2] *Like priests who hear confession, they will whisper secretly*

[3] *Beware then the part of the tally stick kept by the creditor (i.e., beware the debt you incur with marriage)*

	And yet summe wyves wol fallen to consent	*incline*
170	Men to be maistres, so wommen have her will;	*as long as; their*
	That must nede be, or elles harm shal be hent.	*suffered*
	The husband must his wyves wille fulfill;	*wife's desire*
	And whoso geveth counsel but not thertille,	*thereto*
	She maketh hym werer, for sume haten ful sore	*wary*
175	Such as ther husbondes loven and no man more.[1]	

	Ther was a wife that seven husbandes hadde,	
	And for six she wepte nat whan thei deied;	
	But for the sevent she wept and was ful sadde,	
	Wherefore hir neighbures merveyled, and hir preied	
180	To telle the cause, and thus to hem she seied, —	
	"I may wele weep and cause I have therto	
	To care and moorne, with me standeth so:	*[it] stands so with me*

	"Of six husbandes whan thei were on bere,	*bier*
	Was never none that passed unto grave,	
185	But I was purveied, whil he lyved here,	*provided*
	Of a newe one; but now, so God me save!	
	I am onpurveyed, and wot never whom to have;	*unprovided [for]; know*
	Thus must I moorne, for I am destitute,	
	For now no man to me maketh ony sute!"	

190	Lo! lo! my frend, take tent to this womman	*give a thought to*
	That sex tymes had such purveyaunce	*provision*
	Siker betymes, as many of them can,	*Certainly early enough*
	And namely in this case of chevysaunce.	*provision (arrangement)*
	Make thou no doute but thou may leed the daunce	
195	Of Makabre, and the menewhile thi wife	*Death*
	Is syker of such as she loved in thi life.	*accrued*

	She wol perhappous maken hir avowe	*make a solemn promise*
	That she wol take the mantle and the ryng	

---

[1] Lines 173–75: *And whoever gives counsel [to the husband] contrary thereto (i.e., to the wife's will), / She makes him (i.e., that counselor) anxious, because some [wives] sorely hate / Those whom their husbands love, and no man more so*

Whil thou levest, whan she knoweth wel ynowe,   *remain; enough*
200 Thou shalt be dede and have thi buryeng;
But yet she taketh the man and eek the thynge,   *nevertheless; possessions*
And hir husband disceyveth — allas! meschaunce! —
Til she be siker of goode to hir pleasaunce.   *possessions*

Thi wif wol be ful wyly, douht it nouhte,
205 She loketh aboute whil thou lyvest here
Where hir acquytaunce is; it shal be souhte,   *acquittance (satisfaction); sought*
Most goodly persone, most leve and dere,   *esteemed*
That hir best liketh; and whan thou art on bere,   *pleases her most; bier*
She thynketh wel that one is yet alyve
210 That she mowe truste wol have hir unto wyve.   *may*

Thus is she redy, whanever it shal befall,
Ther is hir mynde til mariage be made.
Par case thi men in mynde she kepeth hem all.   *Perchance*
Perhappous one is loved that wol not fade;   *weaken*
215 She cherissheth hym, to hym hir hert is glade.   *encourages*
He bideth, she bideth, at last the knot is knyt,   *waits*
Thei have thi good; lewde man, wher is thi wytte?   *foolish*

Puraventure thou hatest thi servaunt,   *Perhaps*
Puraventure thi wife she loveth hym best,
220 Puraventure with good she wol hym daunt.   *subdue*
And meryly he shal slepe in thy nest;
Whan thou art dead, in thi bed shal he rest;
And he and she shal have lond, fee, and foode:
Avaunt, rebel, of thy sore goten goode!   *Begone; evil*

225 He is a persone, she thynketh, of fair figure, —
A yong rotour, redy to hir pleasier;   *one who plays the rote*
Hyr eyen she fyxeth on hym, this is ful sure,
And lokketh hym in hir herte hoote as fier, —   *locks*
And seeth the olde, hir colde and cowherand syer;   *boils; cowering sire*
230 Thou gost thi ways into a fer cuntré,
Thi lewde servaunt thi successour shal be.

110

She wol ordeyn by menes ful dyvers,
That the kyng, or som gret lord, shal wryte
To hir lettres, hir hert ful sore to pers,   *pierce*
235   Coriously and craftly to endyte   *write*
For hym, to whom was hir appetite
Beforn goven, peraventure, many a day,   *given*
Askauns she may nat to the lettres sey nay.   *Pretending that*

This is the wyle of the womman wyly,
240   For she wol have hir wille at al hir lust;
Thou wenest wel but she is ful gyly, —   *expect; guileful*
Thou art deceyved whanne thou best gynnest to trust;
Thou thynkest hir pollisshed whan she is ful of rust.
Whil thou art here in hert she cherissheth other,
245   As thouhe it were hir cosyn or hir brother.

But be wel ware of feyned cosynage,
And gossiprede, and myght of mayntenaunce,[1]
And lordes lettres, and ravisshing, and rage,   *forcible abduction; horseplay*
For these are coloures and menes of myschaunce,   *tricks; trouble*
250   Wherby thi wife shal have to hir pleasaunce
One or other, such as she list to have   *desires*
In dyverse wise, whan thou art gone to grave.

To make herof a confirmacioun,
Lo! here a tale, and prynte it in thi mynde,   *hear; imprint*
255   Of a riche man who, by commoun relacioun,
Had gret power and myhte, both lose and bynde,[2]
In his cuntree; yet, after cours of kynde,   *nature*
He was aged, and drouhe unto dotage,   *grew old; drew*
As olde men done that drawe to mariage.   *move toward*

---

[1] Lines 246–47: *But be very wary of supposed cousins, / Or god-relations, or the maintenance of retainers*

[2] Lines 255–56: *Of a rich man who, according to everyone, / Had great power and might, both [to] loosen and [to] bind [others in servitude]*

260	At last ther was one aspied oute,	*spied*
	Goodly of port, that had experience	*appearance*
	Wel of the world, that semed ful devoute,	
	Humble, sobre, nortured with reverence, —	
	A fair womman, save that indigence	*except that [of] poverty*
265	She was sumdele; that is for to say,	*somewhat*
	She was nat riche and she was nat to gay.	

	This man was called Decembre of name,	
	And gan to feble moch as age it wolde,	*began to become feeble much as age requires*
	But the woman kept hir out of blame	*And; disgrace*
270	Ful wilyly, riht lusty, and not olde;	
	Hir name was July, hardly she was not colde	*indeed*
	By cause of age, and feat was hir array,	*comely*
	And after good she longed nyht and day.	

	He had knowlage of hir bi his espyes,	*spies*
275	And gat leiser to se hir prevylye,	*privately*
	And spak with hir ynowh onys or twyes,	*enough once; twice*
	And askid hir if she myht feithfullie	
	Luf hym of herte, and morover, fynallye	
	Become his wife, by spousayle fortunate,	
280	Notwithstandyng his richesse and estate.	

	And with that worde she fel ful humbely
	Unto the grounde, and seid, "Wold God of myht
	I had be born, by influence hevenly,
	So fortunate, that I myht of riht
285	Do trewe servyce, as ancille ever in siht
	Unto hir lord, and spare for non age,
	Which was never apt to such a mariage!¹

---

¹ Lines 282–87: *Onto the ground, and said, "Would [to] God of might / [That] I had been born, by heavenly influence, / So fortunate, that I might justly / Do true service, as a female handmaiden ever in sight / Unto her [watchful] lord, and never refrain regardless of age, / [I] who was never [thought] apt (appropriate) to such a marriage [as you propose]"*

"For to be coupled to so hih astate
I am unable, I am not apt thereto   *unworthy*
290   So to presume, but that erly and late   *always*
It sitteth me wele in other wise to do;   *It becomes me well*
That if ye had a wife, yf it were so,
That gelousye wold not me disdeyne,   *Who would not scorn me because of jealousy*
I wolde hir serve and you and hir obeyne."   *obey*

295   Whan this was seide, his hert began to melt,
For veray sweme of this swemeful tale;   *sorrow; piteous*
Aboute his hert he thoughte he gan to swelt,   *grow faint*
So loved he hir, he wex bothe colde and pale;
And from his eyen the terys fel cleere and smale,
300   As aged men wol lightly weep for routhe,   *easily; pity*
And seid, "My luf, gramercy, up my trouthe,

"Save for thre thinges that I am gylty inne,
Shulde never erdely thyng maw make me lette,   *earthly; be able to; forbear*
But that I wolde our mariage begynne,
305   Which thre thynges have me aside so sette
Fro al spousail with whech never yet I mette,
So that as yet alle wedlok I denye,   *do without*
For which thre thynges I can no remedye."   *know*

"No remedy," quod she, "God it forbede,
310   That were mervail and a wonder thyng;
Unto a sore with salve men must take hede,   *take care*
And for sikenesse men medycyne must bryng.
I praye you, lorde, yf it be your likyng,
Telle me alle thre, and a confortatif   *medicine*
315   And remedye I shal make, up my lif."   *upon*

And with this worde he wex glad in his hert,
And wex mery and bolde to telle alle oute,
As Sampson did, whil he was hole and quert,   *healthy*
When Dalida compassed hym aboute,
320   That Philistees ran in upon a route,   *[So] that; crowd*
And for al strengthe that Gad gaf hym before,   *gave*
Thei hym captived, whereby he was y-lore.   *lost*

113

This man for trust of femynyne promysse
Wolde telle out alle, in semblable wise,   *in the same manner*
325   "Forsothe," quod he, "two thynges ther been amysse
That I wol telle, bene of a sory syse: *[that] be of a sorry kind*
I am sone wroth and angry, this my guyse;   *quickly wrathful; nature*
The secund is ful wroth withoutyn cause.
These tweyne foul thynges are closid in a clause."   *brief statement*

330   Quod she, "Good lorde, can ye no remedye   *know*
For these two poyntes, that bene easy and smale?
In good feith, sire, I cane ful sone aspye
Salve for such sores; she is a feble female,
That lakketh such read; good lorde, telle on your tale   *council*
335   Of your thrid poynt, myn herte mery to make,
And up my soule I shal al undirtake."   *upon*

"The thridde," quod he, "nay, I may not for shame."
"Why, sir," quod she, "seith on, upon my life."
"Forsothe," quod he, "as touchynge chambre game,
340   It were ful hard for me to have a wife;
But I were able, we shuld ever stond in strife,   *Unless*
And wel I wote that I am impotent.   *But*
Thus must I nedes, allas! be contynent."   *chaste*

And with that worde she cauht hym in hir armes
345   And halsed hym and kissed hym ful swete;   *embraced*
Lo! suche bene the wyly wommens charmes,
And with his berde he frusshed hir mouthe unmete.   *rubbed; exceedingly*
Thus sone agen she fel doun at his fete,   *again*
And seide, "Dere lorde, this is the laste of alle
350   Your seid thre poyntes, that miht hereaftyr falle?"   *hereafter occur*

"Ya," quod he. "Ya, syr, upon my feith,"
Quod she, "drede nat; I undertake these thre;   *take up*
 Chiefly of alle for the thrid poynt," she seith,
"I make warant, for ful onwise is she   *guarantee; unwise*
355   That cannot counsel in such juparté.   *difficulty*
 Myn own dere lorde, take me unto your grace,
To stande in favoure of your weel-favoured face."

114

"Now than," quod he, "in this condicion,
To you, dere herte, my veray trouth I pliht   *pledge*
360   As to my spouse." And, withoute more sermone,   *speech*
Thei drouhe handes, as wedding asketh of riht;   *clasped*
What shuld I lenger tary? Soone was diht   *accomplished*
Al that wedlok asketh and spowsayles,   *wedding festivities*
Al was redy to plesaunt apparailes.   *preparations*

365   The day was comen of the solempnyté;
What shulde I speke of the feest and array?
It were to gret a laboure unto me,
And my paper it conteyne ne may;   *document (writing page)*
But that at laste forth passed was the day,
370   And nyht cam on, and ech man took his leve,
And unto bed them must whan it was eve.

The worthi man, as it cam hym of age,   *being old*
He toke a slepe; al nyhte he was in rest   *went to sleep*
With wery bones, but his wife of corage   *sexual desire*
375   Wolde have be fed, as brid in the nest.
She het his bak, to halse hym thouht hir best,   *hit; embrace*
But al for nouht was al hir contenaunce,   *action*
The man was of a gentle governaunce.   *self-discipline*

And a man of sadde religioun,
380   He kept the nyhte in peas and silence;
He brak no covenaunt nen condicioun,   *nor*
That he with hir made first by his prudence,
But sobrely he kept his contynence.   *chastity*
I dare wel sey ther was no speke y-broke,   *word spoken*
385   Nor wrestelyng wherby he was y-wroke.   *avenged*

But also pleyn was his bedde at the morwe   *as undisturbed*
As at even, so was he nortured wele,   *disciplined*
But the womman was woo, I dare be borwe,   *saved*
For cherisshyng was withdrawe every dele;   *wholly*
390   She was hungry and wold have had hir mele,
As appetyt ran on in hir corage,
For she smelled flesshe, thouhe it was of age.

115

	Whan it was day and liht the chambre spradde,	*light; spread throughout*
	She hir bethouht and seide, "Good syr, awake."	
395	She rogged on hym, and was nothyng adradde,	*pulled*
	And badde hym turne hym for his wives sake.	
	"What, syr," quod she, "wol ye no merthes make	
	Of cherisshyng, as other men doon alle,	
	When such neightes of mariage befalle?"	

	He turned hym and herd al hir entente,	
400	Merveillyng that she such mater meved.	*mentioned*
	Not disposed to ony turnemente,	*tournament*
	He was agast, and in hert was agreved.	
	"What, wife!" quod he, "I wend I had beleved	
405	And myht have trusted to your thre remedyes	
	And trewe covenaunt, withoute flateryes."	*agreement; deceptions*

	"Flateries!" quod she, "Nay, syr, not soo,	
	It is of ernest that I to you seid;	
	I wol you tell, or that ye ferther goo,	*before*
410	Al that I mente, I am nothing dismayd.	*perturbed*
	I have you nat begyled nen betrayd.	
	As to your poyntes thre, thynges spoken in fere,	*together*
	I shal rehersen pleynly myne answere.	

	"Ye seide to me that ye wolde sone be wroth,	
415	I seide ageyn I cowde a remedye;	*knew*
	That is to sey, be ye never so loth,	*displeasing*
	I wol myself be moch more angrye;	
	Sette one agens anothre hardilye,	
	And se aboute of that that may you greve,	
420	For I gef nat of al that wreth may meve.[1]	

	"And where ye sey ye wol be wroth also	
	Withouten cause, hardily it shal not nede.	*it shall not be necessary*
	Ye shal have cause ynouh where so ye go,	*enough*

---

[1] Lines 419–20: *And look about for that which may grieve you, / Because I could not care less what [your] anger might cause [you to do]*

In thouht and worde ye shal not faile indede!   *lack*
425   How long agoo lerned ye, Crist crosse me spede!   *save*
Have ye no more lernyd of youre a b c?
Whan that ye list ye shal have cause plenté.   *listen*

"To the thrid poynt of which ye gan to meve,
That was grettest to your jugement,
430   And me thouht it, if ye wol me beleve,
It the leste of alle that were y-ment;   *referred to*
Of chambre werk we carped of assent,   *spoke of mutual agreement*
And wel ye wote by holy chirches lawe,
Dette must be payd by oth, soth is this sawe.

435   "But good fayre sir, God hath you endued   *provided*
With gret richesse, silver, gold, and fee,   *movable property*
That if payment of dette be so remewed   *relieved*
For noun power that it wol not be,   *destitution*
Ye may, by godes of your prosperyté,
440   Hire one that may fulfille al that in dede;
Thus shal we never lak help at al oure nede.

"Was this your wytte?" quod the cely man,   *foolish*
"Ya, sir," quod she, "these oure remedies,
Now also mot I thryve." And the saide he than,   *as I may prosper*
445   "I cannat se, for alle wittes and espies,   *[my] powers of observation*
And craft and kunnyng, but that the male so wryes,   *the thing turns out*
That no kunnyng may prevail and appere   *do harm*
Agens a wommans wytt and hir aunswere."

"Allas," quod he, "this is an insolible;   *dilemma*
450   If I strogel, slaundred shal I be;   *disagree*
To satisfye it is but impossible:
It may not be parformed as for me.
What eyled me, lord, maryed for to be,
Or for to trust to promysse femynyne,
455   Sith not is golde al that as golde doth shyne.

"Appeles and peres that semen very gode,
Ful ofte tyme are roten by the core.

117

I myht be ware, if I hadde not be wode,   *have been mindful; crazed*
Of Adam, Sampson, and other me before;
460   Davyd, Salamon, in liche wyse were y-lore;   *a similar way; lost*
Eve, Dalida, beauteous Bersabé,   *Bathsheba*
And concubynes, they myht have warned me.

"But now ther is no more to saye,
I se Dame July must nedes haf hir wille!
465   If I dissente, and if I make affray,   *trouble*
I have the wers, thouhe I have rihte and skylle;
I must hir wille agens my wylle fulfille,
Evyr leve in shame, and that is al my woo,
Farewele, fortune, my joye is al agoo!"   *gone*

470   Nowe is this tale done, and brouhte to ende,
Of Januaries brother, and olde Decembre,
And of Dame July; wherefore, myn olde dere frende,
This counseil I, that ye you wol remembre,
That if ye mowe chastise your carnal membre.   *may discipline*
475   For to leve soul and keep you contynent,   *remain alone; chaste*
Ne weddeth not at al be myn assent.   *would be my opinion*

And as for yssu and heyres to youre goode,   *issue; heirs; possessions*
Ther are ynowe, thouh ye have none at alle,   *enough*
Selle youre godes for coigne that is to goode,   *coin*
480   Do almesse dedes where nede is speciall;
And elles, my frende, sey who is he that shall
Make you yssu and begete you an heyr,
That ye your lif ne shorte nen yt appeyr?   *nor make worse*

And he that may not keep hym contynent,   *chaste*
485   As seith Seynt Poule, lat hym wedded be;
For better is rather than to be brent
To be wedded. But, frend, I trowe that ye
Have no more nede to such fragilité
In this youre age, if ye wel discerne,
490   Than hath a blynde man of a briht lanterne.

And ever thynk wel on this proverb trewe,
Remembring on age by ony weye,
That veray dotage in olde age wol thee sewe,   *follow*
That the first yere wedlokk is called pleye,
495   The second, dreye, and the thrid yere, deye.   *trouble; death*
This is a mery lif to have amonge;   *continually*
It is ful fayre, if ye abide so longe.

This is the ende of trewe relacioun: *purpose; account*
If thou wol wedde, and so be sette amys,   *amiss*
500   If thou therto have gret temptacioun,
Lifte up thyn handes, and with thi fingres blysse
And praye to God, that thou mut thenk on this   *be allowed*
Litel lessoun, and keepe it in thi mynde,
And hardly it shal away as wynde.   *scarcely it shall disappear*

L'envoye

505   Go, pety quaier, and war where thou appere,   *little book; beware*
In aunter that thou tourne unto displesaunce   *In case*
Of joly bodies, that labouren fer and neer
To bryng olde men to her mortal myschaunce   *their*
To that entente: that after variaunce   *purpose; change*
510   Fro lif to deth, withinne a litle stounde,   *short time*
By sotyl crafte, a morsel or pitaunce,
A rustiler shal sone be redy founde.   *a little bit*

Thy wordes, quayer, ar trewe, this no dowte,   *book*
Wherbi wise men, if thei wol, may be ware
515   And for popholy and vyce loke wel aboute,   *both for hypocrisy (pope holy)*
That rybaudy wol calle thi wordes bare.   *ribaldry; plain*
Laboure thiself for to kepe out of snare
Cely dotardes, lat this be thyne entent;   *Foolish*
Farewel and worcke as ferforthe as thou dare,   *far*
520   That life and godes take none abreggement.   *lessening*

Explicit

119

Select Bibliography and Notes to John Lydgate (?), *Prohemy of a Mariage Betwixt an Olde Man and a Yonge Wife, and the Counsail*

[The initial editing of this poem was done by Mary Elizabeth Ellzey and Douglas Moffatt.]

Manuscript

British Library MS Harley 372, fols. 45a–51a (1440–60).

Editions

Halliwell, James Orchard. *A Selection from the Minor Poems of Dan John Lydgate*. London: Printed for the Percy Society by C. Richards, 1840. Pp. 27–46. [Under the title *Advice to an Old Gentleman Who Wished for a Young Wife*. The work was first printed by Caxton as *The Complainte of Them That Ben To Late Maryed*.]

Notes

Abbreviations: **MS**: British Library MS Harley 372, fols. 45a–51a; **Ha**: Halliwell.

Incipit   The title appears in the upper right margin of the MS, separated from the body of the text.

1   *philosophre*. Here *philosophre* probably means "scholar, learned man; wise man" rather than anything more specific.

           clerk seculer. The term probably refers to a priest who has not taken vows of a religious order or rule: "secular" as opposed to "regular," from Latin *regula* "rule."

3   *such*. Ha adds final *-e*.

23–35   All the major characters of Chaucer's The Merchant's Tale are mentioned in these lines: Justinius, Placebo, January, May, Damian, Pluto, and Proserpina.

24   *The long cart offte hath hevy cariage.* The meaning of this proverb is not transparent. It probably refers here to the heavy responsibility of marriage since it was imagined to last a lifetime. *Cariage* is defined in Whiting as "burden." See C55.

30   There seems to be something missing from this line. *Descryveth* is demanded by the rhyme, but the apparent subject, *Chauuceres*, is genitive. However, to add a word like book, tale, or Merchant would seem to make the line overlong. Perhaps the adjective *mayster*, so commonly appended to Chaucer's name in the fifteenth century, was a later insertion that led to the subsequent omission of the verb's original subject.

43–49   This is a difficult series of analogies. Here is one interpretation. The first two lines describe the woman playing the stereotypical beloved; the last line states that her behavior is really a means of entrapment and does not represent her true nature. The philosopher states that beasts of ignoble stature (kite and cur) are wary of entrapment while noble beasts (hawk and greyhound) are easily caught. The old friend would be inclined to align himself with the noble beasts particularly as a lover; he would tend to think of himself as a hawk rather than a kite. The philosopher shows his old friend the consequence of following his noble nature in this case: captivity, i.e., marriage. The philosopher is attempting to undermine the romantic love games that the old man wants to play and, according to the philosopher, the young girl can play only too well.

53–56   The philosopher is fond of puns. What is being said is that many an old rooster appears to be in charge of his flock, but in fact the hens are being served by younger cocks. What is more, the eggs (and chicks) are the young cock's progeny, not the old rooster's.

67   *cache.* MS: *cachche.* Ha: *cache.*

80   *inowe.* Ha: *I nowe.*

91   *astaunche.* The MED has only this example for *astaunchen* meaning "satisfy (sexual desire)." The more common *staunchen* frequently means "satisfy (hunger, thirst, greed, etc.)," so it seems likely that the poet has extended that primary meaning to sexual desire. Hence the use of *appetite* as the verb's object.

121

92–95   The stomach was often viewed as the seat of sexual passion in the Middle Ages. The idea that the old man's cold belly might be covered and remedied by a warm young woman perhaps relates to old Januarie's remarks on "bely-naked" Adam, for whom God created Eve as his comfort(er):

> The hye God, whan he hadde Adam maked,
> And saugh him al allone, bely-naked,
> God of his grete goodnesse seyde than,
> "Lat us now make an helpe unto this man
> Lyk to hymself"; and thanne he made him Eve.
> Heere may ye se, and heerby may ye preve,
> That wyf is mannes help and his confort. (*CT* IV[E]1325–31)

96   *juvencle*. This word derives from Latin *iuvencula* (youth).

104   This is the first of a number of references to the "battle of the sexes."

106   Compare The Merchant's Tale (IV[E]1248–55):

> And sixty yeer a wyflees man was hee,
> And folwed ay his bodily delyt
> On wommen, ther as was his appetyt,
> As doon thise fooles that been seculeer.
> And whan that he was passed sixty yeer,
> Were it for hoolynesse or for dotage
> I kan nat seye, but swich a greet corage
> Hadde this knyght to been a wedded man.

113–15   *pank . . . male de flank*. *Pank* is a word of obscure origin attested only here. The MED entry for *pank* n. speculates on the term as "coinage to rime with flanke," *mal de flanke*, which suggests "inordinate sexual desire." *Male de flank* is a term more widely attested.

132   *them*. The couple the philosopher has just described is the referent of *them*.

144   *junesse*. The noun means "youth" or "youthfulness." See note to line 96.

152–54   *than thouh . . . .* The syntax here is difficult. It seems the wife has the potential to swink her husband to death in a manner made famous by the Wife of Bath.

161   *countertaile*. The tally stick was a means by which debtor and creditor each kept a record of their transaction. The amount of the debt was recorded on both ends of the stick, which was then broken in two, each party receiving half. The *countertaile* must refer to the tally of acquittance held by the creditor, which could be offered as proof of debt to the debtor, or to a court in case of legal action. The idea of marriage partners incurring a "debt" becomes crucial in the story of July and December; see lines 433–41. Of course, the possibility of punning on *countertaile* should not be overlooked. Compare The Wife of Bath's Prologue (III[D]152 ff.) and 1 Corinthians 7:3–4.

162–68   Compare The Wife of Bath's Tale (III[D]1258–64):

> and Jhesu Crist us sende
> Housbondes meeke, yonge, and fressh abedde,
> And grace t'overbyde hem that we wedde;
> And eek I praye Jhesu shorte hir lyves
> That noght wol be governed by hir wyves;
> And olde and angry nygardes of dispence,
> God sende hem soone verray pestilence!

167   *mydnythe, matynes, evensong, prime, and houres*. The canonical hours. Note that the wife plays the role of the monk.

169–75   Compare The Franklin's Tale (V[F]744–52 ff.):

> And for to lede the moore in blisse hir lyves,
> Of his free wyl he swoor hire as a knyght
> That nevere in al his lyf he, day ne nyght,
> Ne sholde upon hym take no maistrie
> Agayn hir wyl, ne kithe hire jalousie,
> But hire obeye, and folwe hir wyl in al,
> As any lovere to his lady shal,
> Save that the name of soveraynetee,
> That wolde he have for shame of his degree.

176   Compare the situation of the Wife of Bath, who has had only five husbands.

183–86   Compare The Wife of Bath's Prologue (III[D]564–71, 587–92):

> I seye that in the feeldes walked we,
> Til trewely we hadde swich daliance,
> This clerk and I, that of my purveiance
> I spak to hym and seyde hym how that he,

123

> If I were wydwe, sholde wedde me.
> For certeinly — I sey for no bobance —
> Yet was I nevere withouten purveiance
> Of mariage, n'of othere thynges eek.
> . . . .
> Whan that my fourthe housbonde was on beere,
> I weep algate, and made sory cheere,
> As wyves mooten, for it is usage,
> And with my coverchief covered my visage,
> But for that I was purveyed of a make,
> I wepte but smal, and that I undertake.

198   *mantle and the ryng.* The mantle and the ring are signs of widowhood. Compare similar collocations in the MED's entry for *mantel* n. 1(g).

199   *Whil thou levest.* MS: there is a word crossed out before *levest*.

213   The situation insinuated here is reminiscent of Damian and May in The Merchant's Tale.

223   *And he and she shal have lond.* MS: the word preceding *have* is crossed out.

224   *Avaunt, rebel, of thy sore goten goode.* MS: *sore* is written above *grete*. This line appears to be addressed to the servant-lover in much the way that Chaucer's Merchant breaks the fictive framework of his narrative to scold Januarie and Damian (e.g., IV[E]1869–74, 2107–10).

232–38 This stanza refers to letters of introduction that the wife receives from high personages that will provide a pretext for her dealing with her lover. The ruse seems to be that the letters plead with the wife to take pity on the man in question, who is in fact already her lover.

246–49 The philosopher here provides a catalogue of tricks by which young wives and their lovers hoodwink old husbands. The *lordes lettres* (line 248; compare lines 232–38) are mentioned again along with pretended kinship, apparent abduction, horseplay, and (perhaps) the need to have retinue (*myght of mayntenaunce,* line 247). *Cosynage* (line 246) meaning "kinship" with a pun on *cozenage* ("cuckoldry") appears three times in Chaucer's The Shipman's Tale (VII[B^2]1226, 1329, 1599).

254 *Lo! here a tale.* Compare the Wife of Bath's "wol ye heere the tale?" (III[D]951), as she introduces the story of Midas and his wife.

260, 274 Compare The Merchant's Tale (IV[E]1410–14):

> And I wol fonde t'espien, on my syde,
> To whom I may be wedded hastily.
> But forasmuche as ye been mo than I,
> Ye shullen rather swich a thyng espyen
> Than I, and where me best were to allyen.

264 *indigence.* The adjective *indigente* would be better, but it ruins the rhyme.

279–80 Although the old man seems to be asking if she will marry him not simply because of his wealth — *by spousayle fortunate, / Notwithstandyng his richesse and estate*, that is, by a marriage which is fortune in and of itself even without his properties — he is really asking if she will marry him despite his age.

334 *lakketh.* Ha: *talketh.*

347 Compare The Merchant's Tale (IV[E]1823–27):

> He lulleth hire; he kisseth hire ful ofte;
> With thikke brustles of his berd unsofte,
> Lyk to the skyn of houndfyssh, sharp as brere —
> For he was shave al newe in his manere —
> He rubbeth hire aboute hir tendre face.

358–61 This is the plighting of troth, which is the heart of the wedding ceremony. For a discussion of the English customs of trothplight and wedding, see George Caspar Homans, *English Villagers of the Thirteenth Century* (Cambridge, MA: Harvard University Press, 1941; rpt. 1942, 1960, 1975), pp. 160–76.

362 *What shuld I lenger tary.* MS: the line begins with two words crossed out.

365–68 *The day was comen . . . And my paper it conteyne ne may.* Compare The Merchant's Tale (IV[E]1709, 1732–39):

> Thus been they wedded with solempnitee. . . .
> Hoold thou thy pees, thou poete Marcian,
> That writest us that ilke weddyng murie
> Of hire Philologie and hym Mercurie,
> And of the songes that the Muses songe!

125

> To smal is bothe thy penne, and eek thy tonge,
> For to descryven of this mariage.
> Whan tendre youthe hath wedded stoupyng age,
> Ther is swich myrthe that it may nat be writen.

Or The Squire's Tale (V[F]61, 63–64, 72):

> And halt his feeste so solempne and so ryche . . .
> Of which if I shal tellen al th'array,
> Thanne wolde it occupie a someres day . . . .
> Ther nys no man that may reporten al.

371   *And.* Ha: *An.*

372–75 Lydgate's amusing account of the husband's indolence and the wife's desire to be *fed* (line 375) resonates well against Chaucer's presentation of Januarie on his wedding night. Unlike Lydgate's *worthi man . . . of age* (line 372) old Januarie at least makes a feeble show of virility on his wedding night as he takes May "faste in armes" and "kisseth hire ful ofte" and rubs her face with the "thikke brustles of his berd unsofte," then "laboureth" till day break (see IV[E]1821–42); May, however, finds his playing not "worth a bene" (IV[E]1854). In the next account of his would-be-love-making he is more like Lydgate's old man as he kisses her and then goes to sleep, "and that anon" (IV[E]1946–49). May, however, does not poke his back and ask for it, as in Lydgate; rather she simply settles on Damyan.

378   *of a gentle governaunce.* MS: word crossed out before *gentle*.

385   *ywroke.* The MS reads *ywroke*, which if it is the authorial reading, would seem to pick up the "sexual intercourse as combat" motif used elsewhere in the poem. However, *ywoke*, "awakened" is a defensible emendation.

391   *As appetyt ran on in hir corage.* MS: *in hir* is preceded by two crossed-out words.

402   *turnemente.* This is likely another euphemism for sexual intercourse.

404–06 It would appear that December expected either an immediate cure for his three points or, at least, no recrimination until the cures have been effected. He accuses her of breaking their agreement.

406   *covenaunt.* Ha: *covenawt.*

414–16   July's remedy for the first point is that no matter how wrathful he gets, she will be more wrathful still. She seems to suggest in lines 418–19 that nothing else will ever cause him to be angry again, because her anger will be so fierce that it will supersede all other possible irritants. Compare the Wife of Bath's treatment of her older husbands and Jankyn.

421–27   The remedy for the second point is that he will not be angry without cause, because she will give him plenty of cause. This may be in reference to how she will act generally or to how she will "cure" his first point. However, the cause may well be the "cure" for the third point, which she is about to explain. *List* in line 427 is ambiguous. If it means "desire," then the second "cure" will be effected at no specific time. However, if *list* means "listen, hear," then the last line reads: "When you hear [what I am about to say], you shall have plenty of cause."

435–41   The "cure" for the third point depends upon the idea, expressed in Church doctrine and more generally, that marriage partners must engage in sexual intercourse just as debtors must pay their debts. One alternative might be for the partners to agree to a chaste marriage. December is relieved, *remewed* (line 437), of his marriage debt to July, because of *noun power* (line 438) "destitution," which of course refers to the impotence he revealed earlier. This is his third point. But July reasons that the debt can still be paid, if other assets can be liquidated to that end. Therefore, she proposes that December use his considerable other assets, silver, gold, and fee, to hire someone who can pay this particular debt to her in his stead. The "cure" is such that not only will December remain impotent, he will hire his own cuckold as well.

438   *noun power*. MED defines as "lack of power," "weakness," and "destitution."

444   *the* might mean "then," in which case it is superfluous. It may well be a textual corruption.

446   *that the male so wryes*. A common saying; see MED *male* n.2 (c). However, a pun on *male* "male, i.e., man" and a reading of *so wryes* as "but the man so twists" or, perhaps, "is twisted" is not out of the question in this poem. N.b. The Wife of Bath's Prologue: "how soore I hym twiste" (III[C]494). The scribe crosses out two words preceding *that the*.

447–48   Compare Proserpyne's retort in The Merchant's Tale (IV[E]2265–67):

127

> Now by my moodres sires soule I swere
> That I shal yeven hire suffisant answere,
> And alle wommen after, for hir sake.

451–52 It seems to be a reference to the marriage debt.

455 *Sith not is golde . . . golde doth shyne.* Proverbial; see Whiting G282.

456–57 *Appeles and peres . . . roten by the core.* Proverbial; a variant of "under fair cheer poison is often hid" (Whiting C177).

477–83 The question at the end of this stanza can be interpreted in at least two ways. *Who is he* in line 481 can be read in a rather vague, generalized way as "who is the one." One might expect *she* here rather than *he*, given the actions described in the following line, but *he* can have vague gender specificity: "tell who is the person who can make you an issue (i.e., a child) and beget you an heir who will not shorten and worsen your life?" The question for the philosopher is rhetorical; no woman, who could fulfil the requirements of line 481, would not also bring about the calamities mentioned in line 482. An alternative interpretation, which can only be sketched here, provides a positive answer to the question. The injunction in lines 477–80 for the old friend to give alms raises the question of bequests and wills, which among the rich, always included considerable benefactions for religious houses and institutions of various kinds, which were considered to be acts of almsgiving. Furthermore, the giving of alms to the poor would often have been done most easily through the offices of a Church institution. And in the first clause in almost all medieval wills the testator bequeathed his soul to Christ. That is, for what is most important, his soul, the old friend does have a true benefactor, Christ who will give him eternal life, in answer to line 483. One might argue further that God the Father answers to the requirements of line 482, since he begat the true issue and heir, his Son, for the old friend's benefit. It seems unnecessary to prove that men of some substance in late medieval England would have been familiar with the formulaic structure of the opening clauses of wills, so the philosopher can afford to be subtle here.

485–87 *As seith Seynt Poule . . . .* From 1 Corinthians 7:9.

494–95 Compare The Merchant's Tale (IV[E]1562): "Ye shul nat plesen hire fully yeres thre." *Deye* (line 495) is an unusual noun form for "death."

504   *And hardly it shal away.* MS: two words crossed out before *shal away.*

505   Compare *Troilus and Criseyde* 5.1786 and The Clerk's Tale (IV[E]1177–212, and also lines 1142–76), where the Clerk deflects possible criticism from the Wife of Bath and others for his portrayal of Griselda. The poet realized that his poem will displease women, because it claims that their sole intention in marrying is to acquire goods, even if only a small amount. "Mortal myschaunce" (line 508) may refer to something more than misery and death; the implication may be that women endanger men's souls as well. However, unlike the Clerk, this poet does not try to appease "jolly bodies" by restricting the applicability of his work.

515–16 The poet here attacks those who would accuse him of ribaldry, i.e., lack of decorum and even licentiousness, because of the plainness of his language. Any who make these accusations are to be regarded as hypocrites. Compare The General Prologue to *The Canterbury Tales*, lines 725–42, and The Miller's Prologue (I[A]3167–86); however, note that Chaucer coyly abjures responsibility for the language of his poems by claiming that he is only repeating the words of others, while this poet boldly takes responsibility for what he has written.

The Meaning of Marriage

    Ther was an old batchleor maried to a young girle, and efter maried he went to bed with the girle everie night for six months time togither, never minding nor understanding what he ought to doe to his wife at night, bot fell asleep when he went to bed at night, and got up in the morning, and went abroad to his busines; and all the time understanding that he

5   hadd nothing to doe with a wife but for dressing his victuals and keeping a clean house and his back wearme all night, bot never minded the onlie and cheif thing the poor young girle wanted. So efter long times patience, or rather impatience, the poor girle went to the preist of the parosh, and compleaned on her housband John, and sayes, "God forgive yow, Sir, for marieing me to a man that understands not mariadge! Therfor, pray, Sir, tell him what

10   he ought to doe, or let us be pairted, for I cannot comand natur longer; and ye wold taiken it ill to me to gon and satisfied nature the wrong way, and mad me sit on the pillar of repentance." The preist replyed that he wold be at her dwelling the nixt day, and speak to John; and acordingly cam, and asked John how he cam to be so unkind to his wife; who replyed that, "Non could be kinder to wife nor he was; never had he disobeyed her, or

15   given her a froward word." "Bot John," say the preist, "ye ar wanting in another thing of greater consequence;" and tell that mariadge was ordained for procreatione of children, for satisfieing nature, and avoiding of fornicatione, with a great manie more arguments: bot, by all, he culd not come to understand what he ought. So the preist says: "Poor girle, I pittie thy caise! for this man is verie dull; bot I think it best yow and I go to bed, and I will

20   shew him how and what to doe." Who replyed she was willing with all her heart; and to bed they went. And the preist got on the top of her, and spok in Irish tongue (as all the rest of the forgoing storie was) MUSSHO VETICH, that is to say, doe this way. So when the preist had don what he was able to do, the poor girl was so weel pleased with the game, that she says, "Oh, Sir, our John is verie forgetful! Pray doe it over again!"

                                            Vale.

25

        [on the back is written]
        scottch stor. . .
        McBaire . . .

131

Select Bibliography and Notes to *The Meaning of Marriage*

Manuscript

British Library MS Sloane 1983 B, leaf 13 (seventeenth century ?).

Edition

Furnivall, Frederick J., ed. *Jyl of Breyntfords Testament . . . and Other Short Pieces*. London: Printed for private circulation by Taylor & Co., 1871. Pp. 40–41.

Notes

Abbreviations: **F**: Frederick J. Furnivall; **MS**: British Library MS Sloane 1983 B, leaf 13.

1   *with*. MS: *wt*. The scribe abbreviates three words: "with," "that," and "sir." F has added the missing letters, as have I.

2   *understanding*. MS: *undestanding*. F has provided the missing consonant.

4–7   The husband's lack of sexual interest which sets up the joke constitutes a denigration of conjugal duty; in medieval marriage both partners are obligated by their vow of consent to pay the conjugal debt even when the other is unwilling. See Chaucer's The Parson's Tale on the second cause of "assemble": "Another cause is to yelden everich of hem to oother the dette of hire bodies, for neither of hem hath power of his owene body" (X[I]940).

6   *the₂*. MS: *te*.

7   *wanted*. MS: *wnted*.

10   *let us be pairted*. The marriage could be annulled for one partner's neglect of the other's sexual needs. Sexual abstinence between spouses (spiritual marriage)

132

needed to be mutually agreed upon as in the case of Cecilia and Valerius in Chaucer's The Second Nun's Tale or the marriage contract between Mary and Joseph in the Corpus Christi plays.

10–11   *taiken it ill to me*. That is, "you would think ill of me if I satisfied nature in the wrong way."

11–12   *pillar of repentance*. A public means of humiliation for allegedly unfaithful wives.

14   *could*. MS: *ould*. F's emendation.

16–17   The three goods of marriage — procreation, satisfaction of nature, and avoiding fornication — are named as evidence of the extent of the husband's neglect. Compare The Parson's Tale (X[I]939–42) on the three goods of marriage, the first two of which are chaste.

21   *they*. MS: *the*.

22   *forgoing*. MS: *forging*. I have followed the emendation made by F to maintain sense and syntax.

         MUSSHO VETICH. This phrase may be understood as it is translated in the narrative, i.e., *doe this way*. It is also quite possible that it is nonsensical, a phrase meant to implicate the Irish. It appears in the printed edition in capital letters.

25   *Vale*. A Latin term meaning "farewell."

26–27   *McBaire*. F: *Mr Baire*. Whether this is a narrative originating in Scotland and attributed to someone named McBaire is unclear. The ellipses replicate those found in F's edition.

William Dunbar, *The Tretis of the Twa Mariit Wemen and the Wedo*

	Apon the Midsummer evin, mirriest of nichtis,	*evening; nights*
	I muvit furth allane in meid as midnicht wes past,	*walked; meadow*
	Besyd ane gudlie grein garth, full of gay flouris,	*beautiful; garden; brightly colored*
	Hegeit of ane huge hicht with hawthorne treis;	*Hedged; height*
5	Quhairon ane bird on ane bransche so birst out hir notis	*Whereupon; poured*
	That never ane blythfullar bird was on the beuche hard.	*more joyful; bough heard*
	Quhat throw the sugarat sound of hir sang glaid,	*Partly through; sweet*
	And throw the savour sanative of the sueit flouris,	*curative; sweet*
	I drew in derne to the dyk to dirkin efter mirthis;	*furtively; wall; lurk; revelry*
10	The dew donkit the daill and dynnit the feulis.	*moistened; valley; sang loudly; birds*
	I hard, under ane holyn hevinlie grein hewit,	*heard; holly tree; green hued*
	Ane hie speiche at my hand with hautand wourdis:	*loud; haughty words*
	With that in haist to the hege so hard I inthrang	*hedge; pushed in*
	That I was heildit with hawthorne and with heynd leveis.	*covered; pleasant*
15	Throw pykis of the plet thorne I presandlie luikit,	*spikes; intertwined thorns; presently*
	Gif ony persoun wald approche within that pleasand garding.	*If; pleasant garden*
	I saw thre gay ladeis sit in ane grein arbeir,	*green arbor*
	All grathit into garlandis of fresche gudlie flouris.	*arrayed in; goodly*
	So glitterit as the gold wer thair glorius gilt tressis,	*wire; tresses [of hair]*
20	Quhill all the gressis did gleme of the glaid hewis;	*Till; green plants*
	Kemmit war thair cleir hair and curiouslie sched,[1]	
	Attour thair schulderis doun schyre schyning full bricht,	*Over; glorious*
	With curches cassin thair abone of kirsp cleir and thin.[2]	
	Thair mantillis grein war as the gres that grew in May sessoun,	*cloaks*
25	Fetrit with thair quhyt fingaris about thair fair sydis.	*Secured; white*
	Of ferliful fyne favour war thair faceis meik,[3]	
	All full of flurist fairheid as flouris in June —	*flourishing loveliness*

---

[1] *Well-combed was their gleaming hair and carefully parted*

[2] *With kerchiefs thrown above of fine fabric clear (bright) and thin*

[3] *Of wonderfully fine appearance were their faces (countenances) gentle (of submissive or pliant disposition)*

	Quhyt, seimlie, and soft as the sweit lillies,	*White, seemly*
	Now upspred upon spray, as new spynist rose;	*stretched up; tree twigs; newly opened*
30	Arrayit ryallie about with mony riche vardour,	*richly; much; greenery*
	That nature full nobillie annamalit with flouris,	*enameled*
	Of alkin hewis under hevin that ony heynd knew,	*every color; courteous [person]*
	Fragrant, all full of fresche odour, fynest of smell.	
	Ane cumlie tabil coverit wes befoir tha cleir ladeis,[1]	
35	With ryalle cowpis apon rawis, full of ryche wynis.	*cups in orderly setting*
	And of thir fair wlonkes twa weddit war with lordis,	*beautiful creatures two wedded*
	Ane wes ane wedow, iwis, wantoun of laitis.[2]	
	And as thai talk at the tabill of mony taill sindry,	*different stories*
	They wauchtit at the wicht wyne and waris out wourdis;[3]	
40	And syne thai spak more spedelie and sparit no matiris.	*then; spoke; spared; matters*
	"Bewrie," said the wedo, "ye woddit wemen ying,	*Reveal; wedded; young*
	Quhat mirth ye fand in maryage sen ye war menis wyffis.[4]	
	Reveill gif ye rewit that rakles conditioun,	*rue; imprudent contract*
	Or gif that ever ye luffit leyd upone lyf mair	*living man more*
45	Nor thame that ye your fayth hes festinit for ever,	*them; fastened*
	Or gif ye think, had ye chois, that ye wald cheis better.	*choice; choose*
	Think ye it nocht ane blist band that bindis so fast,	*blessed bond*
	That none undo it a deill may bot the deith ane?"[5]	
	Than spak ane lusty belyf with lustie effeiris;	*beautiful woman; lively expression*
50	"It, that ye call the blist band that bindis so fast,	
	Is bair of blis, and bailfull, and greit barrat wirkis.	*naked; wretched; strife*
	Ye speir, had I fre chois, gif I wald cheis bettir?	*You ask*
	Chenyeis ay ar to eschew; and changeis ar sueit:[6]	
	Sic cursit chance till eschew, had I my chois anis,	*Such; for once*
55	Out of the chenyeis of ane churle I chaip suld for evir.	*boor; escape*
	God gif matrimony wer made to mell for ane yeir!	*grant; copulate*

---

[1] *A beautiful table covered [with a cloth] was before those fair ladies*

[2] *One was a widow, certainly, of amorous behavior*

[3] *They quaffed at the strong wine and let out words*

[4] *What mirth you found in marriage since you were men's wives*

[5] *That none may undo it in the smallest part except death alone*

[6] *Chains are always to be avoided; and changes are sweet*

It war bot merrens to be mair, bot gif our myndis pleisit:[1]
It is agane the law of luf, of kynd, and of nature,
Togidder hairtis to strene, that stryveis with uther:[2]

60   Birdis hes ane better law na bernis be meikill,   *than men by far*
       That ilk yeir, with new joy, joyis ane maik,   *consorts with a mate*
       And fangis thame ane fresche feyr, unfulyeit, and constant,   *embraces; energetic*
       And lattis thair fulyeit feiris flie quhair thai pleis.   *worn out mates go where; please*
       Cryst gif sic ane consuetude war in this kith haldin!   *such; custom; country held*

65   Than weill war us wemen that evir we war fre;   *well [off] were*
       We suld have feiris as fresche to fang quhen us likit,[3]
       And gif all larbaris thair leveis, quhen thai lak curage.   *give impotent men their leave*
       Myself suld be full semlie in silkis arrayit,   *very beautifully; arrayed*
       Gymp, jolie, and gent, richt joyus, and gent.   *Slender, very happy; elegant*

70   I suld at fairis be found new faceis to se;   *faces*
       At playis, and at preichingis, and pilgrimages greit,   *sermons*
       To schaw my renone, royaly, quhair preis was of folk,   *show; renown; gathering*
       To manifest my makdome to multitutde of pepill,   *comeliness*
       And blaw my bewtie on breid, quhair bernis war mony,[4]

75   That I micht cheis, and be chosin, and change quhen me lykit.   *[So] that; choose*
       Than suld I waill ane full weill, ovr all the wyd realme,   *choose; rightly; wide*
       That suld my womanheid weild the lang winter nicht;   *womanliness use potently*
       And quhen I gottin and ane grome ganest of uther,   *[have] gotten; fellow more fit than*
       Yaip, and ying, in the yok ane yeir for to draw;   *Keen; young; yoke*

80   Fra I had preveit his pitht the first plesand moneth,[5]
       Than suld I cast me to keik in kirk, and in markat,   *look about in church*
       And all the cuntré about, kyngis court, and uther,   *elsewhere*
       Quhair I ane galland micht get aganis the nixt yeir,   *gallant; again; next*
       For to perfurneis furth the werk quhen failyeit the tother;   *perform; weakened; other*

85   A forky fure, ay furthwart, and forsy in draucht,[6]

---

[1] *It was but a nuisance to be a longer time (more), unless we so desired*

[2] Lines 58–59: *It is against the law of love, of nature, and of natural law, / Together hearts to force, that contend with each other*

[3] *We should have mates (companions) as fresh to embrace whenever it pleased us*

[4] *And make widely known my beauty abroad, where lovers were many*

[5] *After I had tested his vigor the first pleasant month*

[6] *A vigorous (powerful) man, always up front, and forceful in draftsmanship (tilling, plowing)*

Nother febill, nor fant, nor fulyeit in labour,   *Neither; faint; weak*
But als fresche of his forme as flouris in May;   *stature*
For all the fruit suld I fang, thocht he the flour burgeoun.   *take; flower cause to expand*
I have ane wallidrag, ane worme, ane auld wobat carle,
90   A waistit wolroun, na worth bot wourdis to clatter;[1]
Ane bumbart, ane dron bee, and bag full of flewme,   *lazy fellow; drone; phlegm*
Ane skabbit skarth, ane scorpioun, ane scutarde behind;[2]
To see him scart his awin skyn grit scunner I think,   *scratch; own; great disgust*
Quhen kissis me that carybald, than kyndillis all my sorow;[3]
95   As birs of ane brym bair, his berd is als stif,   *bristles; furious bear*
Bot soft and soupill as the silk is his sary lume;   *sorry tool*
He may weill to the syn assent, bot sakles is his deidis.   *harmless is his performance*
With gor his tua grym ene ar gladderrit all about,[4]
And gorgeit lyk twa gutaris that war with glar stoppit;   *choked; gutters; filth*
100   Bot quhen that glowrand gaist grippis me about,   *glowering ghost*
Than think I hiddowus Mahowne hes me in armes;   *hideous Mahomet has*
Thair ma na sanyne me save fra that auld Sathane;   *may; sign [of the Cross]; old Satan*
For, thocht I croce me all cleine, fra the croun doun,   *cross myself; completely*
He wil my corse all beclip, and clap me to his breist.   *body; embrace; press*
105   Quhen schaiffyn is that ald schalk with a scharp rasour,   *shaven; aged man*
He schowis on me his schevill mouth and schedis my lippis[5]
And with his hard hurcheone skyn sa heklis he my chekis,   *hedgehog skin; scratches*
That as a glemand gleyd glowis my chaftis;   *gleaming coal; chin (jaws)*
I schrenk for the scharp stound, bot schout dar I nought,   *cower; sharp pain*
110   For schore of that auld schrew, schame him betide![6]
The luf blenkis of that bogill, fra his blerde ene,   *leers; hobgoblin; bleary eyes*
As Belzebub had on me blent, abasit my spreit;   *As [if]; looked, cast down; spirit*

---

[1] Lines 89–90: *I have a slovenly fellow, a worm, an old hairy rustic, / A used up stray boar, good for nothing but words to clatter (i.e., grunt)*

[2] *A scabby monster, a scorpion, a filthy (shitty) behind*

[3] *When that repulsive wretch kisses me, then kindles all my sorrow*

[4] *With slime his two angry (dirty/ugly) eyes are smeared all about*

[5] *He showers on me his twisted mouth and parts my lips*

[6] *For threatening demeanor of that malignant rascal, shame him beset!*

And quhen the smy one me smyrkis with his smake smolet,
He fepillis ike a farcy aver that flyrit one a gillot.[1]

115 "Quhen that the sound of his saw sinkis in my eris,   *speech; ears*
Than ay renewis my noy, or he be neir cumand: *vexation, before; coming near*
Quhen I heir nemmyt his name, than mak I nyne Crocis,
To keip me fra the cummerans of that carll mangit,[2]
That full of eldnyng is and anger and all evill thewis.   *jealousy; traits*
120 I dar nought luke to my luf for that lene gib,   *because of; scrawny tomcat*
He is sa full of jelusy and engyne fals;   *ingenuity*
Ever ymagynyng in mynd materis of evill,
Compasand and castand cacis a thousand   *Contriving; tricks*
How he sall tak me, with a trawe, at trist of ane othir:[3]
125 I dar nought keik to the knaip that the cop fillis,   *glance; groom; cup*
For eldnyng of that ald schrew that ever one evill thynkis;   *jealousy*
For he is waistit and worne fra Venus werkis,   *acts of love*
And may nought beit worth a bene in bed of my mystirs.   *bean; sexual needs*
He trowis that young folk I yerne yeild, for he gane is,   *believes; eagerly; impotent*
130 Bot I may huke all this yer, or his yerd help.   *itch; before; penis*
"Ay quhen that caribald carll wald clyme one my wambe,   *monstrous man; belly*
Than am I dangerus and daine and dour of my will;   *reluctant; haughty; unwilling*
Yit leit I never that larbar my leggis ga betueene,   *allow; impotent wretch*
To fyle my flesche, na fumyll me, without a fee gret;   *fill; nor fumble with*
135 And thoght his pené purly me payis in bed,   *though; penny/penis poorly; gratifies*
His purse pays richely in recompense efter:
For, or he clym on my corse, that carybald forlane,   *body; worthless monster*
I have conditioun of a curche of kersp allther fynest,   *kerchief; all the finest fabric*
A goun of engranyt claith, right gaily furrit,   *scarlet cloth; trimmed with fur*
140 A ring with a ryall stane, or other riche jowell,   *royal stone; jewel*
Or rest of his rousty raid, thoght he wer rede wod:
For all the buddis of Johne Blunt, quhen he abone clymis,

---

[1] Lines 113–14: *And when the knave simpers at me with his narrow rogue's mouth, / He dribbles like a diseased horse that leers at a mare (see note)*

[2] Lines 117–18: *When I hear mentioned his name, than I make nine crosses (i.e., the sign of the Cross nine times), / To keep me from the annoyance (trouble) of that imbecilic fool*

[3] *How he shall catch me, by means of some trick, [while I] rendezvous with another*

	Me think the baid deir aboucht, sa bawch ar his werkis;[1]	
	And thus I sell him solace, thoght I it sour think:	
145	Fra sic a syre, God yow saif, my sueit sisteris deir!"	*From; man; sisters*
	Quhen that the semely had said her sentence to end,	*lovely [one]; speech*
	Than all thai leuch apon loft with latis full mery,	*laughed aloud; behavior*
	And raucht the cop round about full of riche wynis.	*passed; cup*
	And ralyeit lang, or thai wald rest, with ryatus speche.	*jested; riotous*
150	The wedo to the tothir wlonk warpit thir wordis:	*widow; lovely [lady] directed*
	"Now, fair sister, fallis yow but fenyeing to tell,	*it befalls; without deceit*
	Sen man ferst with matrimony yow menskit in kirk,	*favored in church*
	How haif ye farne be your faith? confese us the treuth:	*have; fared; confess*
	That band to blise or to ban, quhilk yow best thinkis?	*bond; curse; to you seems*
155	Or how ye like lif to leid into leill spousage?	*as a faithful wife*
	And syne myself ye exeme one the samyn wise,	*afterwards; examine in; same*
	And I sall say furth the south, dissymyland no word."	*truth, dissembling*
	The plesand said, "I protest, the treuth gif I schaw,	*agreeable [woman]; if*
	That of your toungis ye be traist." The tothir twa grantit;	*trustworthy; agreed*
160	With that sprang up hir spreit be a span hechar.	*spirit; about five inches higher*
	"To speik," quoth scho, "I sall nought spar; ther is no spy neir:	*near*
	I sall a ragment reveil fra rute of my hert	*long discourse; depths*
	A roust that is sa rankild quhill risis my stomok[2]	
	Now sall the byle all out brist, that beild has so lang;	*bile; burst; swollen [with rage]*
165	For it to beir on my brist wes berdin ovr hevy:	*endure; breast; burden*
	I sall the venome devoid with a vent large,	*cast out; discharge*
	And me assuage of the swalme, that swuellit wes gret.	*swelling; swollen*
	"My husband wes a hur maister, the hugeast in erd,	*whoremaster; earth*
	Tharfor I hait him with my hert, sa help me our Lord!	*hate*
170	He is a young man ryght yaip, bot nought in youthis flouris;	*nimble*
	For he is fadit full far and feblit of strenth:	*faded; feeble*
	He wes as flurising fresche within this few yeris,	*flourishing; these*
	Bot he is falyeid full far and fulyeid in labour;	*failed; weakened*
	He has bene lychour so lang quhill lost is his natur,	*lecher; sexual power*
175	His lume is waxit larbar and lyis into swonne:	

---

[1] Lines 141–43: *Or rest of his clumsy (rusty) ride, though he were furiously angry (stark-raving mad):* / *For all the bribes of Stupid John, when he above climbs, / I think the delay dearly bought, so bungled are his deeds*

[2] *A canker that is so festered it makes me sick*

The Tretis of the Twa Mariit Wemen and the Wedo

Wes never sugeorne wer set na one that snaill tyrit,[1]
For efter seven oulkis rest, it will nought rap anys; *weeks; penetrate once*
He has bene waistit apon wemen, or he me wif chesit, *before; chose*
And in adultré, in my tyme, I haif him tane oft: *taken (discovered)*

180 And yit he is als brankand with bonet one syde, *as proud; cap*
And blenkand to the brichtest that in the burgh duellis, *glancing at the fairest; lives*
Alse curtly of his clething and kemmyng of his hairis, *courtly; combing; hair*
As he that is mare valyeand in Venus chalmer; *valiant; bedchamber*
He semys to be sumthing worth, that syphry in bour, *cipher in bower*

185 He lukis as he wald luffit be, thocht he be litill of valour;[2]
He dois as dotit dog that damys on all bussis, *stupid; makes; bushes*
And liftis his leg apone loft, thoght he nought list pische; *aloft; unable to piss*
He has a luke without lust and lif without curage; *look; stamina*
He has a borme without force and fessous but vertu,[3]

190 And fair wordis but effect, all fruster of dedis; *without efficacy; worthless*
He is for laydis in luf a right lusty schadow, *appearance*
Bot into derne, at the deid, he sal be drup fundin;[4]
He ralis, and makis repet with ryatus wordis, *rails; uproar; riotous*
Ay rusing him of his radis and rageing in chalmer; *boasting; rides; sexual vigor*

195 Bot God wait quhat I think quhen he so thra spekis, *knows; boldly*
And how it settis him so syde to sege of sic materis.[5]
Bot gif himself, of sum evin, myght ane say among thaim, *evening*
Bot he nought ane is, bot nane of naturis possessoris. *nature's possessors*
 "Scho that has ane auld man nought all is begylit; *deceived*

200 He is at Venus werkis na war na he semys; *no worse than*
I wend I josit a gem, and I haif geit gottin;[6]
He had the glemyng of gold, and wes bot glase fundin. *found glass*
Thought men be ferse, wele I fynd, fra falye ther curage, *fierce; after[wards] fails*
That is bot eldnyng and anger ther hertis within. *jealousy*

---

[1] Lines 175–76: *His instrument is exhausted and lies in [a] swoon: / Was never [a] sojourn (rest period) worse expended than on that sluggard*

[2] *He looks as [if] he were capable of love-making, though he be of little endurance (physical strength)*

[3] *He has a fair shape without force and appearance without power*

[4] *But in secret, at the deed, he shall be drooping discovered*

[5] *And how it becomes him so widely [to boast] to men of such matters*

[6] *I believed I possessed a gem, and I here had gotten an amber jewel (geit=jet: see note)*

205	Ye speik of berdis on bewch: of blise may thai sing,	*birds; branch*
	That, on Sanct Valentynis day, ar vacandis ilk yer;	*free [to take mates] each*
	Hed I that plesand prevelege to part quhen me likit,	*Had; privilege; depart*
	To change, and ay to cheise agane, than, chastité, adew!	*choose; farewell*
	Than suld I haif a fresch feir to fang in myn armes:	*should; young [man]; clasp*
210	To hald a freke, quhill he faynt, may foly be calit.	*hold a man; foolish*
	"Apone sic materis I mus, at mydnyght, full oft,	*muse*
	And murnys so in my mynd I murdris myselfin;	*mourning; slay*
	Than ly I walkand for wa, and walteris about,	*awake; grief; toss and turn*
	Wariand oft my wekit kyn, that me away cast	*Cursing; wicked*
215	To sic a craudoune but curage, that knyt my cler bewté,[1]	
	And ther so mony kene kynghtis this kenrik within:	*There [being]; fierce; kingdom*
	Than think I on a semelyar, the suth for to tell,	*one more attractive (seemlier); truth*
	Na is our syre, be sic sevin; with that I sych oft:	*Than; by seven times; sigh*
	Than he ful tenderly dois turne to me his tume person,	*Then; feeble*
220	And with a yoldin yerd dois yolk me in armys,	*an exhausted; force me to surrender*
	And said, 'My soverane sueit thing, quhy sleip ye no betir?'	*why*
	Me think ther haldis yow a hete, as ye sum harme alyt.'	*fever; distress suffered*
	Quoth I, 'My hon, hald abak, and handill me nought sair;	*painfully*
	A hache is happinit hastely at my hert rut.'	*ache; root*
225	With that I seme for to swoune, thought I na swerf tak;	*faint; do not swoon*
	And thus beswik I that swane with my sueit wordis:	*deceive; lowly man*
	I cast on him a crabit e, quhen cleir day is cummyn,	*ill-tempered (crabby) eye*
	And lettis it is a luf blenk quhen he about glemys.	*feign; love glance; looks*
	I turne it in a tender luke, that I in tene warit,	*look; anger [had] put on*
230	And him behaldis hamely with hertly smyling.	*behold him intimately; warmth*
	"I wald a tender peronall, that myght na put thole,	
	That hatit men with hard geir for hurting of flesch,[2]	
	Had my gud man to hir gest; for I dar God suer,	*as her guest; swear*
	Scho suld not stert for his straik a stray breid of erd.[3]	
235	And syne I wald that ilk band that ye so blist call	*same bondage*
	Had bund him so to that bryght, quhill his bak werkit;	*bound; pretty [girl]; ached*

---

[1] *Who bound my bright beauty to such an impotent coward (gloss by Bawcutt 1996)*

[2] Lines 231–32: *I would that a young woman, who might not [the pain of] a thrust (putt) endure, / Who hated men with erect implements because of hurting of flesh*

[3] *She should not flinch at his stroke, a straw's breadth of ground (gloss by Bawcutt 1996)*

	And I wer in a beid broght with berne that me likit,	*bed; lover; pleased*
	I trow that bird of my blis suld a bourd want."[1]	
	Onone, quhen this amyable had endit hir speche,	*Forthwith; amiable [woman]*
240	Loud lauchand, the laif allowit hir mekle:	*laughing; rest praised; greatly*
	Thir gay wiffis maid game amang the grene leiffis,	*These; made sport; leaves*
	Thai drank and did away dule under derne bewis;	*cast off sorrow; dark boughs*
	Thai swapit of the sueit wyne, thai swan quhit of hewis,	*tossed off; those white swans*
	Bot all the pertlyar, in plane, thai put out ther vocis.	*saucier, frankly; poured out*
245	Than said the Weido, "Iwis ther is no way other;	*Widow; indeed*
	Now tydis me for to talk; my taill it is nixt:	*it is time; tale*
	God my spreit now inspir and my speche quykkin,	*invigorate*
	And send me sentence to say, substantious and noble;	*wisdom; weighty*
	Sa that my preching may pers your perverst hertis,	*pierce; wayward (perverse)*
250	And mak yow mekar to men in maneris and conditiounis.	*more meek; dispositions*
	"I schaw yow, sisteris in schrift, I wes a schrew evir,	*show; confession; scold*
	Bot I wes schene in my schrowd, and schew me innocent;	*bright; gown; appeared*
	And thought I dour wes and dane, dispitous, and bald,[2]	
	I wes dissymblit suttelly in a sanctis liknes:	*disguised cleverly in likeness of a saint*
255	I semyt sober, and sueit, and sempill without fraud,	*seemed meek; simple*
	Bot I couth sexty dissaif that suttilar wer haldin.	*could beguile; more crafty*
	"Unto my lesson ye lyth, and leir at me wit,	*listen; learn from my wisdom*
	Gif you nought list be forleit with losingeris untrew:	*wish; abandoned; flatterers*
	Be constant in your governance, and counterfeit gud maneris.	*behavior*
260	Thought ye be kene, inconstant, and cruell of mynd;	*fierce*
	Thought ye as tygris be terne, be tretable in luf,	*tigers; ferocious; tractable*
	And be as turtoris in your talk, thought ye haif talis brukill;[3]	
	Be dragonis baith and dowis, ay in double forme,	*dragons both; doves, always*
	And quhen it nedis yow, onone, note baith ther strenthis;[4]	
265	Be amyable with humble face, as angellis apperand,	*appearing*
	And with a terrebill tail be stangand as edderis;	*deadly; stinging; adders*
	Be of your luke like innocentis, thoght ye haif evill myndis;	*look*
	Be courtly ay in clething and costly arrayit,	
	That hurtis yow nought worth a hen; yowr husband pays for all.	*not a whit*

---

[1] *I believe that the girl [with regard to] my [alleged marital] bliss would have cause for laughter*

[2] *And though I was stubborn and haughty, contemptuous, and bold*

[3] *And be as turtledoves in your talk, though you have fragile (readily yielding) tails*

[4] *And when you need it, forthwith, employ both their strength*

270	"Twa husbandis I have had, thai held me baith deir,	*Two; both dear*
	Thought I dispytit thaim agane, thai spyit it nathing:	*despised; in return; observed*
	Ane wes ane hair hogeart, that hostit out flewme;[1]	
	I hatit him like a hund, thought I it hid prevé:	*hated; hound; secretly*
	With kissing and with clapping I gert the carill fone;	*fondling; made; boor foolish*
275	Weil couth I keyth his cruke bak, and kemm his cowit noddill,	
	And with a bukky in my cheik bo on him behind,[2]	
	And with a bek gang about and bler his ald e,	*curtsy walk; blur his aged eye*
	And with a kynd contynance kys his crynd chekis;	*countenance; shriveled cheeks*
	Into my mynd makand mokis at that mad fader,	*derisive gestures*
280	Trowand me with trew lufe to treit him so fair.	*Believing; love*
	This cought I do without dule and na dises tak,	*could; lament; distress*
	Bot ay be mery in my mynd and myrth full of cher.	
	"I had a lufsummar leid my lust for to slokyn,	*more lovable youth; satisfy*
	That couth be secrete and sure and ay saif my honour,	*Who; dependable*
285	And sew bot at certayne tymes and in sicir placis;	*follow [me]; certain; safe*
	Ay quhen the ald did me anger with akword wordis	*old [man]; ill-tempered*
	Apon the galland for to goif it gladit me agane.	*gallant; gaze*
	I had sic wit that for wo weipit I litill,	*such skill; wept*
	Bot leit the sweit ay the sour to gud sesone bring.	*good relish*
290	Quhen that the chuf wald me chid, with girnand chaftis,[3]	
	I wald him chuk, cheik and chyn, and cheris him so mekill,	*fondle, cheek; cherish*
	That his cheif chymys he had chevist to my sone,	*split manor house; provided*
	Suppos the churll wes gane chaist or the child wes gottin:[4]	
	As wis woman ay I wrought and not as wod fule,	*crazy fool*
295	For mar with wylis I wan na wichtnes of handis.	*more; wiles; won than strength*
	"Syne maryit I a mercheand, myghti of gudis:	*Since then married*
	He was a man of myd eld and mene statur;	*middle age; low social status*
	Bot we na fallowis wer in frenschip or blud,	*equals; kinship; blood*
	In fredome, na furth bering, na fairnes of persoune,	*generosity; conduct*
300	Quhilk ay the fule did forghet, for febilnes of knawlege,	*intelligence*
	Bot I sa oft thoght him on, quhill angrit his hert,	*caused him to think of*

---

[1] *One was a gray-haired, tired-out old man, who coughed out phlegm*

[2] Lines 275–76: *Well could I rub his crooked back (i.e., do his back a favor) and comb his cropped pate, / And with tongue in cheek make a face behind his back (see note)*

[3] *When the churlish one would chide me, with snarling jaws*

[4] *Although the churl had become "chaste" (i.e., impotent) before the child was begotten*

144

	And quhilum I put furth my voce and pedder him callit;	*sometimes; pedlar*
	I wald ryght tuichandly talk be I wes tuyse maryit,	*affectingly; twice*
	For endit wes my innocence with my ald husband.	
305	I wes apperand to be pert within perfit eild;	*appearing; clever; maturity*
	Sa sais the curat of our kirk, that knew me full ying:	*curate (priest); church; young*
	He is ovr famous to be fals, that fair worthy prelot;	*too reputable; prelate*
	I sal be laith to lat him le, quhill I may luke furth.	*shall be loath; tell lies; look around*
	I gert the buthman obey, ther wes no bute ellis;	*make; shopkeeper; remedy*
310	He maid me ryght hie reverens, fra he my rycht knew;	*respect; right (privilege)*
	For, thocht I say it myself, the severance wes mekle	*difference*
	Betuix his bastard blude and my birth noble.	
	That page wes never of sic price for to presome anys[1]	
	Unto my persone to be peir, had peté nought grantit.	*equal; compassion*
315	Bot mercie into womanheid is a mekle vertu,	*in womanhood; great virtue*
	For never bot in a gentill hert is generit ony ruth.	*engendered; pity*
	I held ay grene into his mynd that I of grace tuk him,	*fresh*
	And for he couth ken himself I curtasly him lerit:	*teach; educated*
	He durst not sit anys my summondis, for or the secund charge,[2]	
320	He wes ay redy for to ryn, so rad he wes for blame.	*come running; afraid*
	Bot ay my will wes the war of womanly natur;	*worse*
	The mair he loutit for my luf, the les of him I rakit;	*humbled himself; esteemed*
	And eik, this is a ferly thing, or I him faith gaif,	*also; strange; before*
	I had sic favour to that freke, and feid syne forever.	*man; hostility subsequently*
325	"Quhen I the cure had all clene and him ourcummyn haill,	*overcome wholly*
	I crew abone that craudone, as cok that wer victour;	*crowed above; coward*
	Quhen I him saw subjeit and set at myn bydding,	*submissive*
	Than I him lightlyit as a lowne and lathit his maneris.	*despised; loon; detested*
	Than woxe I sa unmerciable to martir him I thought,	*grew; pitiless; torment*
330	For as a best I broddit him to all boyis laubour:	*beast; goaded; menial labor*
	I wald haif ridden him to Rome with raip in his heid,	*halter*
	Wer not ruffill of my renoune and rumour of pepill.	*impairment; reputation*
	And yit hatrent I hid within my hert all;	*hatred*
	Bot quhilis it hepit so huge, quhill it behud out:[3]	
335	Yit tuk I nevir the wosp clene out of my wyde throte,	*stopper*

---

[1] *That low-class person was never of such worth to presume at any time*

[2] *He never once dared disregard my summons, for before a second command*

[3] *But at times it accumulated so huge, till it needed (behooved) to issue out*

Quhil I oucht wantit of my will or quhat I wald desir.   *anything lacked*

Bot quhen I severit had that syre of substance in erd,   *deprived; fellow; wealth*

And gottin his biggingis to my barne, and hie burrow landis,[1]

Than with a stew stert out the stoppell of my hals,   *stink started; bung; throat*

340 That he all stunyst throu the stound, as of a stele wappin.   *astounded; shock; weapon*

Than wald I, efter lang, first sa fane haif bene wrokin,   *[a] delay; gladly; avenged*

That I to flyte wes als fers as a fell dragoun.   *scold; fierce; cruel*

I had for flattering of the fule fenyeit so lang,   *fool feigned*

Mi evidentis of heritagis or thai wer all selit,[2]

345 My breist, that wes gret beild, bowdyn wes sa huge,   *swollen [with rage], inflamed*

That neir my baret out brist or the band makin.[3]   *trouble; bond*

Bot quhen my billis and my bauchles wes all braid selit,[4]

I wald na langar beir on bridill, bot braid up my heid;   *be restrained; tossed*

Thar mygjt na molet mak me moy, na hald my mouth in: *curb bit; submissive*

350 I gert the renyeis rak and rif into sondir;   *made the reins strain; split*

I maid that wif carll to werk all womenis werkis,   *womanish man*

And laid all manly materis and mensk in this eird.   *buried; dignity; earth*

Than said I to my cumaris in counsall about,   *female friends*

"Se how I cabeld yone cout with a kene brydill!   *fastened; colt*

355 The cappill, that the crelis kest in the caf mydding,   *horse; baskets; dung heap*

Sa curtasly the cart drawis, and kennis na plungeing,   *knows; violent leaping*

He is nought skeich, na yit sker, na scippis nought one syd":   *spirited; restive; skips*

And thus the scorne and the scaith scapit he nothir.   *humiliation escaped; neither*

   "He wes no glaidsum gest for a gay lady,   *happy guest*

360 Tharfor I gat him a game that ganyt him bettir;   *obtained; sport; suited*

He wes a gret goldit man and of gudis riche;   *wealthy*

I leit him be my lumbart to lous me all misteris,   *Lombard (banker); free*

And he wes fane for to fang fra me that fair office,   *glad; take*

And thoght my favoris to fynd through his feill giftis.   *many gifts*

365 He grathit me in a gay silk and gudly arrayis,   *adorned; clothing*

In gownis of engranyt claith and gret goldin chenyeis,   *crimson cloth; chains*

In ringis ryally set with riche ruby stonis,

Quhill hely raise my renoune amang the rude peple.   *highly*

---

[1] *And given his buildings to my child, and tall tenements in the burgh*

[2] *My legal proofs of documents of inheritance before they were all sealed*

[3] *That my anger nearly burst out before the drawing up of the contract (gloss by Bawcutt 1996)*

[4] *But when my legal documents and my denunciations were all amply sealed*

	Bot I full craftely did keip thai courtly wedis,	*those; clothes*
370	Quhill efter dede of that drupe that docht nought in chalmir[1]	
	Thought he of all my clathis maid cost and expense,	*garments*
	Aneothir sall the worschip haif, that weildis me eftir;	*honor; possesses*
	And thoght I likit him bot litill, yit for luf of otheris,	
	I wald me prein plesandly in precius wedis,	*preen*
375	That luffaris mycht apone me luke and ying lusty gallandis,	*lovers; young*
	That I held more in daynté and derer be ful mekill	*esteem; costlier; much*
	Ne him that dressit me so dink: full dotis wes his heyd.	*Than; finely; stupid*
	Quhen he wes heryit out of hand to hie up my honoris,	*plundered excessively; raise*
	And payntit me as pako, proudest of fedderis,	*adorned; peacock; plumes*
380	I him miskennyt, be Crist, and cukkald him maid;	*disregarded; cuckold; made*
	I him forleit as a lad and laithit him mekle:	*rejected; serving man; loathed; greatly*
	I thoght my self a papingay and him a plukit herle;	*parrot; plucked heron*
	All thus enforsit he his fa and fortifyit in strenth,	*gave strength to; enemy; enhanced*
	And maid a stalwart staff to strik himselfe doune.	
385	"Bot of ane bowrd into bed I sall yow breif yit:	*cause for amusement; tell*
	Quhen he ane hal year wes hanyt and him behuffit rage,[2]	
	And I wes laith to be loppin with sic a lob avoir,	*reluctant; mounted; loutish old horse*
	Alse lang as he wes on loft, I lukit on him never,	*on top; looked*
	Na leit never enter in my thoght that he my thing persit,	*vulva pierced*
390	Bot ay in mynd ane other man ymagynit that I haid;	*imagined; had*
	Or ellis had I never mery bene at that myrthles raid.	*mirthless ride*
	Quhen I that grome geldit had of gudis and of natur,	*man; castrated*
	Me thoght him gracelese one to goif, sa me God help:	*unattractive; gaze*
	Quhen he had warit all one me his welth and his substance,	*expended*
395	Me thoght his wit wes all went away with the laif;	*remainder*
	And so I did him dispise, I spittit quhen I saw	*spat*
	That super spendit evill spreit, spulyeit of all vertu.	*overspent; despoiled*
	For, weill ye wait, wiffis, that he that wantis riches	
	And valyeandnes in Venus play, is ful vile haldin:	*valor; held*
400	Full fruster is his fresch array and fairnes of persoune,	*useless*
	Al is bot frutlese his effeir and falyeis at the up with.[3]	
	I buskit up my barnis like baronis sonnis,	*dressed; children; baron's sons*

---

[1] *While after [the] death of that wretched [fellow] who was of no account in the bedchamber*

[2] *When he a whole year was restrained and he needed to take sexual pleasure*

[3] *His equipment is all but fruitless and fails at the climax*

	And maid bot fulis of the fry of his first wif.	*fools; progeny*
	I banyst fra my boundis his brethir ilkane;	*banished; lands; brethren every one*
405	His frendis as my fais I held at feid evir;	*foes; enmity ever*
	Be this, ye belief may, I luffit nought himself,	*loved*
	For never I likit a leid that langit till his blude:	*liked a person; belonged*
	And yit thir wisemen, thai wait that all wiffis evill	*know; women's*
	Ar kend with ther conditionis and knawin with the samin.[1]	
410	"Deid is now that dyvour and dollin in erd:	*Dead; bankrupt; buried*
	With him deit all my dule and my drery thoghtis;	*dies; sorrow*
	Now done is my dolly nyght, my day is upsprungin,	*mournful*
	Adew dolour, adew! my daynté now begynis:	*delight*
	Now am I a wedow, iwise, and weill am at ese;	*indeed; well at ease*
415	I weip as I were woful, but wel is me forever;	*weep as [if]*
	I busk as I wer bailfull, bot flith is my hert;	*dress; sad; blithe*
	My mouth it makis murnyng, and my mynd lauchis;	*mourning; laughs*
	My clokis thai ar caerfull in colour of sabill,[2]	
	Bot courtly and ryght curyus my corse is ther undir:	*very beautiful my body*
420	I drup with a ded luke in my dule habit,	*droop; lifeless appearance; mourning clothes*
	As with manis daill I had done for dayis of my lif.[3]	
	"Quhen that I go to the kirk, cled in cair weid,	*mourning clothes*
	As foxe in a lambis fleise fenye I my cheir;	*fleece; pretend; cheer*
	Than lay I furght my bright buke one breid one my kne,	*forth; book wide open*
425	With mony lusty letter ellummynit with gold;	*many; illuminated*
	And drawis my clok forthwart our my face quhit,	*over; white*
	That I may spy, unaspyit, a space be me syd:	
	Full oft I blenk by my buke, and blynis of devotioun,	*glance away from; cease*
	To se quhat berne is best brand or bredest in schulderis,	*youth; muscled; broadest*
430	Or forgeit is maist forcely to furnyse a bancat	*built; muscularly; furnish; banquet*
	In Venus chalmer, valyeandly, withoutin vane ruse:	*bedchamber; vain boasting*
	And, as the new mone all pale, oppressit with change,	*moon; afflicted*
	Kythis quhilis her cleir face through cluddis of sable,	*Reveals at times; clouds*
	So keik I through my clokis, and castis kynd lukis	*peep; cast*
435	To knychtis, and to cleirkis, and cortly personis.	

---

[1] *Are recognized by their dispositions and known by the same*

[2] *My clothes they are mournful in color of black (sable) (i.e., mourning clothes)*

[3] *As if with sexual intercourse I was finished for the remainder of my life*

"Quhen frendis of my husbandis behaldis me one fer,   *behold me from afar*
I haif a watter spunge for wa, within my wide clokis,   *water sponge; woe*
Than wring I it full wylely and wetis my chekis,   *stealthily; cheeks*
With that watteris myn ene and welteris doune teris.   *eyes; stream down*

440 Than say thai all, that sittis about, "Se ye nought, allace!
Yone lustlese led so lelely scho luffit hir husband: *joyless [creature]; faithfully*
Yone is a peté to enprent in a princis hert,   *pity; imprint*
That sic a perle of plesance suld yone pane dre!"   *suffering endure*
I sane me as I war ane sanct, and semys ane angell;   *sign myself; saint*

445 At langage of lichory I leit as I war crabit: *lechery; behave; ill-natured*
I sich, without sair hert or seiknes in body;   *sigh; sore heart; illness*
According to my sable weid I mon haif sad maneris,[1]
Or thai will se all the suth; for certis, we wemen   *truth; certainly*
We set us all for the syght to syle men of treuth:[2]

450 We dule for na evill deid, sa it be derne haldin.   *mourn; so long as it be kept secret*
  "Wise wemen has wayis and wonderfull gydingis   *ways of acting*
With gret engyne to behaip ther jolyus husbandis;   *ingenuity; deceive; jealous*
And quyetly, with sic craft, convoyis our materis   *conduct our business*
That, under Crist, no creatur kennis of our doingis.   *knows*

455 Bot folk a cury may miscuke, that knawledge wantis,[3]
And has na colouris for to cover thair awne kindly fautis;   *disguises; natural defects*
As dois thir damysellis, for derne dotit lufe,   *young women; secret foolish*
That dogonis haldis in dainté and delis with thaim so lang,[4]
Quhill all the cuntré knaw ther kyndnes and faith: *understand*

460 Faith has a fair name, bot falsheid faris bettir: *falsehood*
Fy one hir that can nought feyne her fame for to saif!   *Fie on; deceive; reputation*
Yit am I wise in sic werk and wes all my tyme;
Thoght I want wit in warldlynes, I wylis haif in luf,   *lack; worldly matters; cunning*
As ony happy woman has that is of hie blude: *noble blood*

465 Hutit be the halok lase a hunder yeir of eild!   *Mocked; guileless girl; hundred*
  "I have ane secrete servand, rycht sobir of his toung,   *paramour; trustworthy*
That me supportis of sic nedis, quhen I a syne mak: *sign*
Thoght he be sympill to the sicht; he has a tong sickir;   *innocent; sight; secure*

---

[1] *In accordance with my black raiment I must have sad manners*

[2] *We direct us all for show to deceive men away from the truth*

[3] *But folk a cooked dish may spoil, who lack understanding*

[4] *That worthless fellows hold in favor and have to do with them so long*

Full mony semelyar sege wer service dois mak: *more handsome person; worse*

470 Thought I haif cair, under cloke, the cleir day quhill nyght, *anxiety; until*

Yit I have solace, under serk, quhill the sone ryse. *chemise; until*

"Yit am I haldin a haly wif out all the haill schyre, *holy woman throughout; county*

I am so peteouse to the pur, quhen ther is persounis mony. *compassionate; poor; many*

In passing of pilgramagis I pride me full mekle, *great*

475 Mair for the prese of the peple na ony perdoun wynyng. *praise; obtaining of pardons*

"Bot yit me think the best bourd, quhen baronis and knychtis, *sport*

And othir bachilleris, blith blumyng in youth, *young knights*

And all my luffaris lele, my lugeing persewis, *faithful; lodging enter*

And fyllis me wyne wantonly with weilfair and joy: *pours out for me*

480 Sum rownis; and sum ralyeis; and sum redis ballatis; *whisper; race; read poems*

Sum raiffis furght rudly with riatus speche: *rant forth rudely; riotous*

Sum plenis, and sum prayis; sum prasis mi bewté, *lament; pray; praise*

Sum kissis me; sum clappis me; sum kyndnes me proferis; *embrace*

Sum kerffis to me curtasli; sum me the cop giffis; *carve [at table]; cup*

485 Sum stalwardly steppis ben, with a stout curage. *boldly march within*

And a stif standand thing staiffis in my neiff; *erect; thrusts; fist*

And mony blenkis ben ovr, that but full fer sittis, *glances; seated far apart*

That mai, for the thik thrang, nought thrid as thai wald. *crowd; prosper*

Bot, with my fair calling, I comfort thaim all: *welcome*

490 For he that sittis me nixt, I nip on his finger;

I serf him on the tothir syde on the samin fasson; *serve; same fashion*

And he that behind me sittis, I hard on him lene;

And him befor, with my fut fast on his I tramp; *tread*

And to the bernis far but sueit blenkis I cast. *young men fair; glances*

495 To every man in speciall I speik sum wordis,

So wisly and so womanly, quhill warmys ther hertis.

"Thar is no liffand leid so law of degré *living person; low of status*

That sall me luf unluffit, I am so loik hertit; *warm-hearted*

And gif his lust be so lent into my lyre quhit, *inclined; face white*

500 That he be lost or with me lig, his lif sall nocht danger.[1]

I am so mercifull in mynd and menys all wichtis, *take pity on; witches*

My sely saull sal be saif, quhen sabot all jugis. *innocent; so long as shoe (see note)*

Ladyis leir thir lessonis and be no lassis fundin: *learn; ignorant girls*

This is the legeand of my lif, thought Latyne it be nane." *legend (saint's life); Latin*

---

[1] *That he be lost or with me lie (in the carnal sense), his life shall not be endangered*

505   Quhen endit had her ornat speche, this eloquent wedow,

Lowd thai lewch all the laif, and loffit hir mekle;   *Loud; laughed; others; praised*

And said thai suld exampill tak of her soverane teching,   *superior*

And wirk efter hir wordis, that woman wes so prudent.   *act according to*

Than culit thai ther mouthis with confortable drinkis;   *cooled*

510   And carpit full cummerlik with cop going round.   *talked like gossips; cup*

    Thus draif thai ovr that deir nyght with danceis full noble.   *spent*

Quhill that the day did up daw, and dew donkit flouris;   *dawn; drenched*

The morow myld wes and meik, the mavis did sing,   *song-thrush*

And all remuffit the myst, and the meid smellit;   *passed away; meadow*

515   Silver schouris doune schuke as the schene cristall,   *fell; shining*

And berdis schoutit in schaw with thair schill notis;   *birds chirped; wood; shrill*

The goldin glitterand gleme so gladit ther hertis,

Thai maid a glorius gle amang the grene bewis.   *made; melody; boughs*

The soft sowch of the swyr and soune of the stremys,   *murmuring; valley; sound*

520   The sweit savour of the sward and singing of foulis,   *birds*

Myght confort ony creatur of the kyn of Adam,

And kindill agane his curage, thocht it wer cald slokynt.   *extinguished by cold*

    Than rais thir ryall rosis, in ther riche wedis,   *arose; roses*

And rakit hame to ther rest throgh the rise blumys;   *proceeded; brushwood blossoms*

525   And I all prevely past to a plesand arber,   *secretly*

And with my pen did report thair pastyme most mery.   *entertainment*

    Ye auditoris most honorable, that eris has gevin   *ears*

Oneto this uncouth aventur, quhilk airly me happinnit;   *strange; in the early hours*

Of thir thre wantoun wiffis, that I haif writtin heir,   *these*

530   Quhilk wald ye waill to your wif, gif ye suld wed one?   *choose*

Select Bibliography and Notes to William Dunbar, *The Tretis of the Twa Mariit Wemen and the Wedo*

Manuscripts

Maitland Folio (Pepys Library, Magdalene College, Cambridge MS 2553) (1570–86).

Early Printed Edition

Chepman and Myllar (National Library of Scotland, Edinburgh), pp. 177–89 (c. 1507).

Editions

Bawcutt, Priscilla, and Felicity Riddy, eds. *Selected Poems of Henryson & Dunbar*. Edinburgh: Scottish Academic Press, 1992.

Bawcutt, Priscilla, ed. *William Dunbar: Selected Poems*. London: Longman, 1996.

————. *The Poems of William Dunbar*. 2 vols. Glasgow: Association for Scottish Literary Studies, 1998.

Conlee, John. *The Works of William Dunbar*. Kalamazoo, MI: Medieval Institute Publications, forthcoming.

Craigie, W. A., ed. *The Maitland Folio Manuscript, Containing Poems by Sir Richard Maitland, Dunbar, Douglas, Henryson, and Others*. Scottish Text Society n.s. 7. Edinburgh: W. Blackwood and Sons, 1919. Pp. 98–115.

Kinsley, James, ed. *The Poems of William Dunbar*. Oxford: Clarendon Press, 1979.

Laing, David, ed. *The Poems of William Dunbar, Now First Collected. With Notes and a Memoir of His Life*. Edinburgh: Laing and Forbes, 1834.

Select Bibliography to The Tretis of Twa Mariit Wemen and a Wedo

MacKay, Colin Edward. *The Poems of William Dunbar: A Descriptive and Critical Analysis.* Ph.D. Diss., Brown University, 1957.

MacKay MacKenzie, William, ed. *The Poems of William Dunbar.* London: Faber & Faber, 1932; rpt. 1966. Pp. 85–97.

Rickly, Patricia. *William Dunbar's Tretis of the Tua Mariit Wemen and the Wedo: A Critical Edition.* Ph.D. Diss., University of Rhode Island, 1980.

Schipper, J., ed. *The Poems of William Dunbar.* Vienna: Kaiserliche Akademie der Wissenschaften, 1894.

Small, John, ed. *The Poems of William Dunbar.* Scottish Text Series, first series 2. Edinburgh and London: W. Blackwood and Sons, 1893.

Wood, Harriet Harvey, ed. *William Dunbar: Selected Poems.* Manchester: Fyfield Books, 1999. Pp. 68–83.

Related Studies

Bawcutt, Priscilla. "Dunbar's *Tretis of the Tua Mariit Wemen and the Wedo* 185–187 and Chaucer's *Parson's Tale.*" *Notes and Queries* 11 (1964), 332–33.

———. *Dunbar the Makar.* Oxford: Clarendon Press, 1992.

Bentsen, Eileen, and S. L. Sanderlin. "The Profits of Marriage in Late Medieval Scotland." *Scottish Literary Journal* 12.2 (Nov. 1985), 5–18.

Bitterling, Klaus. "*The Tretis of the Tua Mariit Wemen and the Wedo*: Some Comments on Words, Imagery, and Genre." *Scottish Studies* 4 (1984), 337–58.

Burness, Edwina. "Female Language in *The Tretis of the Tua Mariit Wemen and the Wedo.*" *Scottish Studies* 4 (1984), 359–68.

Dobson, E. J., and Patricia Ingham. "Three Notes on Dunbar's *The Tua Mariit Wemen and the Wedo.*" *Medium Ævum* 36 (1967), 38–39.

Ebin, Lois. "Dunbar's Bawdy." *The Chaucer Review* 14 (1980), 278–86.

Evans, Deanna Delmar. "Dunbar's *Tretis*: The Seven Deadly Sins in Carnivalesque Disguise." *Neophilologus* 73 (1989), 130–41.

Fradenburg, Louise. "Spectacular Fictions: The Body Politic in Chaucer and Dunbar." *Poetics Today* 5 (1984), 493–517.

Fries, Maureen. "The 'Other' Voice: Woman's Song, Its Satire and Its Transcendence in Late Medieval British Literature." In *Vox Feminae: Studies in Medieval Woman's Songs*. Ed. John Plummer. Kalamazoo, MI: Medieval Institute Publications, 1981. Pp. 155–78.

———. "Medieval Concepts of the Female and Their Satire in the Poetry of William Dunbar." *Fifteenth-Century Studies* 7 (1983), 55–77.

Hope, A. D. "'The two mariit wemen and the wedo': Protest or Satire?" In *Proceedings of the Ninth Congress of the Australasian Universities' Languages and Literature Association, 19–26 August 1964*. Ed. Marion Adams. Melbourne: University of Melbourne Press, 1964. P. 48.

Kinsley, James. "*The Tretis of the Tua Mariit Wemen and the Wedo*." *Medium Ævum* 23 (1954), 31–35.

McCarthy, Shaun. "'Syne maryit I a Marchand': Dunbar's *Mariit Wemen* and Their Audience." *Studies in Scottish Literature* 18 (1983), 138–53.

Parkinson, David. "Prescriptions for Laughter in Some Middle Scots Poems." In *Selected Essays on Scottish Language and Literature*. Ed. Steven R. McKenna. Lewiston: Edwin Mellen Press, 1992. Pp. 27–39.

Pearcy, Roy. "The Genre of William Dunbar's *Tretis of the Tua Mariit Wemen and the Wedo*." *Speculum* 55 (1980), 58–74.

———. "William Dunbar's *Tretis of the Tua Mariit Wemen and the Wedo*." *Studies in Scottish Literature* 16 (1981), 235–39.

Reiss, Edmund. "The Ironic Art of William Dunbar." In *Fifteenth-Century Studies: Recent Essays*. Ed. Robert F. Yeager. Hamden, CT: Archon, 1984. Pp. 321–31.

Ridley, Florence. "A Plea for the Middle Scots." In *The Learned and the Lewed: Studies in Chaucer and Medieval Literature*. Ed. Larry D. Benson. Cambridge, MA: Harvard University Press, 1974. Pp. 175–96.

————. "Studies in Douglas and Dunbar: The Present Situation." In *Fifteenth-Century Studies: Recent Essays*. Ed. Robert F. Yeager. Hamden, CT: Archon, 1984. Pp. 93–117.

Ross, Ian S. *William Dunbar*. Leiden: E. J. Brill, 1981.

Roth, Elizabeth. "Criticism and Taste: Readings of Dunbar's *Tretis*." *Scottish Literary Journal* sup. 15 (1981), 57–90.

Singh, Catherine. "The Alliterative Ancestry of Dunbar's *The Tretis of the Tua Mariit Wemen and the Wedo*." *Leeds Studies in English* 7 (1974), 22–54.

————. "Line 124 of William Dunbar's *The Tretis of the Tua Mariit Wemen and the Wedo*." *Notes and Queries* 21 (1974), 163.

————. "'Sabot' and 'Saull' in Line 502 of Dunbar's *The Tretis of the Tua Maritt Women and the Wedo*." *Forum-for-Modern-Language Studies* 21 (1985), 185–86.

Explanatory Notes

Abbreviations: **B₁**: Priscilla Bawcutt (1996); **B₂**: Priscilla Bawcutt (1998); **B&R**: Priscilla Bawcutt and Felicity Riddy; **C**: W. A. Craigie; **DOST**: *Dictionary of the Older Scottish Tongue*; **HW**: Harriet Harvey Wood; **Ki**: James Kinsley; **Mac**: William MacKay MacKenzie; **MS**: Maitland Folio (Pepys Library, Magdalene College, Cambridge MS 2553); **Sm**: John Small.

Incipit: *Here beginnis the tretis of the twa mariit wemen and the wedo, complyit be Maister William Dunbar* [found in the Maitland Folio]. The Maitland Folio is a handwritten compilation of 366 pages dated between 1570 and 1586 and owned by Sir Richard Maitland. According to Priscilla Bawcutt, the Folio "was not written by Sir Richard himself, who was blind in old age, but seems to have originated in family piety" (B₂, p. 8). The Maitland Folio, now housed in the Pepys Library at Cambridge University, is the most significant repository of Dunbar's work, containing over sixty poems now attributed to him.

1   *Midsummer evin*. This marks a specific day and time, i.e., St. John's Eve (23 June) which was traditionally celebrated with revelry, hence the *mirriest of nichtis*. The nativity of John the Baptist was 24 June and because of that date the celebration became associated with festivities connected to the summer solstice. The festivities were later condemned (1577) for promoting superstition.

21–25   Many scholars have suggested that the flowing hair and exquisite clothes worn by the women in the garden point to romance and its heroines. The women are also connected to Nature and in this sense their presence indicates otherworldliness. A. D. Hope sees a parallel to a scene from an earlier Breton lay, *Sir Orfeo*. See *A Midsummer Eve's Dream: Variations on a Theme by William Dunbar* (New York: Viking Press, 1970).

26   *thair faceis meik. Meik* is used here as a courtly term meaning "gentle," "quiet," "obedient," "unaggressive," "kind," "sweet," "demure," "lowly," "humble," "submissive," "docile," "amenable," "soft," "supple," "pliant." (See MED *mek* adj.) I have glossed the phrase "faces (countenances) gentle (of pliant disposition)" to focus attention on the courtly fantasy of the protagonist as he looks upon the lovely faces of the women, which leads him to his self-indulgent voyeurism. The joke is, of course, how unpliant, ungentle, independent, and disobedient to men these boisterous women are, if seen from the other side of the hedge — hardly "warm wex" that men may "with handes plye," to borrow Januarie's fantastic notion (The Merchant's Tale IV[E]1430).

58–63   *agane the law of luf, of kynd, and of nature.* Natural law, discussed by scholastics in the thirteenth century, referred to natural phenomena as implanted in Nature by the Creator. The laws of Nature were imagined to be discernible by rational creatures to do good and avoid evil through the "right" use of reason. Ki notes that Dunbar's immediate model for the complaint against the repeal of nature is Lydgate's *Floure of Curtesey*, but the ultimate source is Ovid's *Metamorphoses*, Book X, lines 32 ff. (trans. Frank Justus Miller [Cambridge, MA: Harvard University Press, 1916; rpt. 1984]) and the retelling of the Orpheus and Eurydice myth in which Orpheus speaks to Hades:

> . . . I beg of you, unravel the fates of my Eurydice, too quickly run. We are totally pledged to you, and though we tarry on earth a little while, slow or swift we speed to one abode. Hither we all make our way; this is our final home; yours is the longest sway over the human race. . . .

60 ff.   Birds were said to take mates on St. Valentine's Day as in line 206. Chaucer's *Parliament of Fowls* makes a narrative of nature's selection process.

67   *curage.* B&R point out that this word has a range of meaning including "spirit," "vigor," and "courage," as well as "sexual desire." However, its association with male impotence seems most likely to indicate an emphasis on male sexuality.

70–72   *I suld at fairis.* The peregrinations of the widow are reminiscent of Chaucer's Wife of Bath. Lydgate also mentions such wanderings of women in "Payne and Sorowe of Evyll Maryage":

They hem rejoise to see and to be sayne,	*seen*
And to seke sondry pilgremages,	*various*
At grete gaderynges to walken upon the playne,	*plain (open spaces)*
And at staracles to sitte on hie stages.	*plays; raised seats*
(Lines 106–09)	

A "staracle" is a public entertainment, a pageant, spectacle, or play.

85   *A forky fure.* Mac takes *forky* to be a variant of *forsy.* When describing *fure,* which later means "man," the phrase translates to "forceful man." Ki prefers *fortly,* meaning "forward," "enterprising," or "bold." Two emendations are possible based on this interpretation: 1) *Fortly to fure* with *fure* understood as a verb "to bear, go, fare" or as a noun, "furrow," or 2) *Forthy in fure* which Ki prefers because of the equine images that follow and the popular medieval metaphor for sexual intercourse as "ploughing." But it might also simply mean one with good legs as in the verbal sense to *forken,* meaning to stride swiftly or vigorously.

89–92   *wallidrag . . . ane scutarde behind.* B&R identify this contemptuous portrait of the husband as belonging to the *senex amans* (elderly lover) tradition. Chaucer's old John the Carpenter or Januarie along with John Gower's Amans in the *Confessio Amantis,* may be the most explicit sources for Dunbar. But Dunbar is more graphic than either of his predecessors. *Scutarde* suggests defecation, as B₁ observes; thus *scutarde behind* suggests something like "shitass." Ki glosses the term as "skitterer" (n.b. *skit,* meaning "shit" as in the expletive Noah hurls at Gill — "We! hold thi tong, ram-skyt" — in the Towneley Noah play, line 313). If this is the gloss, there is perhaps an aroma of incontinence about the old man.

94   *carybald.* Ki notes the obscurity of this word's origin, though its connotation in the context of the poem is pejorative.

101   *Mahowne.* A colloquial form of a Saracen god, possibly Mohammed himself. The name also occurs in late medieval English romances, such as *Bevis of Hampton,* where it is equated with all that is non-Christian and, therefore, considered evil. In the Corpus Christi plays it equates with tyranny and is the god by which Pharaoh, Caesar, Herod, and their minions swear.

111   *bogill*. Hobgoblin, perhaps the original bogeyman. According to DOST, this term is "of uncertain origin; in northern English dialect as boggle. A supernatural being of an ugly or terrifying aspect; a bugbear" (p. 296).

112   *Belzebub*. A derogatory form of the Syrian deity, Baal-zebul. He appears as one of the fiends in the cycle plays.

113   *smake smolet*. For this obscure phrase, E. J. Dobson and Patricia Ingham offer an explanation: "since the context requires the sense 'mouth' for *smolet*, and since *smake* is properly a noun meaning 'rogue' . . . it is possible that we should read *smake[s]* and emend the second word to *mol[l]et*," a diminutive form of *mull* or "lip." See "Three Notes on Dunbar's *The Tua Maritt Wemen and the Wedo*," p. 38.

128   *nought . . . worth a bene*. I.e., utterly worthless, with some phallic overtones. Compare May's scorn of old Januarie, whose "pleyying" is "nat . . . worth a bene" (*CT* IV[E]1854). B₂ has *worght*.

132   *dangerus*. Alluding to the porter of the *Roman de la Rose* whose name is Danger, this term is taken to mean "resistance." However, recent scholars have questioned this singular meaning particularly in the context of The Wife of Bath's Prologue where it is also found. There it accrues meanings of risk and potential bodily harm. See Elaine Tuttle Hansen, "'Of his love daungerous to me': Liberation, Subversion, and Domestic Violence in the Wife of Bath's Prologue and Tale," in *Geoffrey Chaucer: The Wife of Bath*, ed. Peter G. Beidler (Boston: St. Martin's Press, 1996) and Eve Salisbury, "Chaucer's 'Wife,' the Law, and the Middle English Breton Lays," in *Domestic Violence in Medieval Texts*, ed. Eve Salisbury, Georgiana Donavin, and Merrall L. Price (Gainesville: University of Florida Press, 2002).

135–36 *pené . . . purse*. The sexual economy here is not only similar to that found in Chaucer's The Wife of Bath's Prologue in which Alisoun makes it clear that she has gained financially from having "swynked" (*CT* III[D]202) her first three elderly husbands to death with her "nether purs" (*CT* III[D]44b), but it is also a motif found in The Shipman's Tale as well as in "The Complaint of Chaucer to His Purse." Both the *pené* and *purse* motifs derive from the idea that conjugal debt was a marital obligation to be rendered or "paid" by each spouse. B severs the final -*e* in *pené* and points out the "monetary pun on *recompense*" (B₂, p. 289).

139   *engranyt claith*. A cloth "ingrained" or dyed in scarlet or crimson derived from the berry or grain of a plant. B₂ has *claight*.

141 *rousty raid*. The OED defines *rousty* as an obsolete form of "rusty." Ki (p. 267) suggests that this may mean "clumsy" or a "foray with a rusted weapon," particularly when understood in relation to *raid* (sexual foray, ride; rod), the noun it modifies.

142 *Johne Blunt*. A pejorative term impugning a man's intellectual capability, social situation, or, perhaps, his sexual ability, if his "instrument" be blunt. Contrast the idiom "kene swerd" as a metaphor for sexual prowess.

185–87 There is a parallel between these lines and a passage in Chaucer's The Parson's Tale. In the section on lechery the Parson uses a similar image of the impotent lover. This may be a common image Bawcutt says, though she has "not encountered its use elsewhere. Dunbar is clearly emulating Chaucer in the construction of *The Tretis*, and it seems likely that this is an instance of direct indebtedness to one of the more striking (and probably original) passages of the Parson's Tale" (p. 333). See "Dunbar's *Tretis of the Tua Mariit Wemen and the Wedo* 185–187, and Chaucer's *Parson's Tale*," pp. 332–33.

201 *geit*. Ki glosses as "jet bead"; B₁ simply says "jet." Normally the implication is "glossy black" and might imply something or someone gleaming or fashionable like Chaucer's Pardoner, who "thoughte he rood al of the newe jet" (*CT* I[A]682). Line 202 says the husband "had the glemyng of gold," which might mean that initially he seemed a golden-haired prize (or it might simply mean that he was rich or had the glow of success). But, although the term with reference to gems usually means black, the MED cites a passage in Trevisa which says "Gete . . . is double, that is to seye ʒelow and black," to suggest that there might also be "yellow jet, ?amber" (*get* n. 2[c]). So, given the suggestion of line 202, I have hesitantly glossed the term "amber jewel." On the other hand, if it simply means "fashionable black," *haif geit* might simply mean "have black hair," while the gleaming gold of the next line signifies that he is wealthy.

206 *Sanct Valentynis day*. St. Valentine's Day celebrated now in popular culture was once an official feast day commemorating the martyrdom of one of two possible saints — either a Roman priest martyred under Emperor Claudius circa 269 A.D. or a Bishop of Terni martyred at about the same time. It is possible that the legend of St. Valentine conflates both into a singular entity. St. Valentine's Day may also have its origins in the mid-February pre-Christian festival of Lupercalia, a celebration of courtship and fertility. See also explanatory note to lines 60 ff.

231–34   The point is that even if he were trying to copulate with a tender virgin, for whom sex might be painful, she would not wince a bit, since his equipment would be non-functional.

262   *turtoris*. Turtledoves symbolize marital fidelity and affection. B₂ notes a sarcastic use of the turtle dove in *Reson and Sensuallyte*, lines 6855–90 (p. 291).

269   *nought worth a hen*. "Not a bit." A hen may be worth more than a bean, but it is still worth very little. Compare Chaucer's monk, who "yaf nat of that text a pulled hen, / That seith that hunters ben nat hooly men" (*CT* I[A]177–78).

275   *keyth*. DOST cites *keyth* as a verb meaning "to do a favour"; hence "rub" his crooked back. B₁ and B₂ emend to *claw*, which is glossed as "scratch gently"; that gloss is in keeping with Chaucer's drunken cook who is so pleased with the bawdry of The Reeve's Tale that "he clawed him [the Reeve] on the bak" (*CT* I[A]4326). One gets the impression that there is nothing particularly "gentle" about his action, however. Ki emends to *krych*, which he glosses as "scratch." *Krych* is the emendation proposed by E. J. Dobson and Patricia Ingham, "Three Notes on Dunbar's *The Tua Maritt Wemen and the Wedo*," p. 38.

290   *chuf*. "Churlish fellow"; a boor. But perhaps also a pun on "chough," the jackdaw or rook, said to announce adultery. N.b. The Wife of Bath's ability to prove to her jealous husband that "the cow is wood" (III[D]232).

316   *For never bot in a gentill hert is generit ony ruth*. Compare Chaucer's Knight's "For pitee renneth soone in gentil herte" (*CT* I[A]1761), the most repeated line in *CT*. See also The Man of Law's Tale (*CT* II[B¹]660); The Merchant's Tale (*CT* IV[E]1986); and The Squire's Tale (*CT* V[F]479).

351   *carll*. B₂ suggests that the "sexual role reversal, latent in the Widow's references to herself (e.g., 326, 371, 379), is here explicit" (p. 293).

384   *maid a stalwart staff*. B₁ suggests an allusion to the proverb: "to make a rod with which to beat oneself (Whiting S652)" (p. 356). Whiting lists Dunbar's line as well as references to use of the proverb in *Cursor Mundi*, Chaucer, Gower, the Knight of La Tour Landry, Froissart, and many others (see Whiting).

424   *my bright buke*. B&R suggest that this is an illuminated Book of Hours. Ki notes that this indicates membership in the upper classes.

160

465 *a hunder yeir of eild*. B₁'s gloss is to the point: "May the woman who reaches the age of a hundred, but remains a foolish girl, be publicly derided" (p. 357). She cites J. A. Burrow, *The Ages of Man* (Oxford: Oxford University Press, 1986), pp. 155–56, who suggests a perversion of Isaiah 65:20 (*puer centum annorum morietur, et peccator centum annorum maledictus erit*) in this "boldly feminized version."

502 *sabot*. A later hand has inserted *sall not*. Many editors find this word obscure and disturbing. B₁ notes that "the most ingenious but not wholly convincing suggestion [for meaning] is that this means 'God', from the Biblical *Dominus Sabaoth*, 'Lord of Hosts'"(p. 240). Ki agrees with this interpretation while Catherine Singh offers another possibility, i.e., that *sabot* is "a sort of shoe rather like a present-day Dr. Scholl's or a wooden clog. They were known as 'sabots' or 'saparts' in Trinidad. . . . What exactly the Middle Scots *sabot* looked like is a matter for conjecture or further research but it is apparent that it was some form of sandal or shoe and that the Widow in the poem is simply being flippant about her chances of a safe passage to heaven: 'My innocent sole (or soul) shall be safe, when the shoe is judge of all'"(p. 186). See "'Sabot' and 'Saull' in Line 502 of Dunbar's *The Tretis of the Tua Mariit Wemen and the Wedo*," pp. 185–86. Another possibility is that *sabot*, or "shoe," has a sexual connotation, like "*bele chose*" (*CT* III[D]447) in the Wife of Bath's remarkable vocabulary; see *CT* III[D]492–94, where she passes judgment on her fourth husband's promiscuity by making the shoe fit ill. See also The Merchant's Tale, *CT* V[E]1553.

504 *legeand*. B&R suggest that this term refers to a saint's life, a popular form of narrative written in both Latin and the vernacular in the late Middle Ages.

530 *Quhilk wald ye waill to your wif, gif ye suld wed one*. B&R suggest that the posing of such a question was "both a literary game and a social pastime" (p. 241). Formally called *demande d'amour*, this marks a satiric response to the earlier question posed by the Widow. The implicit rhetorical opposition between the narrator and the Widow links this part of the poem to *flyting*, the informal art of argumentation and debate often associated with the English alliterative tradition, a genre in which Dunbar thrives.

Textual Notes to *The Tretis of the Twa Mariit Wemen and the Wedo*

1   *Midsummer evin.* MS: *missummer evin.*

2   *in meid.* MS: *in* is omitted.

21   *war.* MS: *war.* All editors agree, except Mac, who emends to *was.* *cleir.* B₂ has *clier.*

34   *cleir.* Most editors agree, except Sm, who reads *thre,* and B₂, who has *clier.* This portion of the MS is faded and difficult to read.

36   *twa.* MS: *wyth tua.*

40 ff.   Immediately following this line is a Latin directive: *Aude viduam iam cum interrogatione sua.* ("Hear now the widow with her question.") Latin interjections at various points in the poem appear in the MS: after lines 48, 149, and 244.

48 ff.   *Responsio prime uxoris ad viduam.* ("Response of the first wife to the widow.")

65   *we war fre.* MS: *we war.* HW, Ki, Mac: *we war fre*; B₁: *we war born.* All emendations complete the line, though B₁ differs from the others.

66   *feiris.* MS: *freiris.*

69   *jolie, and gent, richt joyus, and gent.* To avoid the repetition, Mac emends to *joyus, and gentryce.* Others oppose.

98   *gor his.* MS: *gor is his.* Ki, B₁: *gor his.* HW: *gor is.*

104   This is the point where CM begins.

106   *schowis on me.* MS: *chowis me.* B₁: *schowis on me.* Ki, HW, Mac: *schowis one me.*

106   *schedis.* MS: *scheddis.* B₂ has *schendis,* departing from past editors.

109   *the.* MS: *that.*

111   *bogill.* MS: *bugill.*

113   *smake smolet.* The phrase appears as *smakes molet* in Ki's edition. See also explanatory note to this line.

115   *sound of.* MS: *soundis.*

123   *cacis.* MS: *cassis.* B₁, Ki: *cacis.* HW, Mac: *casis.*

124   *trawe, at trist.* MS: *trew atryst.* From the OE *thrawan* meaning "turn," "twist," "trick." Catherine Singh suggests an emendation from *trawe* to *traine,* "a word used elsewhere by Dunbar in its variant forms trane and trayne." See "Line 124 of William Dunbar's *The Tretis of the Tua Maritt Wemen and the Wedo,*" p. 163.

125   *keik.* MS: *luik.*

129   *yerne yeild, for.* MS: *warne ӡeild quhair.*

131   *Ay.* MS: *And.*

135   *pené.* MS: *pen.* HW, Mac, Ki read *pene,* while B₁ and C read *pen.* *in bed.* MS: *in to bed.*

138   *have.* MS: *have ane.* *curche.* MS: *curchef.*

139   *claith.* B₂ has *claight.*

141   *wod.* MS and CM: *wmyod.*

149 ff.   *Hic bibent et inde vidua interrogat alteram mulierem et illa respondet ut sequitur.* ("Here they drink and from there the widow questions the other wife and she responds as follows.")

152   *man.* MS: *men.*

152 *menskit.* MS: *mensit*; CM: *menkit.*

155 *leill.* B₁, HW, and Ki emend to *lell.*

157 *dissymyland.* MS: *dissembland.*

160–61 Transposed in MS.

162 *fra rute.* MS: *the rute.*

164 *so.* MS: *bein.*

166 *devoid.* MS: *avoyd.*

167 *the swalme.* MS: *that swalne.*

172 *as.* MS: *ane.*

177 *rap.* MS: *ryd.*

182 *kemmyng of his hairis.* MS: *kemmit his hair is.* B₁: *kemmyng of his haris.* HW, Ki, Mac: *kemmyng of his hair.*

183 *As.* MS: *And.* Also occurs in variant forms in lines 186, 187, 263, 457, and 489.

184 *semys.* MS and CM: *sunys.*

193 *ralis.* MS: *railʒeis.*

196 *sege.* MS: *segis.*

197 *say.* MS: *sa.*

201 *josit.* MS: *had chosin.*
      geit. MS: *ane geit.*

204 *and.* MS: *ot.* B₁: *and.* HW, Mac, Ki emend to *or.*

218 *sych.* MS: *sicht.* B₁ has *syth.*

219 *Than.* MS: *That.*

221 *no betir.* MS: *nocht betir.*

223 *Quoth.* B₁ has *Quod.*

224 *is happinit.* MS: *hes happinit.*

227 *e, quhen.* MS: *and quhen the.*

229 *warit.* MS: *waryit.*

233 *my gud man.* MS and CM: *man gud my.*

237 *a beid.* MS: *beid.*

240 *Loud lauchand.* So B₁ and MS. HW, Ki: *ludly lauchand.* Mac: *loudly lauchand.* CM: *Luly rauthand.*

242 *bewis.* MS: *levis.*

243 *swapit of.* MS: *swappit at.*

244 ff. *Nunc bibent et inde prime due interrogant viduam et de sua responsione et quomodo erat.* ("Now they drink and then the first two question the widow about her response and what it was [meant].")

249 *Sa that.* MS: *Sa.*

251 *sisteris in.* MS: *sisteris in to.*

252 *innocent.* MS: *inicrit*, an abbreviated form of the word.

258 *be forleit.* MS: *befoir be.*

260 *kene.* MS: *kene and.*

263 *ay.* MS: *and.*

265 *angellis.* MS: *angell.*

272 *hogeart.* MS: *hachart.*

278 *chekis.* MS: *cheik.*

282 *be mery.* MS: *mery.*

283 *lufsummar.* MS: *lustiar.*

285 *sicir.* MS: *secreit.*

286–87 B₂ and Ki concur that these lines are defective.

288 *litill.* MS: *lytill.*

289 *gud.* MS: *the.*

292 *chevist.* MS: *I wist.*

295 *wichtnes.* MS: *vertuousnes.*

296 *marcheand.* CM: *nichand.*

302 *furth.* B has *furtht.* Also in line 308.

303 *tuichandly.* MS: *twichand.*

309 *buthman.* MS: *bicheman.*

310 *my rycht.* MS: *me rycht.*

311 *severance.* MS: *soueranis.*

315 *mercie.* CM: *nicy.*
      mekle. MS: *greit.*

327 *subjeit.* MS: *subiectit.*
      set. CM: *soit.*

329 *unmerciable.* MS: *vnmercifull.*

331 *raip.* MS: *ane raip.*

334 *hepit.* MS: *hapnit.*

334 *behud.* MS: *be hid.*
340 *throu the.* MS: *of that.*
345 *beild.* MS: *beild and.*
347 *bauchles.* MS: *bauchlis.* CM: *bauthles.*
351 *carll.* Omitted in MS. C omits the term, while Ki, B₁, Mac, and HW include it.
351 *werkis.* MS: *laubouris.*
352 *laid.* MS: *laid doun.*
     mensk. MS: *mens.*
356 *drawis.* MS: *drew.*
360–61 These lines are omitted in MS.
362 *my lumbart.* MS: *lumbart.*
     me all. MS: *all my.*
363 *fra me.* MS: *fre.*
368 *hely.* MS: *all helie.*
373 *luf.* MS: *the luif.*
378 *honoris.* MS: *honour.*
389 *Na.* MS: *And.*
391 *had I.* MS: *I had.*
     at. MS: *of.*
396 *saw.* MS: *saw him.*
398 *weill.* Omitted in MS.
     that he. MS: *for he.*
399 *valyeandnes.* MS: *falʒeit anis.*
401 *effeir.* MS: *affect.*
403 *bot.* MS: *his.*
405 *held.* MS: *had.* Mac's emendation, followed by Ki and HW. B₁ reads MS as *heid*, glossing *heid at feid* as "despised." B₂ reads MS as *had.*
408 *thir.* MS and CM: *ther.*
     thai. Not in MS.
412 *dolly.* MS: *dullit.*
417 *it makis.* MS: *makis.*
419 *ryght.* Not in MS.
     my corse is. MS: *is my corps.*

421 *I.* MS: omits, but supplied by all modern editions.
     had done. MS: *done had.*
423 *fleise.* MS: *flesche.*
429 *brand or.* MS: *branit in.*
442 This line is not in MS.
449 *for.* MS: *fra.*
451 *wemen.* MS and CM: *men.*
452 *behaip.* MS: *begaik.*
453 *convoyis.* MS: *gydis.*
457 *As dois.* MS: *And dois.*
461 *hir.* MS: *hir awin.*
     feyne. MS: *fenye.*
465 *the.* MS: *that.*
466 *sobir.* B₂ reads *sovir.*
470 *quhill.* MS: *to the.*
473 *persounis.* B₂ reads *person is.*
475 *perdoun.* B₂ reads *pardon.*
479 *And.* MS: *Sum.*
480 *rownis.* MS and CM: *rowis.*
488 *for.* MS: *nocht for.*
     nought. MS: omits.
491 *serf.* MS: *schir.*
492 *hard on him lene.* MS: *hard on him.*
493 *befor.* MS: *before me.*
502 *sabot.* A later hand has inserted *sall not.*
503 *no lassis.* MS: *nocht.*
506 *thai.* MS: *than.*
509 *ther.* Omitted in MS.
516 *in.* MS: *in the.*
     schill. MS: *still.*
517 *gladit.* MS: *glaid.*
518 *the.* MS: *thai.*
523 *thir.* MS: *ryer.*
529 *thir.* MS: *yer.*
Colophon. MS: *Quod maister Williame Dunbar.* CM: *Quod Dunbar.*

Emperator Felicianus
(How a Wife Employed a Necromancer to Cause the Death of Her Husband, and How He Was Saved by a Clerk)

Felician regnyd emperour in the cyté of Rome, in the empeire of whom ther was a knyght that hadde weddid a yong damesell to wif. And withinne fewe yerys this woman lovid by wey of synne another knyght, undir hire husbond, and that so moch, that she ordeyned for hire husbonde to be ded. Happyng that this knyght wold goo on pilgrimage over the see; and therfore he seide to his wif, "Dame, y woll goo on pilgrimage, over the see; and therfore governe thee wele the while til I come home agen." And with that she was glad, and seide, "Sir, with the grace of God all shall be wele y-do." And shortly for to touche this mater he tooke his leve, and yede his wey. Nowe this false quene, his wif, ordeyned for his dethe in all that she cowde, and spake therfore to a nigromauncer in this forme: "Myn husbond," quod she, "is biyende the see; I woll wite, if thou cowde helpe that he were ded by ony crafte. Aske of me what thou wolt, and thou shalt have hit." Then spake he to hyre agen, and saide, "This, forsoth, lady, that I can. That knyght shall dye by my crafte, yn what cuntré of the wordle soever that he be ynne. And y woll have nothing of thee for my travayle but the love of thyne hert." And she it grauntid to him. So this nigromancien dyd make an ymage of erthe, and fastenyd it in the wall afore him. And the knyght, that was gon on pilgrimage, walkyd yn the same day in the stretys of Rome. So ther met with him a clerke, the which hielie beheld him. And when the knyght perceyvid it, he seide to him, "Goode Sir, tell me why and what skile, that thou so beholdest me?" Thenne seid the clerke, "Forsoth, Sir, for thy deth; for douteles thou shalt yn this same day be

5

10

15

20

---

1 regnyd, reigned. **4 ordeyned**, planned; **Happyng**, It just so happened. **5 see**, sea. **8 y-do**, done. **9 yede**, went. **10 cowde**, could; **nigromauncer**, magician. **11 biyende**, across; **wite**, [like to] know. **12 crafte**, magic. **15 travayle**, work. **17 afore**, before. **19 hielie**, familiarly. **20 what skile**, for what reason.

165

ded, but if thou be the better holpyn." And he told the knyght how that his wif
was a strompet, and which purveith in that day that hire husbond shud be ded.
And when the knyght hurde theise wordes, he had grete merveile, and saide, "A!

25 Sir, I knowe well that my wif is an hore, and long tyme hath y-be; but that she
ever pursuyd for my deth, that is unknowe to me, and therfore I pray thee tell me
if ther be ony remedye agenst my deth; and if thou mowe save my lyf; sothly all my
goodys shull be at thyne owne will." "Yys," quoth the clerk, "a remedye ther is, if
thou wolt do aftir my conseil." "Yis, yis," seide the knyght, "I am redy to fulfill all

30 in dede that thou wolt sey unto me." Thenne seide this clerke, "Thy wif," he
seide, "hath this day spoken with a man that can of nigromancye, to sle thee by
his crafte and sotilté; and so the nigromancien hath y-made an ymage, and sette it
in a wall; and anoon he woll take a bowe and arowis, and shete att it. And if he
wounde this ymage, thyne herte shall brest, wheresoever thou be in the wordle.

35 And so thou sholdiste dye; nevertheles do aftir my conseil, and sone I shall save
thi life. Do of alle thy clothis, and be nakid, and go into a bath that I shall make
for thee." And the knyght dyd right as he bad him. And when he was in the bath,
the clerk toke him a myrour in his hond, and seide, "Nowe thou shalt see in this
myrour all that I spake of to thee." And thenne seide he, "Ye, sothly I see all opynly

40 in myne hous, that thou spakist of to me. And now the myster-man takith his
bowe, and woll schete att the ymage." Thenne seide the clerk, "Sir, as thou lovist
this lif, what tyme that he drawith his bowe, bowe thyne hed undir the watir; for
if thou do not certenly thy ymage shall be smytene, and thou both." And when the
knyght sawe him begynne for to drawe his bowe, he dyd as the clerke conseilid

45 him. And thenne seide the clerk, "What seist thou now?" "Forsoth," quoth he,
"now hath he schote an arowe at the ymage; and for that he failith of his strook,
he makith moch sorowe." Thenne seide the clerke, "Ye, that is goode tydyng for
thee; for if he had smyten the ymage, thou sholdist have i-be ded. But loke nowe
on the myrour, and tell me what thou seist." "Now he takith an other arowe, and

50 woll shete agen." "Do thenne," quoth the clerke, as thou dyd afore, or ellis thou

22 holpyn, helped. **24 merveile,** amazement. **25 hore,** whore; **y-be,** been. **27 mowe,**
might. **29 Yis,** Yes. **31 can,** knows. **32 sotilté,** subtlety; **nigromancien,** magician. **33**
anoon, soon; **arowis,** arrows; **shete,** shoot. **34 brest,** burst; **wordle,** world. **35 do aftir,**
follow. **36 Do of,** Take off. **37 bad,** commanded. **38 myrour,** mirror. **40 myster-man,**
sorcerer. **42 bowe,** duck. **43 smytene,** shot. **46 strook,** stroke. **48 i-be,** been.

shalt be ded." And therfore the knyght putte all his hede undir the water. And whenne he had so y-done, he raisid hit up agen, and seyde to the clerke, "He makith sorowe nowe more than ony man woll trowe, for he smot not the ymage; and he cryed to my wif, seiyng, that if I fayle the third tyme, I am but ded my-
55   selfe, and thyne husbond shall lyve; and my wif makith therfor moch lamentacion." "Loke agen," seide the clerke, "and tell me what he doth." "Forsothe," seide he, "he hath bend his bowe and goith ny to the ymage for to shete; and therfor I drede now gretly." "Do therfor," seide the clerke, "do as I bade doo afore, and dred thee nothyng." So the knyght, whenne he sawe the scheter drawe his bowe, he swapte
60   his hed undir the waitr, as he dyd afore; and thenne he toke it up agen, and lokid yn the myrour, and he lowgh with a gret myrth. "I sey," quod the clerke, "whi lawghist thou soo?" "For the archer wold have y-schot at the ymage, and he hath y-schotte himselfe in the lungen, and lyeth ded; and my wif makith sorowe withoute ende, and woll hyde his body by hire beddys syde." "Ye, Sir," quod the
65   clerke, "now thou haste thi lif savid, do yeld to me my mede, and go; farwell." Thenne the knyght gaf him mede as he woll aske. And the knyght went hom, and fond the body undir the bedde of his wif; and he yede to the meyre of the towne, and told him howe his wife hadde don in his absence. Thenne when the meyre and the statys sawe this doyng, they made this wif to be slayne, and hire herte to be
70   departid ynto three parteis, in tokne and emsampill of veniaunce. And the goode man toke another wif, and faire endid his liffe.

Moralitee

Seith nowe, goode men; this emperour I call owre lord Jhesu Criste; the empire is this wordle, in which is moch adversité; for all that is in the wordle other it is fals
75   covetise of flesch, or fals covetise of yen, or prowde of lif. The wif that lovith not hire husbond is thi flesch, that dispisith all werkis that the spirite lovith. Now in speking gostely of this mater, while that a man goith in pilgrimage, serys, that is to sey, in werke of ony goode dede to be fullfilled, thenne the flesh spekith with the

53 trowe, attest to. **59 scheter**, shooter; **swapte**, ducked. **65 mede**, reward. **67 fond**, found; **yede**, went; **meyre**, mayor. **68 howe**, what. **69 statys**, nobles. **70 emsampill**, example; **veniaunce**, sin. **71 faire endid his liffe**, lived out his life well. **74 wordle**, world. **75 yen**, eyes; **prowde**, pride. **77 gostely**, spiritually.

nigromancier, *scil.* the devill; and that he doth as ofte tyme as he grucchith agenst
80   the spirit, and sesith fro werkis of penaunce, wherby the spirit may be slayne. For
it is as the Apostill seith, *Caro concupiscit adversus spiritum, et spiritus adversus
carnem*, this is to undirstonde, the flesch desirith thing that is agenst the spirite,
and the spirit desirith thing agenst the flesch. The clerke that helpith the knyght is
a discrete confessour or a prechour, which techith a man how that he shall defende
85   him agenst the dartys of the devill. This nigromancer that is the devill, biginnith to
schete an arowe att the ymage, — what is that? The reson within a man. But
beware that he hit not him with his arowe, *scil.* envy or avarice, for if he do,
withoute doute he shall dye in evermore lastyng deth. And therfore thou most
putte downe thyn hed — what is that? Thyne old lif of synne, and entre ynto the
90   bath of confession. And thou most hold in thy hond a myrour, *scil.* holy doctrine,
that prelatis and prestis every day shewith, by the which thou shalt see all perilis
that perteynith to thi soule. And also holdyng downe of the hed in the bath is to be
redy to goo undir the yoke of penaunce and submitte thee to it that shall be
enjoyned to thee; and that is not hard, witnessing the saviour himself, wher he
95   seith, *Iugum meum suave, et onus meum leve*, Lo! My yoke, he seith, is swete,
and my charge is light. And if thou do thus, no doute of thou shalt stonde agenst
all the shotis that the devill can shete to thee; and his shotis shall turne to his owne
sorowe, and encresing of his peyne in the bed of hell, wher he shall be buryed.
Now than most a prelate honge the wif — what bymenyth that? Forsoth that
100 consciens and discrecion late the flesh be hongyd on the jebet of penaunce, of the
which maner of living the Apostill spekith this, *Suspendium elegit anima mea*, this
is to sey, my soule hath chosen the jebet, *scil.* doyng of penaunce. And after the
herte is departid unto thre parteys, that is, the flesh is devidid ynto thre, *scil.*
praying, almysded, and fastyng. And thenne thou shalt take a new wif, *scil.* a
105 spirit obediente to a new governaunce; and thenne per consequens thou shalt have
evermore lastyng lif, *Ad quam nos et vos perducat*, &c.

79 *scil.* (scilicet), that is to say; **grucchith**, complains. **84 which**, who. **85 dartys**,
arrows. **91 prelatis**, prelates. **94 enjoyned**, bound. **98 encresing**, increasing; **peyne**,
pain. **99 bymenyth**, means. **100 discrecion**, discretion; **jebet**, gibbet. **103 devidid**, di-
vided. **105 per**, through. **106 Ad quam nos et vos perducat, &c.**, To which He leads us
and you, etc.

Godfridus a Wise Emperoure
(Of the Magic Ring, Brooch, and Cloth, Which an Emperor Left to His Son: How He Lost Them and How They Were Recovered)

Godfridus regnid a wise Emperour in the cetee of Rome, and he had childerin that he lovid moche. And when he laye on his dethebed, he callid to him his eldest sonne and saide to him, "Der sone, the heritage that my fadir lefte and biquathe to me, holly I geve hit to thee." Aftir that he clepid the secounde sone, and saide to him, "Der sone,
5 I have certeyne possessions, londis and tenementes, that come of my purchas, and therfor, sone, I geve al tho, and alle other that I have, withoute my heritage." And he made the thirde to be callid, and seide to him, "Sone, I have noo mevable goodes to geve thee, but only thre jewell, *scil.* a presious ringe, a gay broche, and a riall clothe; and thes thre I bequethe thee. And the vertu of the ringe is this, that whosoever ber
10 hit upon him, he shalle have love of al men. The vertu of the broche is this, that whosoevere ber hit upon his brest, late him thinke what he wolle, and he shalle mete therwith at his likynge. And the vertu of the clothe is swiche that lete a man sitte uppon hit, and he shalle be in what partye of the worlde he wolle desire. And sone, I geve thee thes thre and I charge thee, that thou go to scole, for thow shalt by thes
15 thre, gete god inowhe." When this was seyde, he turnid his body to the walle, and yelde up the gost. The childerin with the moder reverently buryed him, and gret lamentacion was made for his dethe. Then the eldest sone occupied his eritage; the secounde sonne al the purchas. And the Emperes saide to the yongest sone, "Thi fadir gaf to thee a ringe, and a broche, and a clothe; here I take to thee the ringe, that thow
20 go to scole, and lerne; and yf thou do welle, thow shalte be myn owne der harte." The yonge sone receyvid the ringe; and his name was Jonathas; and he yede to an université,

1 **childerin**, children. 3 **biquathe**, bequeathed; **holly**, wholly. 4 **clepid**, called. 5 **tenementes**, properties. 7 **mevable**, movable. 8 *scil.* **(scilicet)**, namely; **riall**, royal. 14 **scole**, school. 15 **god i-nowhe**, goods enough. 18 **purchas**, chattel. 19 **take**, give. 21 **yede**, went.

and there he lernid in a mervelous maner. And as he walkid in a certeyne day ther in
the citee, ther mette with him a faire woman; and whenne Jonathas sawe hir, he was
i-storid to an unlawfull maner of love and spake to hir therof. She grauntid him, and he
25 lay withe hir al nyght, and aftir helde hir stille to his store. And thorow vertu of the
ringe he hadde getyn love of al the université; he made gret festes, and nothinge him
lackid, for they lovid him so moche, that for his love they geve him inowe. This
woman, that was his leman, hight Felicia; and she had gret marvayle that he had alle
thinges to his luste, and at his wille, and for she coude fynde nere ner peny with him.
30 So in a nyght, as thei lay togeder in bed, she saide to him, "Worshipfull sir, ye have
i-had my maydinhode, and ye shulle have me as longe as I live; and as ye coveyte me
to be redye to youre wille, I pray yow tellithe me a petucion that I shalle asked of yow,
scil. how ye make so many festes, and havithe so muche goode, and havithe no
tresoure ne mony, that I can se?" Thenne saide he, "Yf so be that I telle thee my
35 counseill, I trowe that thow woldest discover me." "Nay, sir, God forbede," quod
she, "that ever I shuld do that traytorye to yowe!" Thenne said he, "My fadir hathe
biquethe to me this ringe, that thow seist me have on my finger; and hit hathe swiche
a vertu, that he that berithe hit on his finger, shalle have love of alle men, and so al men
lovithe me therfore so moche, that whatsoever I aske of them thei gevithe me." And
40 then saide she, "Sir, whi wolde thow never telle me this or nowe, for perilis that
myght falle?" "Whi?" quod Jonathas, "What perile myght falle?" Thenne saide Felicia,
"Thou goste ofte tyme in the towne, and ther thow myghtest les hit by some chaunse;
and for to lese swiche a jewelle, hit wer grete harme and perill; and therfore, der birde,
leve me that ringe, and I shalle kepe it." Jonathas gaff goode credense to hir wordes
45 and toke hir the ringe. And when hit was so i-don, the love of the peple bygan to turne
fro him ne ther was noon that wolde eny mor geve him, as thei dud afore. And when
he perceyvid that, and that the cause was for he bare not the ringe, he turnid agene to
his lemman, and saide to hir, that she shulde deliver hit to him agene. And thenne she
beganne to feyne a lesynge, and saide with a loude crie, "Alas! My cheste is i-broke,
50 and the ringe is borne awey!" Thenne Jonathas was hili mevid, and saide, "Alas!

24 i-storid, inspired. **25 stille,** close; **store,** possession. **27 i-nowe,** enough. **28 hight,**
was called. **29 luste,** desire; **coude,** could. **31 coveyte,** want. **32 petucion,** request. **39**
gevithe, give. **40 or,** before. **42 goste,** go; **les,** lose. **43 birde,** love. **45 i-don,** done. **46**
dud, had. **49 feyne,** devise; **lesynge,** lie; **i-broke,** broken into. **50 borne awey,** stolen.
hili mevid, greatly upset.

womman, that ever I saw thee!" And she beganne to wepe, and to make grete sorow; and Jonathas sawe that, and saide, "Wepe not, for God hathe holpin me hedirto"; and he trowid hir right welle. So he wente to his contré, and come to his modir. Whenne the Empresse sawe him, she said to him, "Der sonne whi ert thow come hom so soone fro thi studie?" Thenne seide Jonathas, "A! Modir, I have lost my rynge, by cause that I toke hit to my lemman." Thenne answerd the modir, "Sone, I have ofte tyme saide to thee, that thow sholdeste beware of womman; and now I wolle take thee thi broche, but loke that thow lese not hit." Jonathas resseyvid the broche, and fastenid hit uppon his brest, and yede to the université, as he dude afor. And so, thorowe vertu of the broche, he gate al thinge that he wolde coveite towchinge wordly goodes, inso-muche that the damiselle hadde grete marvayle of hit; and therfore bothe nyght and day she lay aboute him to seye the sothe, how that he made so gret festes, and hadde so deyntefulle metis, but he wolde not telle hir longe tyme. But the shrewe wepte, sighid, and saide, "Thou trowest not me, I see wel; and I wolle bynde my lyf to thee, to kepe thi counseill, and thi jewel eke, yf thou haddist eny." Jonathas trowid hir wordes and tolde hir the vertu of the broche. Thenne she wepte mor faste, and wolde not be stille. And then saide he, "Woman, whi wepist thow, and for what cause sorowest thou?" "For I trowe," quod she, "that thow wolte lese thi broche, and thenne thow lesist al thi thryfte." Thenne saide he, "What wolte thow counsaile me in this cas?" Thenne she saide, "I counseille thee, that thou take hit me to kepe." "I trowe," quod he, "that thou wolte lese hit, as thow loste my ringe." "Iwisse," quod she, "rathir shalle the sowle parte from my bodye or I lese hit." Jonathas undir a grete triste tooke hir the broche; and some aftir the godes bygon to fayle. Thenne Jonathas entirid into the chaumbr, and she began to crye, as she dude afor, and saide, "Allas! The broche is i-stole; I wolle now for woo slee nowe myself!" She drowe oute a knyf and feynid as she wolde have smetin hirselfe. Thenne Jonathas trowid that she wolde have slayne hirselve; he toke the knyf from hir, and saide, "Damiselle, I pray thee, leve thi wepinge, for I forgeve it thee altogedir." Anon by cause of nede he turnid home ageyne, and visitid his moder. And whenne his moder sawe him, she saide to him, "Sey, sone, hast thowe lost thi broche, as thow didest thi ringe?" and he saide,

52 holpin, helped; **hedirto**, before. **53 trowid**, trusted. **59 afor**, before; **thorowe**, by. **60 gate**, acquired; **wordly**, worldly. **62 seye**, discover. **63 deyntefulle metis**, gourmet cuisine. **64 trowest**, trust. **69 thryfte**, wealth. **71 Iwisse**, Indeed. **74 entirid**, entered. **75 i-stole**, stolen. **76 feynid**, pretended; **trowid**, believed. **78 leve**, cease.

"The woman that had the ringe, hadde the broche in the same maner"; but what worthe of hit he ne knew, as he saide. Thenne the modir beinge ivele apayde withe him, she saide, "Sonne, thou wotist welle I have now no mor of thyne but a clothe, and therfore her it is; ches thou wher thow wolte kepe it, or leve it her. But, sone, I warnid thee to

85 beware of women." And Jonathas seide thenne agene, "Sothely, modir yf so be that the clothe be lost, I shalle never mor thenne loke thee in the face." Thenne she deliverid to him the clothe, and he yede agene to scole. And soone aftir his unthrifti lemman mette withe him, as she dude afor, and she made him gode chere and kiste him; and he dide as thowhe he hadde no jewel. Whenne he was in his hostelle, sone he leyde the

90 clothe undir him, and bad his leman sitte downe biside him uppon the clothe; and she knewe not of the vertu of the clothe, and anoon Jonathas thoute, "Lorde! Yf we wer now in fer contrees, wher never man come afore this!" And thenne withe the same thoute they wer bothe reysid up togedir, into the ferrest coste of the worlde, with the clothe with hem. And whenne the woman sawe that, she saide, "Alas! What do we

95 her!" "Her we bethe nowe," quod he, "and her I shalle leve thee, and bestes shulle devoure thee, for that thow hast i-holynd my rynge and my broche." "A! sir, mercy," quod she, "for sothely yf thow wolte brynge me agene to the citee, I shalle geve to thee thi ringe and thi broche, withouten anye agene-stondynge; and but yf I do in dede that I seye, I wolle bynde me to the foulest dethe." Jonathas trowid hir, and saide, "Loke

100 nowe, that thou never do trespas mor, for yf thow do, thou shalt dye." And thenne she saide to him, "For the love of God tel me now how we come hedir!" Thenne saide he, "The vertu of the clothe is, that whosoevere sittithe therupon, shalle be in what coste of the worlde he wolle desire to be ynne." And then he saide, "Forsothe, I hadde lever slepe then al the worldes goode, as me thinkithe; and therefore, I pray thee, ley

105 forthe thi sherte, that I may ligge down, and have a litle slepe." She dude so, and he leyde downe his hede in hir shirte, and byganne stronglye to slepe. Thenne she heringe his grete slepe, she drow the parti of the clothe that was undir him unto hir; and thenne she thowte, "Lord! Yf I wer now wher that I was today!" And anon, sodenly she was browte to the same plase; and Jonathas lay stille slepinge. Whenne he wakid,

110 he saw neithere clothe, ne woman; he wepte bitterly, and saide, "Alas! Alas! What

81 **worthe**, became. 82 **ivele apayde**, very angry. 84 **her**, here. 87 **unthrifti**, untrustworthy. 89 **dide**, pretended; **hostelle**, room. 93 **thoute**, thought; **reysid**, raised; **ferrest coste**, farthest coast. 95 **bestes**, beasts; **shulle**, shall. 96 **i-holynd**, stolen. 99 **trowid**, trusted. 104 **lever**, rather. 105 **ligge**, lie. 109 **and,** but.

shalle I nowe do I wot nevere; and I am worthi al this bale, for I tolde to the woman al my counseill." He lokid abowte on everye side, and sawe nothinge but wilde bestes, and briddis fleing in the heir; and of hem he hadde grete drede in herte. And he rose up, and yede by a certeyne pathe, but he wiste never to what place. And as he yede, ther

115 was a water in his weye, over the whiche he moste nedis goo; and whenne he enterid into the water, it was so hote, that hit brende of the fleshe fro the boone of his legges, for hit drowe awey alle the fleshe that it towchid. And Jonathas hadde ther a crewette, and fillid hit of that water. Tho he yede forthe, tille he saw a tree fulle of frute; and there he gaderid frewte, and ete, thorow the whiche he was made a foule lepre. And thoo for sorowe he fel

120 down, and seide, "Cursid be the day wherin I was borne, and also the hour in which I was conseyvid in my modir!" Aftir this he rose, and yede, and sawe the secounde water; and dradde for to entir. Nevertheles he enterid in, and as the fyrste water drowe of the fleshe of his feet, so the secounde water restorid hit agen. And he filde a cruet therwith, and bare the frute with him also. And as he yede forthe, he sawe the secounde frewte afer, and for

125 he hungerid, he yete of that frute, and anon he was clansid of alle his lepr; and toke of the frute with him, and livid welle withe sustenaunce thereof. Thenne he sawe a feire castell, and in the circuite aboute ful of hedis of lechis. And as he come ny to the castell, there mette two squiers, and thei seid to him, "Der frende, whens erte thowe?" "I am," quod he, "a leche of fer contrees hennys." Thenne saide thei, "The kynge of this castell is a lepr

130 man, and manye lechis comithe to him, and undirtakithe to hele him, up peyne of hir hedis, and thei havithe y-faylid everychone; and therfor thow maiste see hir hedis sitte in the wallis of the castelle. And therefore we telle thee for certeyne, yf thow undirtake my lorde, and not hele him, thou shalte lese thy lyfe." Thenne saide he, "Yis, I shalle hele him." Tho he was browte before him, and he gaf the kynge of his frewte to ete, and also he gafe him

135 of his secounde water to drynke, and anon the kynge was hole. And he gaf to Jonathas riche giftes, and fair, plentefully, and mo behite him, yf he wolde abyde withe him. But he wolde not assent to dwelle withe him. And eche day he usid to go unto the see-syde, that was therin, to aspie yf ther wer enye shippe, that mygt bringe him home. And at the

111 bale, grief. **113 briddis**, birds; **heir**, air. **116 brende of**, burned off. **117 towchid**, touched; **crewette**, cruet. **119 frewte**, fruit; **ete**, ate; **lepre**, leper. **122 of**, off. **125 clansid**, cleansed; **lepr**, leprosy. **128 whens erte thowe**, where do you come from. **129 leche**, physician; **hennys**, hence. **130 lechis**, physicians; **hele**, heal; **peyne of hir hedis**, loss of their heads. **131 y-faylid everychone**, failed everyone. **133 Tho**, Then. **135 hole**, whole. **136 mo**, more; **behite**, asked.

laste, in a certeyne day there come toward thirty shippis, and alle in a morow reysid
140　there. Thenne Jonathas enquerid amonge hem, yf eny shippe wer there redy for to go
to swiche a londe, wher as he hauntid scole.

　　At the last he founde a shippe redy, that wolde to the same contree. Thenne Jonathas
was gladde, and enterid into the shippe, aftir that he hadde take leve of the kynge.
Sone aftir that he was come to the citee, there as was his leman. But ther was noon
145　that had knowleche of him, for longe tyme, that he had be devourid with wilde bestes.
Whenne Jonathas was in the citee, anoon he toke cure of syke peple, and he helid alle.
And by that tyme his leman was the richeste of that citee, by vertu of the rynge and
of the broche, and of the clothe, but she was gretly turmentid withe sikenesse. And
whenne she harde telle, that such a sotill leche was come to the citee, anoon she made
150　messagers to go for him, and that he wolde vouchesaffe to hele hir of hir sykenesse.
Jonathas come to hir, and there he fonde his lemman on bed; and he knewe hir welle,
but she knew not him. And whenne he hadde i-seyne hir uryne, he seide to hir,
"Worthi ladye, thow haste oo sekenesse that may not be helid but by oo way; and yf
thow wolt preve that wey, thowe may be helid." Then seide she, "I am redy to do
155　whatsoever thow comaundist, so that I be hole therby." Jonathas saide to hir,
"Thou moste be clene i-shriven; and yf thou have withedrawe owte fro eny man
with wronge, thow moste restor hit agene, and thenne I shalle warante thee to be
hole; and ellis my medicinis wolle not stonde in stede." And so by cause that she was
grevousely holde withe sekenesse, she made an opyn confession afore al men, how
160　that she had deseyvid the sonne of the Emperoure, as hit is seide afor, and how she
lefte him at the ende of the worlde. Thenne seide he, "Wher ben the thre jewellis that
thou withedrew fro him, *scil.* the ringe, the broche, and the clothe?" And she tolde
him that thei wer at hir beddis fete, in a chest. "And therfor," she saide, "open the
cheste." And there he fonde as she saide, with gret joye to him. And he toke the ringe
165　and put hit on his fynger, he sette the broche on his breste, and toke the clothe undir
his arme. And he toke hir drinke of his firste cruet, *scil.* of that water that drow awey
the fleshe of his fete, and yaf hir to ete of that frute that made him lepr; and whenne

140 enquerid, inquired. **141 hauntid**, attended. **142 wolde**, was going. **144 there as**,
where. **148 turmentid**, tormented. **149 sotill**, skillful. **150 messagers**, messengers; **and**,
[to see] if; **vouchesaffe**, promise. **152 i-seyne**, examined; **uryne**, urine. **153 oo**, one; **but**,
except. **154 preve**, follow. **156 i-shriven**, confessed. **160 deseyvid**, deceived. **163 beddis
fete**, foot of the bed.

she hadde resseyvid hit, she was in swiche a likenesse, that no man wolde no lenger abide with hir, and in that grete angr she yede up the sprite. Thenne aftir hir dethe, 170 Jonathas turnid home to his contree, with gret joye, beryng with hime the ringe, the broche, and the clothe; and in goode pes endid his lyf.

Moralitee

Dere frendes, this Emperoure is oure lord Jhesu Criste, that hathe thre sones. By the firste sone we must undirstonde angelis, to whome God hathe gevin swiche 175 confirmacion and grace that they may not synne; for aftir that aungels weer falle don, God so confermid hem that thei dwelle stille after, that they myght not synne aftire. By the secounde sonne undirstonde prophetes, to whom God gaf the olde lawe of Moyses; the which law was mevable, for it was chaungid by the advent of Criste. And to the thirde sone, *scil.* a Cristen man, he gaf thre jewell — a ringe a broche, and a clothe. By 180 the ringe we muste undirstonde feithe, for that owithe to be rounde like a ringe, and withoute eny twartynge; and he that hathe the ringe of feithe, witheoute eny dowte he shalle have the love of God and of aungles; and therefore seithe oure savioure: *Si habueritis fidem, sicut granum sinapis*, &c. *Ut supra*, this is to seye, yf ye have feithe, as the seed or as the greyene of synevey, as is saide befor. And therfor he that hathe 185 the ringe of feithe, vereliche he shalle have al thinges to his likinge. Also he gaf to the Crysten man a broche, *scil.* the Holy Goste in his herte; and therfore it is seyde, *Mittam vobis spiritum paraclitum et suggeret vobis omnia quecumque dixero vobis*, this is to sey, I shalle sende to yow the Holy Gost, the whiche shall shew in yow all goodis which I shall seye to yowe. And therfor yf we have the Holy Goste in oure 190 hertes, witheoute dowte we shulle have al thinge that shall be prophitable to oure soulis. Also he gaf to Cristin man a presious clothe. The clothe is perfite charité, the whiche God shewithe for us and to us in the Cros; for he lovythe us so muche, that he offirde himselfe to dye for us, for to bringe us to the place that we desire for to come to, *scil.* to hevene. And therfor whoso wille sitte on the clothe of perfite charité, 195 witheoute dowte he may be translatid. Jonathas may be callid every Cristen man that

169 angr, agony; **yede**, gave; **sprite**, spirit. **178 mevable**, transformed. **180 feithe**, faith; **owithe**, ought. **181 twartynge**, opposition. **184 synevey**, mustard. **185 vereliche**, truly. **190 prophitable**, profitable. **191 perfite charité**, love. **193 offirde**, sacrificed. **195 translatid**, transformed.

is fallyn to synne. Thenne his leman metithe with him, *scil.* his wrecchid fleshe, that
stirithe him to synne; and than he lesithe the ringe of feithe that he reseyvid in baptisme;
and thenne the broche, *scil.* the Holy Gost, fleithe from him, for synne; and the
clothe, *scil.* charité, is drawin fro him as ofte tyme as he assentithe to synne; and so
200 the wrecchid man is lefte witheoute helpe amonge the wylde bestes, *scil.* the devil,
the wordle, and the fleshe; and thenne it is gretlye to sorow. Therfore, man, do as
dude Jonathas: arys fro thi slepe of synne, for thow hast slepte to longe in the slepe of
carnalité; and therfor hit is wretin thus, *Surge qui dormis, et illuminabit te Christus*;
this is to sey, aryse thou that slepest, and Criste thee shalle i-liyten. Thenne whenne
205 thou ert up risen fro slepe of synne, and art i-litenyd, and mayste see, entre into the
water that wolle have of the fleshe fro the boone, *scil,* penaunce, the whiche putithe
awey fleshelyche affeccions. Aftir he etithe the frute of sharpenesse, the whiche
chaungithe the cher, in maner of a lepr man; as it is wretin of Crist: *Vidimus eum non
habentem speciem neque decorem*; this is to seye, we saw him not having shappe ne
210 fairnesse. So of the soule, that is in bitternesse for his synnes; and therfor in figur a
sowle is seide to be blak, thogh hit be wel i-shape. Aftir he entrithe the secounde
water, that is i-callid holly comunynge, that is aftir penaunce; and therfor seithe oure
Savioure: *Ego sum fons vite; qui biberit ex aqua hac, non siciet in eternum*; this is to
sey, I am the welle of lyfe and he that drinkithe of this water shalle not thirste. Aftir
215 that, he etithe of the fruyt of the secounde tree, the whiche restorithe al that was
loste; whenne that he is glorefiid in everlasting lyfe, aftir that he hathe helide the
kynge, *scil,* the soule, and so he entrithe into the shippe of holy chirche, and gothe to
his lemman, *scil.* his fleshe, and rechithe to hir the water of contrucion, and the frute
of penaunce, and of sharpnesse, for the whiche the fleshelyche affeccions deyethe.
220 And so by penaunce he takithe of hit his lost goodes, and so he gothe to his contree,
scil. to the kyngdom of hevene. To the whiche He us brynge, that is Kynge everlastinge!
Amen.

197 lesithe, loses. **199 ofte tyme**, many times; **assentithe**, gives in. **201 wordle**, world.
202 dude, did. **203 wretin**, written. **204 i-liyten**, enlightened. **206 have of**, take off. **208
cher**, countenance; **lepr**, leprous. **210 his**, its; **figur**, figura (i.e., metaphorically). **215
etithe**, eats. **217 entrithe**, enters. **218 rechithe**, gives.

The Punished of Adulterers
or The Bawd and the Adulterers

A woman there was some tym alyve, that was a bawde betwene an housbond-man and anothere mannys wife, and ofte sithe had brought hem togedre in the synne of avoutery; and contenued many a day throw help of this bawde. Atte laste this woman, that was bawde, felle seke, and shuld deye. She thought in here

5   herte, how she had ben a synfull wrech, and was sory in here herte that ever she had offendid God, and thought she wolde amende here, as holy chirche wolde; and sente for here criature and was shrevyn and toke here penaunce, as she myght for the tyme, and was in wille never to torne agayne to synne; and wepte faste, and praiede Criste, for the vertue of His blessyd passyon, that He wolde

10   have mercy on here, and also for the prayere of His blessyd modre and all seyntes; and so she passyd oute of this worlde. And sone after, the man and the woman that lyvedyn in synne, deyedyn withoute repentaunce. This womans housbond praide faste for his wife, that was the bawde, that God wolde shewe hym how his wife fared. Afterwarde on a nyght, as he lay in his bedde, his wife aperid to hym,

15   and seide, "Housbond, be not aferde, but rise up, and go with me, for thou shalte se mervayles." He rose, and wente with here, til they come into a fayre playne. Then she seide, "Stond here still, and be not aferde, for thou shalte have no harme, and wisely beholde what thou shalte se." Then she wente a litill way from hym til she come at a grete stone that had an hole in the myddes; and as she stode

20   afore the stone, sodenly she was a longe addre, and putte here hede in at an hole in the myddys of the stone, ande crepte throwe; but she lefte hire hame withoute the

1 **bawde**, procuress. 3 **avoutery**, adultery; **throw**, through. 4 **deye**, die. 4–5 **here herte**, her heart. 5 **synfull**, sinful. 7 **criature**, creator (elements of communion); **shrevyn**, confessed. 8 **torne**, turn. 9 **faste**, profusely. 10 **modre**, mother. 12 **deyedyn**, died. 14 **aperid**, appeared. 15 **aferde**, afraid. 19 **myddes**, middle. 20 **addre**, adder. 21 **lefte**, shed; **hame**, skin; **withoute**, outside.

stone, and anone she stode up a fayre woman. And sone after com two devyls yellyng and broughtyn a cawderon full of hote wellyng brasse, and sette it downe besyde the stone; and after hem came othere two devyls, cryenge, and broughtyn

25 a man; and after hem came othere two devyls, with grete noyse, and broughtyn a woman. Than the two devyls tokyn bothe the man ande the woman that they brought, and caste hem into a cawderon and helde hem there, till the fleshe was sothyn fro the bone. Then they tokyn oute the bonys, and leyde hem beside the cawderon; and anone they were made man and woman. And the devyls caste hem

30 in agayne into the cawderon; and thus were they served many a tyme. And then the devyls wentyn as they comyn thiddere. The woman, that crepte throw the stone, wente agayne to hire housbonde, and seide, "Knewes thou ought this man and this woman?" He seide, "Yee, they were oure neghbores." "Sawe thou," she saide, "what payne they had?" He saide, "Yee, an hideouse payne." "This peyne," she

35 seide, "shull they have in helle ever more, for they lyvedyn in avoutery, and amendid hem nought. And I was bawde betwene hem, and brought heme togedre; and I shuld have bene with hem in the cawderon ever had I nought amendid me in my lyfe, with contricion, confession, and satisfaccion, as I myght, be the mercy of God; and crepte throw the stone, and lefte my hame behynde me." The stone is

40 Criste; the hole is his blessid wounde on His side; and the hame is my synnes that I lefte behynde me, be the merite of Cristes passion; and therfore I shall be savyd. Go thou now home, and bewarre of synne, and amende thee, for thou shalte lyve but a while; and do almesse dedes for thee and for me." Then the housbond wente home, and did as she bade hym; and with in shorte tyme after he deyede and

45 wente to the blisse.

23 **cawderon**, cauldron; **wellyng**, boiling. **28 sothyn**, seethed (boiled). **29 anone**, soon. **32 Knewes thou**, Do you know. **38 be**, by. **39 throw**, through; **hame**, skin. **43 almess dedes**, alms deeds (charity).

Select Bibliography and Notes to Excerpts from the *Gesta Romanorum*

Manuscripts in Middle English

Balliol College Oxford MS 354, fols. 1a–3b (early sixteenth century, East Midlands).

Cambridge University Library MS Kk. 1. 6., fols. 216a–245b (late fifteenth century).

British Library MS Additional 9066, fols. 5a–87b (late fifteenth century). [Base text for *The Punished of Adulterers*.]

British Library MS Harley 7333, fols. 150a–203a (1440–96). [Base text for *Emperator Felicianus* and *Godfridus a Wise Emperoure*.]

Gloucester Cathedral MS 22, pp. 723–87 (late fifteenth century).

Early Printed Editions

de Worde, Wynkyn (1510–15). [Contains an abbreviated number of tales beginning with the story of Atalanta. See Albert E. Hartung and Burke Severs, *A Manual of the Writings in Middle English 1050–1500* (New Haven: The Connecticut Academy of Arts and Sciences, 1967–).]

Robinson, Richard, ed. *Gesta Romanorum: A Record of Auncient Histories Newly Perused by Richard Robinson (1595)*. Delmar, NY: Scholars' Facsimiles & Reprints, 1973. [A revision of Wynkyn de Worde's edition.]

Editions

Herrtage, Sidney, ed. *The Early English Versions of the Gesta Romanorum*. EETS e.s. 33. London: N. Trübner & Co., 1879.

Madden, Sir Frederic, ed. *The Old English Versions of the Gesta Romanorum*. London: Roxburghe Club, 1838.

Oesterley, Hermann J., ed. *Gesta Romanorum*. Berlin: Weidmannsche Buckhandlung, 1872. [The Latin text.]

Sandred, K. I., ed. *A Middle English Version of the Gesta Romanorum*. Uppsala: University of Stockholm, 1971.

Siatkowski, J., ed., assisted by R. Olesch. *Gesta Romanorum Linguae Polonicae (1543): cum fontibus latinis et bohemicis*. Köln: Böhlau, 1986.

Weiske, Brigitte, ed. *Gesta Romanorum*. Tübingen: Max Neimeyer Verlag, 1992.

Selections

B. G., ed. *Evenings with the Old Story Tellers: Select Tales from the Gesta Romanorum, etc*. New York: Wiley and Putnam, 1845.

Brunet, G., ed. *Le Violier des Histoires Romaines: Ancienne Traduction Françoise des Gesta Romanorum*. Paris: P. Jannet, 1858.

Dick, Wilhelm, ed. *Die Gesta Romanorum. Nach der Innsbrucker Handschrift vom Jahre 1342 und Vier Münchener Handschriften*. Amsterdam: Rodopi Editions, 1970.

Komroff, Manuel, ed. *Tales of the Monks from the Gesta Romanorum*. New York: The Dial Press, 1928. [A translation of some of the tales in the Latin text.]

Swan, Charles, ed. *Gesta Romanorum: Entertaining Moral Stories*. London: Routledge & Sons, 1905.

Swan, Charles, and Wynnard Hooper, eds. and trans. *Gesta Romanorum, or Entertaining Moral Stories*. New York: Dover Publications, 1959.

Notes to Emperor Felicianus

Related Studies

Archibald, Elizabeth. *Apollonius of Tyre: Medieval and Renaissance Themes and Variations: Including the Text of the Historia Apollonii Regii Tyri with an English Translation.* Cambridge: D. S. Brewer, 1991.

Brewer, Derek. "Observations on a Fifteenth-Century Manuscript." *Anglia* 72 (1954–55), 390–99.

Loomis, Laura Hibbard. *Mediaeval Romance in England: A Study of the Sources and Analogues of the Non-Cyclic Metrial Romances.* New York: Burt Franklin, 1963.

Marchalonis, Shirley. "Medieval Symbols in the *Gesta Romanorum*." *The Chaucer Review* 8 (1974), 311–19.

Metlitzski, Dorothee. *The Matter of Araby in Medieval England.* New Haven: Yale University Press, 1977.

Palmer, Nigel F. "Exempla." In *Medieval Latin: An Introduction and Bibliographical Guide.* Ed. F. A. C. Mantella and A. G. Rigg. Washington: D.C.: Catholic University of America Press, 1996. Pp. 582–88.

Scanlon, Larry. *Narrative, Authority, and Power: The Medieval Exemplum and the Chaucerian Tradition.* Cambridge: Cambridge University Press, 1994.

Speed, Diane. "Middle English Romance and the *Gesta Romanorum*." In *Tradition and Transformation in Medieval Romance.* Ed. Rosalind Field. Cambridge: D. S. Brewer, 1999. Pp. 45–56.

Notes to Emperor Felicianus
(How a Wife Employed a Necromancer to Cause the Death of Her Husband, and How He Was Saved by a Clerk)

The manuscripts used for the *Gesta Romanorum* excerpts in this edition are Harley 7333 and BL Additional 9066. The first of the narratives — "Emperor Felicianus" — appears in Harley 7333, fols. 150a–151b; "Godfridus" appears in both Harley 7333, fols. 181b–183b, and BL Additional 9066, fols. 20b–24b, and "The Punished of Adulterers" appears only in BL Additional 9066, fol. 67. The number order here is consistent with Sydney Herrtage's EETS edition (see Select Bibliography) which contains the contents of both manuscripts. Unless indicated otherwise, I have followed earlier editions in their interpolations of missing dipthongs, syllables, or individual letters. Abbreviations: **Har**: British Library MS Harley 7333, fols. 150a–151b; **Add**: British Library MS Additional 9066, fols. 20b–24b; **Herr**: Sydney Herrtage.

1   *Felician.* Though the *Gesta Romanorum* was understood by its medieval audience as "history," the emperor's name is not historical. Etymologically related to the Latin *felicitatis* meaning "beatification, or capable of beatification," in English it more generally means "felicity" or "happiness." In the Latin text Titus reigns.

4   *that she ordeyned for hire husbonde to be ded.* This phrase echoes in line 9: "ordeyned for his dethe." Herr cites the Latin text which implies that the husband, knowing of his wife's propensity for infidelity, decides to go on pilgrimage to the Holy Land: *Nec de adulterio desistere volebat. Miles vero cum hoc vidisset, contristatus est valde in animo suo et cogitabat terram sanctam visitare.* ("Nor did she wish to put an end to the adultery. The knight saw this, sorrowed greatly in spirit, and decided to visit the Holy Land.") An amusing parallel of such male defensive practice may be found in Chaucer's The Wife of Bath's Prologue, where her fourth husband goes on pilgrimage, then dies (some say mysteriously) on his return, as if to imply that she is more than he can face.

         Happyng. The meaning of this suggests that the pilgrimage is not coincidental. The Latin text says *Accidit* ("It happened").

10   *nigromauncer.* Necromancer, a term that came to be associated with sorcery and witchcraft, originally referred to someone who prognosticated events by means of communication with the dead. A medieval tradition of necromancers includes not only Merlin, King Arthur's wizard, and Nectanabus, a magician to Alexander the Great, but also the much revered Roman poet Virgil. Virgil's prophecies, like those of Merlin and Nectanabus, were looked upon with suspicion by some medieval writers, in part because of the poet's association with the pre-Christian Sibyl. Other medieval poets, like Dante for instance, extol Virgil's virtues, hence Virgil's association with the realm of the dead makes him an appropriate candidate for guiding Dante the Pilgrim through the *Inferno.* Interestingly enough, though Virgil is not named in this particular *Gesta* narrative, in others included in the Anglo-Latin collection he is explicitly identified. For a comprehensive discussion of the poet's reputation in the Middle Ages, see Domenico Comparetti, *Vergil in the Middle Ages*, trans. E. F. M. Benecke (Hamden, CT: Archer Books, 1966). For a recent

general discussion of necromancy see Richard Kieckheffer, *Forbidden Rites: A Necromancer's Manual of the Fifteenth Century* (University Park: Pennsylvania State University Press, 1997).

16   *dyd make an ymage of erthe.* The Anglo-Latin text says that clerks make images *de cera* (of wax). Image-making by any unauthorized person was considered sacrilege by the church, yet the boundary between devotional "magic" — liturgical prayer and eucharistic practices — and the magic of wizards and necromancers is blurred. According to Richard Kieckheffer, a "'clerical underworld' capable of various forms of mischief, including necromancy . . . seems to have been the primary locus for this explicitly demonic magic" (p. 12). Chaucer's *House of Fame* provides an example of the natural magic or "science" of creating images:

> And clerkes eke, which konne wel
> Al this magik naturel,
> That craftely doon her ententes
> To make, in certeyn ascendentes,
> Ymages, lo, thrugh which magik . . . . (Lines 1265–70)

Natural magic and necromancy also figure prominently in The Franklin's Tale when the lovesick and desperate Aurelius, in order to win Dorigen's love, employs a magician to make Brittany's ominous coastal rocks disappear.

19   *hielie.* Herr points out that this translates the Latin word *intime* ("familiarly"), which suggests that the necromancer knows his client's innermost thoughts.

21   *be.* Har: *by.* The expression *be ded*, according to Herr, is of Eastern origin and occurs repeatedly in this narrative as well in other narratives belonging to the Anglo-Latin group.

23   *purveith.* Herr suggests a verb in the past tense — *purveide* — since the Latin text reads *providit.*

24   *he had grete merveile.* The knight's surprise at learning about his wife's plot against him is consistent with culturally determined attitudes toward wives as being incapable of carrying out criminal acts against their husbands. When women were found guilty of spousal homicide in late medieval England, their punishment went beyond the usual for ordinary homicide; they were not only charged with murder, but with petty treason, making the murder of a husband a crime against the crown.

38   *myrour.* The mirror or *speculum* is a multi-dimensional symbol in the Middle Ages. Most often it referred to the reflection of divine order in the world, or the distortion of it by immoral human action; it also served as an emblem of the Virgin Mary. In necromancy any reflective object — bowls, polished fingernails, crystals — could be useful to conjure up demons. This category of divination was condemned periodically. "In 1311 the bishop of Lincoln instructed one of his officials to investigate conjuring spirits in their fingernails and in mirrors, as well as in stones and rings" (Kieckheffer, p. 97). In the Latin text the *speculum politum* is described as *sacram scripturam.*

54   *cryed.* Herr notes that the Latin text reads *clamat* which has a wider range of meaning including "lamented," "worried," and "complained."

66   *the knyght went hom.* The Latin text complicates the action: *domi venisset, uxor eius obviam ei venit, et cum gaudio eum recepit. Miles vero per plures dies dissimilabat; tandem* . . . ("the knight went home; his wife went to meet him and received him with joy. The knight was not himself for days until finally. . .") [the quote is continued in line 67 following].

67   *the meyre of the towne.* The Latin text — a continuation of the quote above — complicates this scene by substituting the knight's in-laws, other clerics, and a judge for the mayor of the town: *pro parentibus uxoris misit et ait eis: Carissimi, hec est cause, quare misi pro vobis: hec est filia vestra, uxor mea, que adulterium sub me commisit et, quod peius est, in mortem meam machinata est. Illa vero cum iuramento negavit. Miles incepit et totum processum clerici recitavit. Quod si non creditis, venite et videte locum, ubi clericus sepultus est. Eos ad cameram suam duxit et corpus clerici sub lecto eius invenerunt. Iudix est vocatus et sententiam dedit, ut ipsa igni combureretur; et sic factum est, et pulvis post per aerem dispergitur.* ("He called the parents of his wife and said to them: My friends, here is the reason I have sent for you: here is your daughter, my wife, who has committed adultery under me and what is worse has orchestrated my death. She denied this under oath. The knight then began to relate all the actions of the clerk. Should you not believe this, come and see the place where the clerk is buried. He led them to the chamber and dragged the body of the clerk from under his bed. A judge was called and sentenced her to be burned and when done her ashes dispersed into the air.")

69   *herte.* Herr notes that the Latin *corpus,* which more generally means "body," "substance," and "physical matter," is limited to a single body part here.

72   *Moralitee.* The moral differs in the Latin text. The emperor is Jesus Christ, the knight is man; the wife, flesh; the wise man, the clerk; the necromancer, the devil (though he is more often referred to as *clericus*, e.g., *Clericus est diabolus*). The bow is avarice; the arrow, pride. Just as Lucifer has tempted Adam, so too has he tempted the knight; without the help of the wise man, his soul would have been doomed.

79   The equation of the necromancer with the devil derives, Herr thinks, from the Latin *diabolus*.

81–82   *Caro concupiscit* . . . . Galatians 5:17.

85–86   *the devill, biginnith to schete an arowe att the ymage.* According to George Ferguson's *Signs & Symbols in Christian Art* (New York: Oxford University Press, 1954), arrows, though generally used "to suggest a spiritual weapon dedicated to the service of God," also serve as "an instrument of war and death figures in the portrayals of many saints" (p. 304. Sts. Sebastian and Ursula are examples). Here the necromancer equates with both death and fiend. The arrow can also serve as a symbol of the plague. An interesting use of the image of archer, bow and arrows occurs in John Gower's *Vox Clamantis* where the poet takes the position of archer shooting his arrows into the world. Presenting himself as social critic, poet, preacher, and prophet, Gower points out the corruption in late medieval England by shooting his barbs into an image of a world turned upside down. The image of the archer with his bow and arrow also signified the preacher whose responsibility it was to point out his parishioners' sins.

89   *putte downe thyn hed.* Herr notes that this is "a mistake of the translator, or more probably of the transcriber"(p. 445). In the Latin text it reads: *oportet te deponere vestimenta tua* ("it behoves you to lay down your clothes").

101   *Apostill.* The line spoken here, i.e., *Suspendium elegit anima mea* ("My soul hangs suspended"), is not found in the New Testament, according to Herr, but rather in the Book of Job. The quotation is found in 7:15 in the form of a question: *Qua mobrem elegit suspendium anima mea, et mortem ossa mea.* ("For what reason is my soul suspended and my bones dead?")

105   *spirit.* Har: *sprit.*

106   *Ad quam nos et vos perducat*, &c. "To which He leads us and you (and so forth),"
        or, as translated at the end of "Godfridus a Wise Emperoure": "To the whiche He
        us brynge, that is kynge everlastinge" (p. 176). Perhaps this alludes to Tobias 10:11,
        Angelus Domini sanctus sit in itinere vestro, perducatque vos incolumes .... ("And
        the blessed angel of God shall lead you unharmed in your journey.")

Notes to Godfridus a Wise Emperoure
(Of the Magic Ring, Brooch, and Cloth, Which an Emperor
Left to His Son: How He Lost Them and How They Were Recovered)

1   *Godfridus regnid*. This is a fictional emperor of Rome.

2   *on his dethebed*. The tale opens with a deathbed distribution of wealth, a literary
        convention more than a customary practice. Implicit in the scene is a hierarchy
        which appears to render the eldest son primogenitor and therefore the recipient of
        the more important assets, i.e., the "heritage" (line 3). The second son is bequeathed
        the property added by the father to the original estate, while the third son inherits
        the movable goods or personal items. As in other tales of the fortunes of the
        youngest son, ranging from the Joseph story of Genesis to medieval romance, what
        appears to be a disadvantageous position in the family turns out to be the most
        beneficial. Here Jonathas gets a university education while at the same time he
        acquires gifts that let him go beyond the material realm to which his brothers are
        bound.

5   *purchas*. Har: *purchus*. Add: omits both the word and the entire phrase: *My sone,
        dyverse londes and tenementis I have bought, and theym all I yeve to the, what so
        evir thei be, that longe not to the heritage.*

8   *thre jewell*. Har: *þe Iwelle*. Add: *iii. Iewelx.*

        presious ringe. The magic ring has long been a motif in literature and mythology
        (the ring of Gyges in Plato's dialogues, for instance). It often appears in medieval
        romance as a token of the lover's intentions; associated with love and commitment,
        a ring also betokened nuptial bonding.

        gay broche. This decorative ornament, when it was not providing wish-fulfillment,
        functioned to hold a cloak together as it does for Chaucer's Prioress. Chaucer's

description of the brooch in the General Prologue to *The Canterbury Tales* suggests its ability, if not to fulfill desire, then to express it:

> Of smal coral aboute hire arm she bar
> A peire of bedes, gauded al with grene,
> And theron heng a brooch of gold ful sheene,
> On which ther was first write a crowned A,
> And after *Amor vincit omnia.* (I[A]158–62)

The Latin expression — "Love conquers all" — may be read as an expression of human relationship as well as allegorically. That the brooch represents wish fulfillment for Jonathas in the *Gesta* tale prompts a similar reading for the Prioress.

8   *riall clothe.* This may be understood as something analogous to a magic carpet, which suggests Eastern influence, perhaps from *A Thousand and One Arabian Nights.* Even without its ability to fly, a carpet motif inevitably pointed to the Middle East where carpet-making emerged as an important commercial enterprise in the Middle Ages.

28   *Felicia.* The Latin root is *felicitatis*, meaning happiness or beatitude, as it was in the first of the *Gesta* narratives — "Emperator Felicianus." Here it seems to be used ironically since Felicia does not seem to embody many positive attributes.

51   *grete sorow.* This is an interpolation Herr adds based on the Latin text which reads *dolorem ostendare* ("to show sorrow").

82   *ivele.* Har: *Iwele.* Add: omits the mother's angry retort.

85   *women.* Har: *wome.* Add: *womans wyles.*

114   *a certeyne pathe.* Herr interpolates *pathe* from the Latin text which reads *per quandam viam.*

120   *hour.* Har: *honour.* Add: *houre.*

149   *she harde telle.* Har omits the feminine pronoun. I have added it for the sake of clarity.

152   *i-seyne hir uryne.* Medieval physicians frequently examined a patient's urine in their attempts to determine the malady. The urine glass even became a symbol of office; an illustration in the Ellesmere manuscript of Chaucer's Physician shows him

holding the glass urine bottle up to the light as he makes a prognosis. According to Peter Murray Jones, *Medicine in Illuminated Manuscripts* (London: The British Library, 1998), "The skilled physician could make his reputation by accurately foretelling the course of an illness. . . . Later authors, and in particular Galen, linked diagnosis and prognosis to a disease theory based on changes in the balance of the four humours (blood, phlegm, black bile, and yellow bile), signified to the physician by changes in urine or pulse" (p. 43).

156   *Thou moste be clene i-shriven.* The relationship between disease and sin is not as unusual as it may seem. Oftentimes human sin was thought to be physically manifested in the body of the sinner. Leprosy, in particular, was associated with venereal consequences of lechery.

168   *likenesse.* As Herr suggests this could be read as *sikenesse*, though the countenance of the lady is the important factor in her punitive rejection by potential suitors.

174   *angelis.* The hierarchy set up in the beginning of the narrative is followed here. The angels equate with the first son, the prophets with the second, and every Christian man with Jonathas. Reference to the angels follows the Latin text which reads: *angeli mali ceciderunt, firmiter alii Deo adheserunt* ("the wicked angels fell, more firmly adhering to the other God").

179   *he gaf.* Har: *and he.* Add: *he yaf.*

181   *twartynge.* According to the MED, this gerund derives from the verb *thwerten* ("thwart").

183   *Ut supra.* Har: *ut c.* Add: omits the Latin passage entirely.

184   *synevey.* The meaning of this term is the same as the Latin term for mustard, i.e., *sinapis.* It recalls the "litel clergeon" (*CT* VII[B^2]503) of Chaucer's The Prioress' Tale who, despite having his throat cut, sings while a holy grain is in his mouth only to have his soul released from his dead body when it is taken out. It also recalls the parable of the mustard seed told by Jesus in which the kingdom of heaven is compared to the potentiality of the lowly seed: "The kingdom of heaven is like to a grain of mustard seed, which a man took, and sowed in his field. Which is the least indeed of all seeds; but when it is grown up, it is greater than all herbs, and becometh a tree, so that the birds of the air come, and dwell in the branches thereof" (Matthew 13:31; Mark 4:32; Luke 13:19).

191   *Cristin man.* Har: *Cristiman.* Add: *cristen man.*

        perfite. Har: *perfe.* Add: *perfite.*

195   *translatid.* The person practicing perfect charity is promised eternal life. Herr notes a gap in Har after the term is used which is provided by Add: *from this world to heven.*

206   *whiche.* Har: *wiche.* Herr's emendation.

        putithe. Har: *putthe.* Add: *departith.*

208   *wretin.* Har: *wetin.* Add: the Latin passage and its introduction are omitted.

215   *whiche.* Har: *wiche.* Herr restores the *h,* as have I.

Notes to The Punished of Adulterers or The Bawd and the Adulterers

1   *bawde.* As a go-between the bawd is associated with a long tradition of courtly love; as a pander or procuress she is more closely aligned with prostitution. This bawd recalls Dame Sirith, the most famous intermediary of English fabliaux.

1–2   *housbond-man.* "Husband" derives from OE *hus* + *bonden* and refers to the male head of household who is "bound" to his domestic duties.

19   *grete stone.* Since a miracle is about to occur, this may allude to the rock of Exodus through which water passed to quench the thirst of the Israelites during their exile in the desert.

20   *addre.* The snake is a traditional symbol of sin and temptation. But once it sheds its old skin, it is also a sign of Christ the new man, raised on the Cross even as Moses raised the serpent in the wilderness (Numbers 21:4–9; see John 3:14). *The Biblia Pauperum* ·e· juxtaposes Moses raising the serpent with the Crucifixion, where Christ on the Cross makes possible redemption, whereby the sinner, i.e., the serpent, can slough off the old wrapping of sin by passing through the sharp passage of penance. That the bawd is transformed into a "fayre woman" (line 22), like the serpent shedding its old skin, demonstrates her newly acquired state of grace. The

amazing transformations demonstrated here differ from the illusions of magicians and necromancers since they are rendered by someone who has been absolved.

23   *cawderon*. The punishment is reminiscent of those found in Dante's *Inferno*, though cauldrons of boiling oil were also found in the legends of saints. St. John the Evangelist, for instance, was martyred when he was placed in such a vat.

38   *contricion, confession, and satisfaccion*. These acts are prerequisites for absolution. See Chaucer's The Parson's Tale (*CT* X[I]107–09).

John Wyclif (?), *Of Weddid Men and Wifis and of Here Children Also*

Oure Lord God Almyghty spekith in His lawe of tweie matrimoneys or wedlokis. The first is gostly matrimonye, bitwixe Crist and Holy Chirche, that is, Cristene soulis ordeyned to blisse. The secunde matrimoyne is bodily or gostly, bitwene man and womman, bi just consent, after Goddis lawe.

5 Of the first matrimoyne spekith God bi the prophete Osie to Holy Chirche; and to ech persone of Holi Chirche God Himself seith, I schal spouse thee, or wedde thee to me, in rightwisnesse, in dom, in mercy, and in feith; and I schal wedde thee withouten ende. This is the first matrimoyne and best, as God and the soule of trewe men ben betre than mennys bodies. And this beste matrimoyne is broken for a tyme bi brekynge

10 of saad feith, and defaute of rightwis lyvynge. And herefore God seith oft His prophetis, that His peple dide fornicacioun and avoutrie, for thei worschipen false goddis; and Seynt Jame seith that men that loven the world ben gostly avoutreris. For thus writith he: yee avoutreris, wite ye not that frendischipe of this world is enemyté of God? And thus alle men that loven more worldly worschipe or goodis of the world than God and

15 His lawe and trewe life, ben avoutreris gostly, yif thei weren Cristene bifore; and this is worse avoutrie than brekynge of fleschly matrimonye.

Of the secunde matrimoyne, that is bodily, spekith God in the firste bok of Holy Writt, whanne he maade matrimoyne bitwene Adam and Eve in paradis in staat of innocence, bifore that thei synneden. And for that God Hymself made this ordre of

20 matrimoyne, and he not so made thes newe religions, it is betre and more to preise than thes newe ordris. Also Jesus Crist wolde not be borne of the Virgine Marie, ne conseyved, but in verrey matrimoyne, as the gospel of Luc, and Seynt Ambrose, and othere seyntis witnessen. Also Jesus Crist was present in His owene persone with His

---

Title: Here, Their. **2 gostly**, spiritual. **7 dom**, judgment. **10 saad**, true. **11 avoutrie**, adultery. **13 wite ye not**, do you not understand; **enemyté**, enmity. **15 gostly**, spiritually. **22 conseyved**, conceived.

191

modir in bodily matrimoyne, to approve it, as the gospel of Jon techith, whanne He
25 turned watir into wyn. Also the Holy Gost warneth Cristen men, hou in the laste daies
summe heretikis schullen departe fro feith of Goddis lawe, gevenge entente to spiritis
of error, and to techynge of develis, spekynge lesyngis in ypocrisie, forbedynge
men and wymmen to be weddid, and techynge men to abstene hem fro metis, the
whiche God hath maad to be eten of trewe men, with thankyngis and heriyng of God.
30 Also this bodily matrimoyne is a sacrament and figure of the gostly wedlok bitwene
Christ and Holy Chirche, as Seynt Poul seith. Also, this wedlok is nedful to save
mankynde bi generacioun to the day of dom, and to restore and fulfille the noumbre of
aungelis, dampned for pride, and the noumbre of seyntis in hevene, and to save men
and wommen fro fornycacion. And therfore he that forbedith or lettith verrey
35 matrimonye is enemye of God and seyntis in hevene and alle mankynde. And herefore
man ponyschide fornycacion and avoutrie in the olde lawe bi stonynge to deth, and in
the lawe of grace bi dampnynge in helle, but yif men be verrey contrit therfore.

And herefore, sith fornicacioun is so perilous, and men and wymmen ben so frele,
God ordeynede prestis in the olde lawe to have wyves, and nevere forbede it in the
40 newe lawe, neither bi Crist ne bi His apostlis, but rathere aprovede it. But now, bi
ypocrisie of fendis and false men, manye bynden hem to presthod and chastité, and
forsaken wifis bi Goddis lawe, and schenden maydenes and wifis, and fallen foulest
of alle. For many ben prestis and religious, in doynge and othere, for to have lustful lif
and eisy, yong and strong of complexion, and faren wel of mete and drynk, and wolen
45 not traveile, neither in penaunce, ne studie of Goddis lawe, ne techynge, ne laboure
with here hondis; and herefore thei fallen into lecherie in dyverse degrees, and in
synne agenst kynde. For many gentilmennis sonys and doutres ben maad religious
agenst here wille, whanne thei ben childre withouten discrecion, for to have the heri-
tage holly to o child that is most lovyd. And when thei come to age, what for drede of
50 here frendis, and what for drede of povert in cas that thei gon out, and for ypocrise
and flatirynge, and faire bihestis of thes religious, and for drede of takynge of here
bodi to prison, thei doren not schewe here herte ne leven this stat, though thei knowen

26 **heretikis**, heretics. 27 **lesyngis**, falsehood. 28 **metis**, food. 29 **heriyng**, praising.
32 **dom**, judgment. 33 **dampned**, condemned. 34 **lettith**, hinders. 36 **ponyschide**, pun-
ished. 37 **but**, except. 42 **schenden**, shun. 47 **kynde**, nature. 48 **here**, their; **discrecion**,
reason. 50 **povert**, poverty. 51 **bihestis**, promises; **here**, their. 52 **doren**, dare; **leven**,
leave; **stat**, sinful condition.

hemself unable therto. And hereof cometh lecherie and sumtyme mortherynge of many men.

55 Netheles, though matrimonye be good and gretly comendid of God, yit clene virgynité is moche betre, — and wedlok also, as Seynt Poul seith opynli; for Jesus Crist, that lyvede most perfitly, was evere clene virgine, and not weddid bodely, and so was His modir evere virgine, and Jon Evaungelist. Seynt Austyn and Jerom specially witnessen wel this in many bokis. Netheles virgynité is so heye and so noble that Crist comaundid

60 it not generaly, but saide, who may take, take he it. And therefore Poul gaf no comaundement of virgynité, but gaf conseil to hem that weren able therto. And thus prestis that kepen clene chastité in bodi and soule doun best; but many taken this charge not discretly, and sclaundren hemselfe foule bifore God and His seyntis, for newe bondis maade nedeles of synful men. And this is a gret disceit of the fend under

65 colour of perfeccion and chastité. For he stireth men to heighe poyntis of perfeccion, when he knowith or supposith hem unable, not for here goode, but for to falle foulere and depere in more synne, as Seynt Austyn techith. And thus the fend Sathanas transfigureth or turneth hem falsly into an angel of light, to disceyve men bi colour of holynesse.

70 See now how this wedlok owith to be kept in both sides. First this wedlok shulde be maad with ful consent of bothe partis, principaly to the worschipe of God, to lyve clenly in the ordre that He made, and bringe forth childre to fulfille the chosen noumbre of seyntis in blisse, and not to have flescly lustis withoute reson and drede of God, as mulis and hors and swyn that han no undirstondynge. For the angel Raphael warned

75 Tobie, that the fend hath maistrie upon siche men that ben weddid, to have thus lustis of flesch as bestis withoute resoun and drede of God. Also this contract shulde not be maade bitwixe a yonge man and an olde bareyne widewe, passid child-berynge, for love of worldly muk, as men ful of coveitise usen sumtyme, — for than cometh soone debat and avoutrie and enemyté, and wast of goodis, and sorowe and car ynowgh.

80 And it is a gret dispit to God to coloure thus here wickide coveitise, lecherie, and avoutrie bi the holy ordre of matrimoyne. And many men synnen moche, for thei defoulen many wymmen, and letten hem fro matrimoyne, and undon hem in this world, and sumtyme ben cause of here dampnacion; for thei ben maad comyn wymmen,

53 mortherynge, murdering. **63 sclaundren hemselfe,** slander themselves. **64 fend,** fiend. **68 hem,** himself. **70 owith,** ought. **75 siche,** such. **79 enemyté,** enmity. **82 defoulen,** defile; **letten hem,** obstruct them. **83 comyn wymmen,** prostitutes.

whanne thei han lost here frendishipe, and kunnynge no craft to lyve by. Many hote
85 and coragious men wolen not take a pore gentil womman to his wif in Goddis lawe,
and make here a gentil womman, and save here owene soule, but lyven in the develis
servyce al here lif, or the more part; and defoulen many templis of God to gret peril of
here soule, and abiden to have a riche womman for muk, and thanne wasten here
goodis in harlotrie and nyse pride, in avoutrie on gaie strumpatis, and evere lyven in
90 wrathe, and chydynge, and in bondage of synne to the fendis of helle. Also summe
myghtty men marien here children where that here herte consentith not wilfully, but
feynen for drede. For comynly thei loken alle aftir richesse and worthinesse to the
world, and not after goodnesse of virtuous lif. And so God and His side is putte
bihynde, and the devel and the world and the flesch han now here maistrie.

95 For three skillis may a man knowe fleschly his rightful wif, the firste for to geten
children, to fulfille the noumbre of men and wymmen that schullen be savyd; the
secunde to kepe his wif fro lecherie of othere men; the thridde is to kepe himself fro
lecherie of othere wymmen. And no party may kepe him chaste fro the dedis of
wedlok withouten assent of the tother comynly, for the man hath power of the wifis
body, and the wif hath power of the mannys body, as Seynt Poul seith. And yif the
100 partie desire to be chast, suffre he withowten his owene luste the thother part in dedis
of matrimoyne, and he getith him thank of God, bothe for suffrynge of his make, and
for the wille that he hath to chastité; for God takith reward to the goode wille, and not
onely to the dede. Also men seyn yif bothe parties assenten wilfully to perfit chastité,
bothe of wille and dede, that it is betre than to use forth the dedis of matrimonye; and
105 yif thei assenten bothe parties at the begynnynge to lyve evere chast, withouten bodily
knowynge, that it is the best kept matrimoyne of all othere, as diden oure Lady and
Josep, whanne thei ben weddid. Loke that eche partie lyve wel anentis God and the
world, and stire eche othere to charité, rightwisnesse, and mekenesse and pacience,
and alle goodnesse. And be ech man war that he procure no fals devours, for money,
110 ne frendischipe, ne enemye; for Crist biddith no man departe atwyn hem that God
hath joyned; but only for avoutré that part that kepith him clene may be departid fro
the totheris bed, and for noon other cause, as Crist seith hymself. And yit thanne the

84 **kunnynge**, knowing; **hote**, arrogant, proud. 85 **coragious**, lascivious. 88 **muk**, filthy
behavior. 89 **nyse**, foolish. 95 **skillis**, reasons. 100 **the thother**, the other. 101 **make**,
mate. 102 **goode wille**, intent. 107 **anentis**, with respect to. 109 **devours**, divorce. 110
departe atwyn, separate.

clene part myght lyve chast evere while the tother lyveth, or ellis be reconseled agen
to the part. Netheles the clene may dwelle forth with the tother lyveth that forfetis, bi
115 weie of charité. And men supposen that that weie is gret charité, yif there be evydence
that the tother part wolle do wel aftirward.

See now how the wif oweth to be suget to the housbonde, and he owith to reule his
wif, and how thei bothe owen to reule here children in Goddis lawe. First Seynt Petir
biddith that wifis be suget to here housbondis, insomoche that yif ony bileve not bi
120 word of prechynge, that thei ben wonnen withoute word of prechynge bi the holy
lyvynge of wymmen, whanne men biholden the chast lyvynge of wymmen. And thes
wymmen schulden not have withouten forth tiffynge of her, ne garlondis of gold, ne
over precious or curious clothinge, but thei schulden have a clene soule, peisible and
meke and bonere, the whiche is riche in the sightte of God. And sumtyme holy wymmen,
125 hopynge in God, honoureden hem in this manere, and weren suget to here owene
housbondis, as Sara, Abrahamys wif, obeischid to Abraham, clepynge hym lord;
and wymmen wel doynge ben gostly doughtris of Sarra. Alle this seith Seynt Petir.
Also Seynte Poul spekith thus of housbondis and wifis; I wole that men preie in eche
place, liftynge up clene hondis, that is, clene werkis, withouten wraththe and strif.
130 Also I wolle that wymmen ben in covenable abite, with schamefastnesse and sobirnesse
ournynge hem or makynge fair, not in writhen here, ne in gold, ne in margery stones
or perlis, ne in precious cloth, but that that bicometh wymmen bihetynge pité, bi
goode werkis. A womman oweth to lerne in silence, with alle obedience and subjeccioun.
But Poul seith, I suffre not a womman to teche, that is, openly in chirche, as Poul seith
135 in a pistel to Corynthis, and I suffre not a womman to have lordischipe in here
housbonde, but to be in silence or stillnesse. For, as Poul seith in many placis, the
housbonde is heed of the wif; and Poul tellith this skille, that Adam was first formed
and Eve aftirward, and Adam was not disceyved in feith, but the womman was
disceyved in feith, in trespasynge agenst Goddis comaundement. Alle this seith Poul
140 in dyverse placis of Holy Writt. Also Poul biddith that bishopis and prestis techen wifis
to love here housbondis, to be prudent and chaste and sobre, and to have care of the

117 **oweth**, ought; **suget**, subject. **118 here**, their. **122 tiffynge**, adorning; **her**, herself.
123 peisible, peaceable. **124 bonere**, good; **riche**, admirable. **126 clepynge**, calling.
130 covenable abite, appropriate dress. **131 writhen here**, braided hair; **margery stones**,
pearls. **132 bihetynge**, pledging. **137 skille**, reason.

hous, and benynge and underlont, or suget, to here housbondes, — that the word of God be not blasphemyd. And that olde wymmen schullen be in holy abite, not puttynge fals cryme or synne to othere, ne suynge to moche wyn, and to be wel techynge, so

145   that thei teche prudence. Also Poul techith thus, — that wymmen ben underlont, or suget, to here husbondis, as to the Lord. For the husbonde is hed of the womman, as Crist is heed of the Chirche, He is saveour of the body therof, that is, the grete multitude of alle worthi to be savyd. But as Holy Chirche is suget to Crist, so be wymmen sugetis to here housbondis in alle thingis. Husbondis, loveth youre wifis,

150   right as Crist lovede Holy Chirche, and toke Himself wilfully to peyne and deth for Holy Chirche, to make it clene and holy; and made it clene bi waschynge of water in the word of lif, to geve the Chirche glorious to Himself, not havynge wem ne revelynge ne ony siche filthe, but that it be holy and withouten spot other wem. And housbondis owen to love here wifis as here owene bodies, for he that loveth his wif loveth hymself.

155   For no man hatid evere his bodi, but norischith and fortherith it, as Crist doth Holy Chirche. For we ben membris of his body, of his flesch, and of his bones. For this thyng a man schal forsake, or leve, his fadir and his modir, and schal cleve to his wif, and thei schullen be tweiyne in o flesch. This sacrament is greet, but i-saye, seith Poul, in Crist and in Holy Chirche. But forsothe, ye husbondis, eche by hymself, love

160   he his wif as hymself, and drede the wif here housbonde. Ye children, obeischith to youre eldris, fader and thi modir, in the Lord, for this thing is rightful. Worschipe thi fadir and thi modir — that is the firste comaundement in biheste; that Crist be wel to thee, and that thou be longe lyvynge upon erthe. And ye fadris, nyle ye stire youre children to wraththe, but norische hem and brynge hem forth in disciplyne, or

165   lore, and chastisynge of God. Alle this seith Seynt Poul togidre. Also Poul comaundith thus in another pistel: wymmen, be ye underlont to youre husbondis, as it bihoveth in the Lord. Ye men, love youre wifis, and beth not bitter to hem. Children, obieschith to youre eldris bi alle thingis, for this is plesaunt to the Lord. Ye fadris, stireth not youre children to indignacion, lest thei of litel witt offenden, or trespasen, agenst God or

170   man.

    Here sturdy husbondis and cruel fightteris with here wifis, withoute resonable cause, ben blamyd of God. But manye, whanne thei ben drounken, comen hom to here wifis,

142 **benynge**, meek; **underlont**, underling. 144 **suynge**, drinking; **techynge**, informed. 145 **ben underlont**, be subservient. 152 **wem**, blemish. 158 **greet**, noble; **but i-saye**, but [only] visible (expressed). 160 **drede**, fear; **obeischith**, be obedient. 163 **nyle**, refrain. 165 **lore**, law.

and sumtyme fro here cursed strumpatis and jectouris of contré, and chiden and fightten with ther wif and meyné, as thei weren Sathanas brollis; and suffren neither

175   reste, pees, ne charité be among hem. But dere schalle thei abie this bitternesse, for yif thei wolen have mercy of God thei moten have mercy of othere men, though thei hadden discervyd betynge, — amende hem in faire manere.

Of this may weddid men and wifis knowen, hou thei owen lyve togidre, and teche here childre Goddis lawe. For at the bigynnynge a childe may esily be taught, and

180   goode thewis and maneris, accordynge with Goddis lawe, esily be prentid in his herte; and thanne he may esily holden hem forthe, and encresse in goodnesse. And therfore Poul biddith that the fadir norische his children in the lore and chastisynge of God; and God comaundith in the olde lawe that the fadris schulden telle to herre children Goddis hestis, and the woundris and myraclis that he dide in the lond of Egipt, and in the Rede

185   See, and in the watir of Jordan, and in the Lond of Biheste. And moche more ben fadir and moder holden to teche here children the bileve of the Trinyté, and of Jesus Crist, howe He is verray God withouten bigynnynge, and was maad man thorough moste brennynge charité, to save mankynde bi stronge penaunce, hard torment, and bittir deth. And so alle comen in poyntis of Cristene bileve, but thei ben most holden to

190   teche hem Goddis hestis, and the werkis of mercy, and poyntis of charité, and to geverne wel here fyve wittis, and to drede God bifore alle othere thingis, and to love Him most of alle thingis, for His endeles myght, endeles wisdom, endelesse goodnesse, mercy, and charité. And yif thei trespasen agenst Goddis hestis, thei owen to blamen hem therfore scharply, and chastise hem a thousandfold more than for dispit or

195   unkyndenesse don agenst here owene persone. And this techynge and chastisynge schulden in fewe yeeris make goode Cristene men and wymmen, and namely goode ensaumple of holy lif of olde men and wymmen, for that is best techynge to here children.

And Cristene men, aboute many prestis, chargen godfadris and godmodris to techen

200   the children the Pater Noster and the Crede; and this is wel don; but it most nede to teche hem the hestis of God, and geve hem good ensaumple bi here owene lif. For though thei ben cristenyd and knowen the comyn poyntis of bileve, yit thei schullen

---

173 jectouris, boasters; **contré,** strife **174 meyné,** household members; **brollis,** brats. **176 moten,** must. **177 amende,** reprimand. **178 owen,** ought. **180 thewis,** mode of conduct. **184 hestis,** behests. **185 Biheste,** Promise. **186 holden,** obliged. **191 geverne,** govern; **wittis,** senses. **193 hestis,** comandments. **202 knowen,** know.

197

not be savyd withoute kepynge of Goddis hestis, but be ful hard and depe dampynd in
helle, more than hethene men. And it hadde betre be to hem to nevere have reseyved
205   Cristendom, but yif thei enden trewely in Goddis comaundementis, as Seynt Petir
techith pleynly.

    But summe techen here children jeestis of bataillis and fals cronyclis not nedful to
here soulis. Summe techen novelries of songis, to stire men to jolité and harlotrie.
Summe setten hem to nedeles craftis, for pride and coveitise; and summe suffren hem
210   in ydelnesse and losengerie, to breden forth strumpatis and theves; and summe with
grett cost setten hem in lawe for wynnynge and worldly worschipe, and here to
costen hugely in many weies. But in alle this Goddis lawe is putt bihynde, and therof
spekith unnethis ony man a good word to magnifye God and that, and to save mennys
soulis. Sume techen here children to swere and stare and fightte, and schrewe alle
215   men aboute, and of this han gret joie in here herte. But certis thei ben Sathanas techeris,
and procuratouris to lede hem to helle bi here cursed ensaumple and techynge and
norischynge and meyntenynge in synne; and ben cruel sleeris of here owene children,
ye, more cruel than though thei hackeden here children as small as morselis to here
poot or mouth. For bi this cursid technyge and endynge therin, here children bodies
220   and soulis ben dampnyd withouten ende in helle. And though here bodies weren thus
hackid nevere so smale, bothe bodi and soule schal be in blis of hevene, so that thei
kepen trewely Goddis comaundementis. And of siche necligent fadris and modris,
that techen not here children Goddis lawe, and chastisen hem not whanne thei trespasen
agenst Goddis hestis, Seynt Poul spekith a dredeful word. He that hath not care of his
225   owene, and most of his homly in houshod, hath resceyved the feith, and he is worse
than a man out of Cristendom. And siche fadris and modris, that meyntenen wityngly
here children in synne, and techen hem schrewdnesse, ben werse than the cursed
fadris that killeden here children, and offre hem up to stockis, worschipynge false
maunmetis. For tho children in here youghthe weren ded and distried, and diden no
230   more synne; but thes children of cursed fadris and modris, that techen hem
pride, thefte, lecherie, wraththe, coveitise, and glotonye, and meyntenen hem therinne,
ben holden in long lif, and encresen in synne to more dampnacion of eche party. And
thus litel wonder though he take vengaunce on oure peple both old and yong, for alle

207 jeestis, stories. **209 craftis**, skills. **210 losengerie**, debauchery. **213 unnethis**,
scarcely. **217 sleeris**, slayers. **225 homly in houshod**, those belonging to the house-
hold. **229 maunmetis**, pagan idols.

comynly dispisen God, and han joie and myrthe at his dispit and reprovynge. And God
235   mot ponische this synne for his rightful majesté.

But though husbondis han thus power over his wifis bodi, netheles thei owen to use
this doynge in mesure and reson, and sumwhat refreyne here foule lustis, and not take
superfluyté of hot wynes and spised alle and delicat metis to delite hem in this
occupacion, but thenk that thei ben gestis and pilgrimes in the world, and han not here
240   a dwellynge-place forevere. And therfore thei mosten geve hem to holynesse, withouten
whiche no man schal see God; and abstynen hem fro fleschly desiris that fightten
agenst the soule, as Petir and Poul techen bi auctorité of God Hymself; and thenke on
this word of Seynt Poul; — The tyme is schort; the tother part is that thei that han
wifes ben as havynge noon; that is to seie, that thei usen hem for and in drede of God
245   and mesure, not to fulfille here lustis, as bestis withoute undirstondynge; and that thei
have mynde of the dredful comynge of Crist to the laste dom, hou thei schullen thanne
answere for eche dede, eche word, and eche thought, — and eche evyl suffraunce of
here children and meyné, and princypaly of evyl ensaumple to here sugetis. And ne
cavyllacion ne procuratour schal be there, but here owene goode lif to save hem, or
250   cursed lif to dampne hem. And fleschly lustis, and glotonye, dronkenesse, and overe
moche likynge in fleschly dedis and lecherie, maken men most to forgete this dredful
dom. And therfore the gospel seith, that the thridde servaunt that hadde wedded a wif,
seide that he myghtte not come to the soper of Crist, and that servaunt is undirstonden,
he that geveth hym to overe moche likynge in fleischly lustis. And therfore biddith
255   Crist in the gospel, that we take hede that oure hertis ben not chargid with glotonye
and dronkenesse and bisyness of this lif, for the day of dom schal come as a snare, or
grane, upon alle tho that sitten upon the face of alle the erthe.

But ben wifis war that thei stiren not here husbondis to wraththe, ne envye agenst
here neigheboris, ne to falsnesse and overe moche bisynesse of the world, to fynde to
260   costy array. For the wif was made to be an helpere lich to the husbounde, eche to
helpe other in clennesse and holy lif, and trewe anentis God and man. But yif the
husbonde be stired to vengaunce and pride and envye, the wif oweth to stire hym to
penaunce and pacience, mekenesse and charité, and alle good manere of Cristene
lif. And whanne Goddis lawe biddith the husbonde and the wif love eche other, be

238 spised alle, spiced ale. **239 gestis**, guests. **248 meyné**, household. **249 cavyllacion,**
spurious arguments. **257 grane**, trap. **258 stiren**, provoke. **260 costy**, costly. **261**
anentis, concerning.

265   thei war that thei turnen not this love al to fleschly love, and not to love of the soule,
for thei ben holden moche more to love the soule than the body, for God loveth that
more than the bodi, and for the soule Crist diede. And certis love of the body is verrey
hate, but yif it be in helpe to save the soule, and kepe it in holy lif.

    But yit thre grete defautis fallen many tymes in weddid men and wymmen. The firste
270   defaute is, as Seynt Jon with the gildene mouth seith, that thei maken sorowe yif here
children ben nakid or pore, but though here children ben nakid fro virtues in soule, thei
chargen nothing. And with moche traveile and cost thei geten grete richessis and heighe
statis and beneficis to here children, to here more dampnacion ofte tymes, but thei wolen
not gete here children goodis of grace and virtuous lif, ne suffre hem to resceyve siche
275   goodis, frely profrid of God, but letten it as moche as thei may; and seyn, yif here child
drawe hym to mekenesse and povert, and flee coveitise and pride, for drede of synne and
for to plese God, that he schal nevere be man, and nevere coste hem peny, and cursen
hem, yif he lyve wel and techen othere men Goddis lawe, to save mennis soulis. For bi this
doynge the child getith many enemyes to his eldris, and thei seyn that he sclaundrith alle
280   here noble kyn, that evere weren helde trewe men and worschipful.

    The secunde defaute is that wifis geven here husbondis goodis to stronge beggeris and
riche, and othere curleris, to geten hem swete morselis, and sumtyme spende here husbondis
goodis aboute holouris and lecherous, the while here husbondis traveilen fare in ferre
contreies or grevous traveiles. And to holden holy and excuse this wickidnesse, wifis
285   many tymes don a litil almes opynly and fynden ypocritis to seyn massis and maken the
sely husbondis to meyntene siche ypocritis in here falsnesse, to robbe the pore peple and
to lette trewe men to teche Goddis lawe and to favoure false sclaunderis of here brethren.
And yif wifis favouren and meyntenen siche ypocritis and stiren here husbondis therto, for
preve lecherie bitwen hemself and for fals sykernesse that the ypocritis maken to hem,
290   though thei dwellen stille as swyn in synne, it is so mochel the worse.

    The thridde defaute is this: yif Almyghtty God, of His rightwisnesse and mercy, take
here children out of this world bi fair deeth, thes riche wifis wepen, grucchen, and crien
agenst God, as God schulde not do agenst here wille; and axen God whi He takith rathere
here children fro hem than pore mennis, sith thei may betre fynde here children than may
295   pore men heren. See now the woodnesse of this grucchynge! It is gret mercy of God to

268 but yif, unless. **279 sclaundrith**, slanders. **282 curleris**, peddlers. **283 holouris**,
fornicators. **285 ypocritis**, hypocrites, i.e., corrupt priests. **292 grucchen**, lament. **293
axen**, ask. **295 woodnesse**, madness.

take a child out of this world; for yif it schal be saaf, it is delyverid out of woo into blisse, lest malice turnyd the undirstondynge of the child to synne, and that is gret mercy of God, and herefor alle men schulden be glade. Yif it schal be dampnyd, yit it is mercy of God to take hym soone to deth, leste it lyve lengere, and do more synne, and therfore be in more

300   peyne. And sith thei grucchen thus agenst Goddis rightful dom, thei putten on God that He is unrightful, — unwitty, — that He knowith not whanne is best tyme of the child, and out of mercy and charité ponysche so sore the child and his eldris. But certis than thei ben cursed Luciferis children, weiward Anticristis, and unkynde heretikis and blasphemes. Therfore be thei glade, and thanke thei God for al His mercyes, and benefices, and rightful

305   domes. Amen.

   Also loke that eche parti enforce hymself to kepe this ordre maad of God, and breke it not for no temptacion ne likynge of flesch. And hereto helpen many resones. First, for God that is auctour of this ordre loveth it to be kept in clennesse and present in every place, and for His rightwisnesse mot ponyschen hym that brekith it. And no defoulynge therof

310   may askape unpeyned, for He knoweth alle thingis, be thei nevere so prevé; and nothing, be it nevere so myghtty, may agenstonde His ponyschynge. Also thenk hou soone this stenkynge flesch, that now deliteth in lecherie, schal turne alle to aschis, and poudre, and erthe, and wermes mete; and for so schort likynge to lese everelastynge blisse and to gete everelastynge peyne in helle, in body and soule, were a cursed chaunge; and no man wot

315   hou soone he schal die, and in what staat. Also goode angelis, keperis of men and wymmen, schewen to God a grevous pleynt, whanne this holy ordre is thus broken, and Cristene soulis, templis of the Holy Gost, ben thus wickidly bleckid with filthe of synne, and maad liche to the fendis of helle. And for this skille, men and wymmen schulden be wel occupied in goode werkis, and not ydel; for ydelnesse is the develis panter, to tempte men to synne;

320   and lyven in devout preieris and resonable and abstynence of mete, and namely of hote drynkis and myghtty, and visite here pore neigheboris that ben bedrede, and clothe hem, and herberwe hem, to gete remyssion of over moche likynge in fleschly dedis; and evere crie to God with gret desire and good lif, that He graunte hem grace to kepe clenly this holy ordre, and do verrey penaunce for here olde synnes, to ende in perfit charité, and so evere

325   have here verrey spouse, Jesus Crist, in blisse of hevene withouten enden. Amen. Explicit.

300 dom, authority (dominion, judgment). **305 domes**, judgments. **309 mot**, must. **310 askape unpeyned**, escape unpunished; **prevé**, secretive. **311 agenstonde**, stand against. **313 lese**, lose. **314 wot**, knows. **315 staat**, condition. **317 bleckid**, blackened. **319 panter**, snare. **321 bedrede**, bedridden. **322 herberwe hem**, provide lodging for them.

Select Bibliography and Notes to Wyclif (?), *Of Weddid Men and Wifis and of Here Children Also*

Manuscripts

Bodleian Library MS Bodley 938 (*SC* 3054), fols. 62a–73a (early fifteenth century).

Cambridge University Library MS 756, fols. 3a–16a (late fourteenth century).

British Library MS Additional 24202, fols. 29a–33b (late fourteenth century).

Corpus Christi College Cambridge MS 296, fols. 224–35 (late fourteenth century). [Base text for this edition.]

Critical Edition

Arnold, Thomas, ed. *Select English Works of John Wyclif*. Vol. 3. Oxford: Clarendon Press, 1871. Pp. 188–201. [Based on Cambridge MS Corpus Christi 296.]

Selections

Vaughan, Robert, ed. *Tracts and Treatises of John de Wycliffe, D.D. with Selections and Translations from His Manuscripts and Latin Works*. London: Blackburn, 1845. Pp. 58–59.

Winn, Herbert E., ed. *Wyclif: Select English Writings*. Oxford: Oxford University Press, 1929. Pp. 105–07.

Select Bibliography to Of Weddid Men and Wifis and of Here Children Also

Related Studies

Aston, Margaret. "'Caim's Castles': Poverty, Politics, and Disendowment." In *The Church, Politics and Patronage in the Fifteenth Century*. Ed. R. B. Dobson. Gloucester: A. Sutton, 1984. Pp. 45–81.

———. *Lollards and Reformers: Images and Literacy in Late Medieval Religion*. London: Hambledon Press, 1984.

———. "Wyclif and the Vernacular." *SCH Subsidia* 5 (1987), 281–330.

Hargreaves, H. "Sir John Oldcastle and Wycliffite Views on Clerical Marriage." *Medium Aevum* 42 (1973), 141–45.

Hudson, Anne. *The Premature Reformation: Wycliffite Texts and Lollard History*. Oxford: Clarendon Press, 1988.

———. *Lollards and Their Books*. London: Hambledon Press, 1985.

Kenny, Anthony, ed. *Wyclif in His Times*. Oxford: Clarendon Press, 1986.

Lambert, Malcolm. *Medieval Heresy: Popular Movements from Bogomil to Hus*. London: Blackwell, 1977; rpt. 1992.

Matthew, F. D., ed. *The English Works of Wyclif Hitherto Unprinted*. EETS o.s. 74. London: Trübner & Co., 1880. [Does not contain "Of Weddid Men."]

McFarlane, K. B. *Lancastrian Kings and Lollard Knights*. Oxford: Clarendon Press, 1972.

———. *John Wycliffe and the Beginnings of English Nonconformity*. London: The English Universities Press, 1952; rpt. 1966.

Murdoch, Vaclav. *The Wyclyf Tradition*. Ed. Albert Compton Reeves. Athens: Ohio University Press, 1978.

Robson, John Adam. *Wyclif and the Oxford Schools: The Relation of the "Summa de ente" to Scholastic Debates at Oxford in the Later Fourteenth Century*. Cambridge: Cambridge University Press, 1961.

Stacey, John. *John Wyclif and Reform*. London: Lutterworth Press, 1964.

Workman, Herbert B. *John Wyclif: A Study of the English Medieval Church*. Hamden, CT: Archon Books, 1966.

Notes

Abbreviations: **Ar**: Thomas Arnold; **MS**: Corpus Christi College Cambridge MS 296.

1–4   The Wycliffite author reviews an orthodox interpretation of holy wedlock as spiritual bond between Christ and the Church as well as a bond between a man and a woman. While the first form of marriage, described as *gostly* (line 2), is spiritual, i.e., between Christ and Holy Church, the second, used for actual marriage, is described in both physical and spiritual terms, *bodily or gostly* (line 3), leaving room for the possibility of marital chastity, in the manner of Joseph and Mary.

5   *prophete Osie*. See Hosea 1:19. One of the twelve prophets, Hosea was commanded by God to marry Gomer, a prostitute; his prophecy is often understood to be about unhappy marriage both on the literal and figural levels, i.e., Israel's turning away from God as the unfaithful wife turns away from her husband. According to David L. Jeffrey, "Medieval commentary focuses largely on the connection between Gomer's adultery and Israel's idolatry, seeing the main force of the book contained in Hosea's warnings against idols and false gods (e.g., 4:17), a theme associated with Hosea by John Gower in his *Mirour de l'omme*." See *A Dictionary of Biblical Tradition in English Literature* (Grand Rapids, MI: William B. Eerdmans Publishing Co., 1992), pp. 364–65.

8   *first matrimoyne and best*. There is no ambiguity in the author's priorities. He clearly puts spiritual marriage first despite the fact that he supports clerical marriage and speaks extensively about spousal relations and family life.

11   *worschipen false goddis*. It is not surprising that this is mentioned early in the treatise since false images are one of Wyclif's primary objections to orthodox practices.

12   *Seynt Jame seith*. See James 4:4. James is called the "lesser" to distinguish him from James the "greater," famous for pilgrimage to Compostela. The passage is from his epistle: "Adulterers, know you not that the friendship of this world is the

enemy of God? Whosoever therefore will be a friend of this world becometh an enemy of God" (4:4).

25   *turned watir into wyn*. The treatise reads the Wedding of Cana episode in John's Gospel (2:1–11) as an affirmation of the married state.

26   *summe heretikis*. The author seems to think of himself as orthodox on the subject of marriage.

            gevenge. Ar reads *gevinge*.

31   *as Seynt Poul seith*. 1 Timothy 4:1.

31–34   One of the goods of marriage is to procreate enough to maintain the numbers of angels and saints and to prevent fornication.

34   *lettith*. Ar reads *letiith*.

36   *ponyschide*. Ar emends to *poniscide*.

41   *false*. Ar omits final -*e*.

43   *in doynge and othere*. Ar notes that the author does not understand this phrase in the Vulgate. The sense is "in name only."

48–49   *to have the heritage holly*. The treatise implies that children who were not loved were forced into religious life while the heritage went to the favored child, often the firstborn son. The author then explains why forcing children into religious life is a bad practice.

55–56   *clene virgynité is moche betre*. This is the same line of reasoning espoused by other orthodox theologians of the Middle Ages, Jerome, for instance.

58   *Jon Evaungelist*. Traditionally held to be the author of the Book of Revelation, this John is thought also to have been present at the Crucifixion.

            Seynt Austyn and Jerom. Sts. Augustine and Jerome are represented together as promoting the same principle, though Augustine's *The Good of Marriage* is a treatise written to offset Jerome's overemphasis on virginity as a higher state of being. Nonetheless, the ambivalence on the subject of marriage even from Augustine affects later writers. G. G. Coulton remarks in *Five Centuries of Religion*, vol. 1 (Cambridge: Cambridge University Press, 1929), pp. 443–44: "The Augustinian theory of original sin necessarily implied a low view of the marriage state. Augustine forged this theory in the heat of controversy; and medieval orthodoxy frequently followed him into his least flattering conclusions. They held a sort of dualism which, in spite of occasional lip-homage to matrimony, never hesitated to exalt virginity as the nobler state. Here, as on many other points of the monastic ideal, St. Jerome's words are epoch-making and are passed from generation to generation of medieval writers as a classical commonplace: 'Marriage peoples the earth, but virginity peoples heaven' (*Patrilogia Latina*, vol. 23, col. 246)."

60–61   *And therefore Poul gaf no comaundement.* MS: *And therefore gaf no comaundement. Poul* is written in the margin.

69   Ar inserts a chapter break here.

75   *Tobie.* This refers to several passages in the Book of Tobias in which Tobias the younger receives a warning from the angel Raphael: "For they who in such manner receive matrimony, as to shut out God from themselves, and from their minds, and to give themselves to their lust, as the horse and mule, which have not understanding; over them the devil hath power" (6:17).

77   *yonge man and an olde bareyne widewe.* The phrase resonates with Chaucer's Wife of Bath and her fifth husband, Jankyn. Since procreation is a good of marriage, a union in which the widow is old and barren constitutes a perversion of scriptural edicts despite Sara's mature and barren state. Sara, of course, was not a widow.

78   *muk.* The MED points to a range of meanings suggesting a negative opinion of material possession: "animal or human excrement," "dung," "manure," "dirt," "filth," "sewage," "putrescence" merge into "property," "possession," "wealth," "worldly gain." Herbert B. Workman sees this treatise on marriage as "a good specimen of Wyclif's teaching with its emphasis on ethics. . . . Nothing could be better than his protest against the marriage of a young man and an old widow 'for love of worldly muck'. . . ." See *John Wyclif: A Study of the English Medieval Church*, p. 45.

85–86   *to his wif in Goddis lawe, and make here a gentil womman.* This phrase is found at the bottom of the MS, where it is designated an addition by a mark placed in the margin.

91   *myghtty men marien here children.* The meaning of *marien* is to "marry off" or arrange the marriage of children, usually without their consent. The author seems to suggest that this is also a social practice among certain members of the English aristocracy. The passage is perhaps subversive of arranged marriages, where lords give their children in marriage without the children's consent or love, where they "feynen for drede" (line 92), that is, agree with their parents' wishes only out of fear.

97   *to kepe his wif fro lecherie of othere men.* The author's emphasis differs slightly from that of Paul and Augustine when he reminds his audience that a husband's duty is to protect the sexual integrity of his wife.

103–07   Following Augustine and others, the treatise advocates spiritual marriage, using the Virgin Mary and Joseph as the paradigm of marital affection.

109   *fals devours.* Medieval "divorce" differs from modern divorce in that the former means what contemporary family law defines as "separation," though the living arrangement would not allow either to remarry.

116   Ar inserts a chapter break here.

117–18   The relation between husband and wife, i.e., that *the wif oweth to be suget to the housbonde, and he owith to reule his wif,* is scriptural, reiterated by many New Testament writers, including Peter, Paul, and Timothy. See note to lines 145 ff.

118 ff.   St. Peter's sayings derive from 1 Peter 3:1–7:

   1) In like manner also, let wives be subject to their husbands: that, if any believe not the word, they may be won without the word, by the conversations of the wives.
   2) Considering your chaste conversation with fear.
   3) Whose adorning, let it not be the outward plaiting of the hair, or the wearing of gold, or the putting on of apparel:
   4) But the hidden man of the heart in the incorruptibility of a quiet and a meek spirit, which is rich in the sight of God.

> 5) For after this manner heretofore, the holy women also who trusted in God adorned themselves, being in subjection to their own husbands.
> 6) As Sara obeyed Abraham, calling him lord: whose daughter you are, doing well and not fearing any disturbance.
> 7) Ye husbands, likewise dwelling with them according to knowledge, giving honour to the female as to the weaker vessel and as to the co-heirs of the grace of life, that your prayers be not hindered.

120   *wonnen*. MS: *wymmen*. Ar makes the emendation.

128   *Seynte Poul spekith*. 1 Timothy 2:8.

131   *writhen here*. Braided hair. In defining *writhen*, a form of *writh*, the OED cites this text which appears originally in 1 Timothy: "In like manner, women also in decent apparel, adorning themselves with modesty and sobriety, not with plaited hair, or gold, or pearls, or costly attire" (2:9). Note the similarity between this passage and the passage from 1 Peter cited above.

       margery stones. Called "margarite," these "stones" (pearls) are listed in many lapidaries, which were popular in late medieval England. In the *Peterborough Lapidary*, the margarita is described as "chef of al stons þat ben wyȝt & preciose, as Ised [Isidore] seyþ. And it haþe þe name margarita for it is founde in shellis which ben cokelis or in mosclys & in schellfyssh of þe see; þis bredyng is schellfyssh, & it is genderd of þe dewe of heuen, which dewe þe schell fissh receyueþ in certen tymes of þe ȝer of þe which dew margarites comen." The *Peterborough Lapidary* is found in a collection called *English Mediaeval Lapidaries*, ed. Joan Evans and Mary S. Serjeanson, EETS o.s. 190 (London: Oxford University Press, 1933), p. 108.

135   *pistel to Corynthis*. St. Paul's first epistle to the Corinthians: "Let women keep silence in the churches: for it is not permitted them to speak but to be subject, as also the law saith" (14:34). The second passage (lines 145 ff.) reads as follows: "But if they would learn anything, let them ask their husbands at home. For it is a shame for a woman to speak in the church" (14:35).

140   *Writt*. Ar reads *writ*.

145 ff. The marital hierarchy which equates men with Christ, women with Holy Church, is consistent with scriptural metaphors. See especially Ephesians 5:22–33.

Notes to Of Weddid Men and Wifis and of Here Children Also

151   *and holy; and made it clene.* MS: *And holy and made it clene.* The phrase is written at the bottom of the MS with an insertion mark in the margin.

156   *For we ben membris of his body.* The author is referring to the mystic body of Christ, i.e., those who believe and participate in Christianity.

163   *and that thou be longe.* MS: *and that belonge.*

165–66 See Ephesians 5:22 and explanatory note to lines 145 ff. Also Colossians 3:18.

171   *withoute resonable cause.* This phrase was left open to interpretation by writers of canon law. Husbands were expected to govern their wives reasonably.

        Ar inserts a chapter break here, as directed by marks in the MS.

173   *jectouris of contré.* MED cites this particular line under *gettour*, from the verb *getten. Contra* is a scholastic formula for the assertion of opposing arguments.

174   *brollis.* A pejorative term for an unruly child.

178   *togidre.* Ar reads *togedir.*

182   *Poul biddith.* This refers to Ephesians 6:1–3: "Children, obey your parents, for it is just. Honour thy father and thy mother; which is the first commandment with a promise. That it may be well with thee and that thou mayest be long upon the earth."

183   *God comaundith in the olde lawe.* The reference returns to the authority of the Old Testament, which the author elaborates in his explanation of God's promise to Moses to liberate his people (see Exodus 3:3–10).

185   *Lond of Biheste.* Promised Land. The author recalls Exodus to illustrate his point on how a father should go about teaching his children. For a discussion of Lollard education see Anne Hudson, *The Premature Reformation: Wycliffite Texts and Lollard History*, chapter 4.

191   *geverne.* Ar reads *governe.*

224   *Seynt Poul spekith.* 1 Timothy 5:8.

235   Chapter break.

241   *see*. Ar reads *se*.

243   *word of Seynt Poul*. 1 Corinthians 7:29. Ar often includes a final *-e* on Paul's name.

251   *and lecherie*. Ar omits this phrase.

266   *holden*. Ar reads *bolden*.

270   *Seynt Jon with the gildene mouth*. The reference is to John Chrysostom whose rhetorical skills were legendary by Wyclif's time. Another reference to Chrysostom appears in *Prohemy of a Mariage Betwixt an Olde Man and a Yonge Wife, and the Counsail*, also included in this volume.

275   *profrid*. Ar reads *proprid*.

281   *wifis geven here husbondis goodis*. Almsgiving was a charitable activity, but wives, thought to be overly generous to the wrong people, were admonished and advised to use discretion.

282   *othere curleris*. There is a word crossed out before *curleris* in MS.

289   *preve*. Ar has *prive*.

305   *Amen*. This marks the original end of the treatise according to Ar.

306 ff.   A late addition perhaps, this ending emphasizes the necessity for *ordre*. It continues in the same hand.

308   *auctour*. Ar reads *auctor*.

319   *ydelnesse is the develis panter*. A proverbial expression. See Whiting I16 (a long entry). Compare the Prologue to Chaucer's The Second Nun's Tale, especially VIII(G)7–13.

John Lydgate, *Payne and Sorowe of Evyll Maryage*

Take hede and lerne, thou lytell chylde, and se
That tyme passed wyl not agayne retourne,
And in thy youthe unto vertues use thee:
Lette in thy brest no maner vyce sojourne, *heart; vice reside*
5   That in thyne age thou have no cause to mourne *regret*
For tyme lost, nor for defaute of wytte: *failure of knowledge*
Thynke on this lesson, and in thy mynde it shytte. *set (shut)*

Glory unto God, laude and benysoun *praise; blessing*
To John, to Petir, and also to Laurence,
10   Which have me take under proteccioun
From the deluge of mortall pestilence,
And from the tempest of deedly violence, *deadly*
And me preserved I fell not in the rage *insanity*
Under the yoke and bondis of mariage. *obligations*

15   I was in purpose for to take a wiff, *wife*
And for to have wedded without avysenesse, *advice*
A full faire mayde, with hir to have ladde my liff, *her; led; life*
Whom that I loved of hasty wylfulnesse,
With other folys ta lyved in distresse, *fools to [have] lived*
20   As some gave me councell, and ganne me to constreyne *began*
To be partable of ther wofull peyne. *be able to share their*

They lay upon me, and hastid me full sore,
And gave me councell with hem to be bounde,
And ganne to preyse eche day more and more *assess*
25   The wofull lyf in which they did habounde, *abound*
And besy weren my gladnesse to confounde,
Themsilf rejoysyng, both at eve and morowe, *evening; morning*
To have a felowe to lyve with them in sorowe. *misery*

	But of his grace God hath me preserved	*saved*
30	By the wise councell of these aungelis three;	*angels*
	From hell gates they have mysilf conserved,	*saved me*
	In tyme of were when lovers lusty be,	*doubt*
	And bright Phebus was fresshest onto see,	
	In Gemyne, the lusty and gladde seasoun,	*Gemini (June)*
35	Whan I to wedde caught first occasioun.	*was first tempted*
	My joy was sette in especiall	*heart*
	To wedde oon excellyng in fairnesse,	*one*
	And through here beauté have made mysilf thrall,	*her; myself slave*
	Under the yoke of everlastyng distresse;	
40	But God all oonly of his grete goodnesse	*alone*
	Hath be an aungill, as ye herde me tell,	*by*
	Stopped my passage from thylke perelis of hell.	*perils*
	Amonge these aungelis, that were in nombre thre,	
	There appered oon oute of the South,	
45	Which that spake first of all that Trinité	
	All of oon sentence, the mater was well couth;	*known*
	And he was called "John with the gildyn mouth,"	*John [Chrysostom]*
	Which concludith by sentence full notable,	*Who*
	Wyves of custome be gladly variable.	*by habit; unstable*
50	Aftir this John, the story seith also,	
	In confirmacioun of ther fragilité,	*weakness*
	Howe that Petyr called the Corbelio,	*Peter Corbelio*
	Affermyd pleynly, how wyfes gladly be	
	Dyvers of hert, full of duplicité,	*heart*
55	Right mastirfull, hasty, and eke proude,	*also*
	Crabbed of langage when thei lust cry loude.	
	Who takith a wyf receyveth a grete charge,	*responsibility*
	In whiche he is like to have a fall;	
	With tempest possede as is a sely barge;	*tossed; wretched*
60	Wher he was fre, he makith hymsilf thrall.	*Where*
	Wyves of porte been so imperyall,	*imperious*
	Husbondes dare not theyre lustis well gaynsaye,	*desire; oppose*
	But lowly plie, and lowly hem obey.	*grovel*

212

Payne and Sorowe of Evyll Mariage

	The husbond ever abideth in travaile;	*suffering*
65	O laboure passed ther comyth another newe;	*One*
	And every day she gynneth a bataile,	*begins; battle*
	With false compleynyng to chaunge chiere and hewe.	*mood*
	Under suche falsenes she feyneth hir to be triewe,	*feigns herself*
	She makith hir husbond rude as a dul asse,	
70	Owt of whos daunger impossible is to passe.	*Out; stubbornness*

Thus wedlok is an endles penaunce,
Husbondes knowe that have experience,   *who*
A martirdome and a contynuaunce
Of sorowe ay lastynge, a deedly violence;   *deadly*
75 And this of wyves is gladly the sentence
Upon here husbondes when hem list be bold,   *their; they choose to*
Howe they allone governe the housold.   *household*

And if the husbond happe for to thryve,   *happens; prosper*
She saith it is here prudent purviaunce: *[by] her; management*
80 If they go bak ageynward and unthryve,   *do poorly*
She sayth it is his mysgovernaunce.
He berith the wite of all suche ordynaunce;   *blame*
If they be poure and fall into distresse,   *poor*
She sayth it is his foly and his lewdnesse.   *folly; ignorance*

85 And yf so be he be no spereman good,   *no good sex partner (spearman)*
Hit may well hap he shall have an horn,   *It; i.e., be cuckolded*
A large bone to stuff wythall his hood;
A mowe behynde, and fayned chere beforn;   *grimace behind [his back]*
And if it fall that there good be lorn,   *lost*
90 By aventure at even or at morowe,
The sely husbond shall have all the sorowe.   *hapless*

And husbond hath grete cause to care   *reason*
For wyff, for childe, for stuff and for mayné,   *chattel; retinue*
And if ought lacke she woll swere and stare,
95 "He is a wastoure, and shall never the!"   *extravagant spender; thrive*
But Salomon seith ther be thynges thre,
Shrewed wyfes, rayne, and smokes blake   *shrewish*
Makith husbondes there houses to forsake.

213

Wyves been bestes very unstable   *[like] beasts*
100   In ther desires, which may not chaunged be,
Like a swalowe whiche is insaciable
Like perilous Caribdis of the trouble see,   *Charybdis; sea*
A wawe calme, full of adversité,   *wave*
Whoes blandisshyng medled with myschaunce,   *Whose; mixed*
105   Callid Syrenes ay full of variaunce.   *Sirens*

They hem rejoise to see and to be sayne,   *seen*
And to seke sondry pilgremages,   *various*
At grete gaderynges to walken upon the playne,   *plain (open spaces)*
And at staracles to sitte on hie stages,   *plays; raised seats*
110   If they be faire to shewe ther visages;   *show; faces*
If they be fowle of look or countenaunce,   *unattractive*
They can amend it with pleasaunt daliaunce.

Of ther nature they gretly hem delite,   *delight themselves*
With holy face fayned for the nones,   *faked; church service*
115   In seyntuaries ther frendes to visite,   *sanctuaries*
More than for relikkes or any seyntis bones,   *relics; saints'*
Though they be closed under precious stones;
To gete hem pardoun, like there olde usages,
To kys no shrynes, but lusty yong images.   *kiss*

120   And to conclude shortly on reasoun,
To speke of wedlok of foles that be blent,   *fools; blind*
Ther is no more grevous, fell poysoun,   *poison*
Ne noon so dredfull, peryllous serpent,   *Nor none such*
As is a wyfe double of here entent;   *her*
125   Wherfore, yonge men, to eschewe sorowe and care,   *forgo*
Withdrawe your foot, or ye fall in the snare.   *before*

Explicit

Select Bibliography and Notes to John Lydgate, *Payne and Sorowe of Evyll Maryage*

Manuscripts

Bodleian Library MS Digby 181 (*SC* 1782), fols. 7a–8b (sixteenth century).

Cambridge University Library MS Ff. 1.6, fols. 155a–156b (c. 1500).

British Library MS Harley 2251, fols. 45a–51a (1464–83).

Rome Engl. Coll. MS 1306 (also numbered 1127 and A. 347), fols. 80b–82a (1436–56).

Early Printed Edition

de Worde, Wynkyn (1509). [With introductory stanza from Cambridge University Library MS Dd. 4.54, fol. 229b.]

Editions

Collier, J. Payne, ed. *The Pain and Sorrow of Evil Marriage: From an Unique Copy*. In *Early English Poetry, Ballads, and Popular Literature*. Vol. 1. London: Printed for the Percy Society, 1965. Pp. 17–22. [Part 4.]

MacCracken, Henry Noble, ed. *The Minor Poems of John Lydgate, Part II*. EETS o.s. 192. London: Oxford University Press, 1934. Pp. 456–60.

Wright, Thomas, ed. *The Latin Poems Commonly Attributed to Walter Mapes*. London: Camden Society, 1841. [Contains Latin and French sources.]

Related Studies

Boffey, Julia. "Short Texts in Manuscript Anthologies: The Minor Poems of John Lydgate in Two Fifteenth-Century Collections." In *The Whole Book: Cultural Perspectives on the Medieval Miscellany*. Ed. Stephen G. Nichols and Siegfried Wenzel. Ann Arbor: University of Michigan Press, 1996. Pp. 69–82.

Renoir, Alan. "Attitudes Toward Women in Lydgate's Poetry." *English Studies* 42 (1961), 1–14.

Seah, Victoria Lees. "Marriage and the Love Vision: The Concept of Marriage in Three Medieval Love Visions as Relating to Courtship and Marriage Conventions of the Period." Ph.D. Diss., McGill University, 1978.

Notes

Abbreviations: **Mac**: Henry Noble MacCracken; **MS**: Bodleian Library MS Digby 181 (*SC* 1782), fols. 7a–8b; **W**: Wynkyn de Worde.

1–7   This first stanza derives from the Cambridge University MS.

14   *Under the yoke and bondis of mariage.* Each marital partner was obligated to fulfill certain requirements of married life, such as payment of the conjugal debt. Both wife and husband could demand sex from the other at any time with expectations of compliance. The word "husband" refers to a man's ties to his domestic environment, i.e., "bound" to the "house."

16   *wedded without avysenesse.* This phrase suggests that there is no coercion for the narrator to marry as might be the case in real life. Rather, he is compelled by romantic love.

18   *Whom.* MS: *when.*

19   *ta lyved.* MS: *tallowed.*

23   *And gave.* MS: *Gave.*

46   *mater was well couth.* MS: *mater well couth.*

62   *Husbondes dare not theyre lustis well gaynsaye.* MS: *Husbondes dare not well gaynsaye.* Mac's emendation.

64–70   This stanza derives from MS Harley 2251.

75   *And this.* MS: *And thus.*

83   *fall into distresse.* MS: *full in distresse.*

85   *And yf so be he.* MS: *And if be he.* Mac's emendation.

90   *aventure at.* MS: *aventure or at.*

93   *and for mayné.* MS: *and mayne.*

96–98   See the Wife of Bath's version of the adage:

> Thow seyst that droppyng houses, and eek smoke,
> And chidyng wyves maken men to flee
> Out of hir owene houses; a, benedicitee! (III[D]278–80)

Compare also The Tale of Melibee, where Prudence refutes Melibee's charge that "thre thynges dryven a man out of his hous — that is to seyn, smoke, droppyng of reyn, and wikked wyves" (*CT* VII[B^2]1085).

107   *sondry pilgremages.* Lydgate's persona seems to have someone like the Wife of Bath in mind, who has been three times to Jerusalem, as well as to Rome, Bologne, Compostela, and Cologne in search of company.

113–19 This stanza is substituted for four spurious stanzas according to MacCracken's EETS edition. A fifth stanza, not included in his account, appears in Wynken de Worde's printed edition. The five stanzas are as follows:

> And of profyte they take but lytell hede,
>   But loketh soure whan theyr husbandes ayleth ought;
> And of good mete and drynke they wyll not fayle in dede
>   What so euer it cost they care ryght nought;
>   Nor they care not how dere it be bought,
> Rather than they should therof lacke or mysse
> They wolde leeuer laye some pledge ywys.

It is trewe, I tell you yonge men euerychone,
 Women by varyable and loue many wordes and stryfe;
Who can not appease them lyghtly or anone,
 Shall haue care and sorowe all his lyfe,
 That woo the tyme that euer he toke a wyfe;
And wyll take thought, and often muse
How he myght fynd the maner his wyfe to refuse.

But that maner with trouth can not be founde,
 Therfore be wyse or ye come in the snare,
Or er ye take the waye of that bounde;
 For and ye come there youre joye is tourned unto care
 And remedy is there none, so may I fare,
But to take pacyens, and thynke none other way aboute
Then shall ye dye a martyr without ony doute.

Therfore you men that wedded be,
 Do nothynge agaynst the pleasure of your wyfe,
Than shall you lyue the more meryle,
 And often cause her to lyue withouten stryfe;
 Without thou art unhappy unto an euyll lyfe,
Than, yf she than wyll be no better,
Set her upon a lelande, and bydde the deuyll fet her.

Therfore thynke moche and saye nought,
 And thanke God of his goodnesse,
And prece not for to knowe all her thought,
 For than shalte thou not knowe, as I gesse,
 Without it be of her own gentylnesse,
And that is as moche as a man may put in his eye,
For, yf she lyst, of thy wordes she careth not a flye.

123 *dredfull, peryllous serpent.* MS: *dredfull serpent.*

127 *Explicit.* W: *Finis. Here endeth ye payne and sorowe of evyll maryage. Imprynted at London in flete strete at the sygne of the Sonne, by me Wynkyn de Worde, W.*

218

How the Goode Wife Taught Hyr Doughter

	Lyst and lythe a lytell space,	*Listen; be attentive*
	Y schall you telle a praty cace,	*pretty story*
	How the gode wyfe taught hyr doughter	
	To mend hyr lyfe, and make her better:	*amend*
5	"Doughter, and thou wylle be a wyfe,	*if you*
	Wysely to wyrche in all thi lyfe	*work; your life*
	Serve God, and kepe thy chyrche,	*support; church*
	And myche the better thou shalt wyrche.	
	To go to the chyrch, lette for no reyne,	*i.e., rain or shine*
10	And that schall helpe thee in thy peyne.	
	Gladly loke thou pay thy tythes,	*see to it; tithes*
	Also thy offeringes loke thou not mysse;	*do not miss*
	Of pore men be thou not lothe,	*disdainful*
	Bot gyff thou them both mete and clothe;	*give; food; clothing*
15	And to pore folke be thou not herde,	*hard*
	Bot be to them thyn owen stowarde;	*your own steward*
	For where that a gode stowerde is,	*good*
	Wantys seldome any ryches.	*seldom [is there] lack of*
	When thou arte in the chyrch, my chyld,	
20	Loke that thou be bothe meke and myld,	*See to it; humble; gracious*
	And bydde thy bedes aboven alle thinge,	*pray with your beads*
	With sybbe ne fremde make no jangelynge.	*kinfolk nor strangers; gossip*
	Laughe thou to scorne nother olde ne yonge,	*neither*
	Be of gode berynge and of gode tonge;	*good behavior; careful talk*
25	Yn thi gode berynge begynnes thi worschype,	*begins your honor*
	My dere doughter, of this take kepe.	*[advice] take heed*
	Yf any man profer thee to wede,	*offers to wed you*
	A curtas answer to hym be seyde,	*courteous reply*
	And schew hym to thy frendes alle;	*introduce him*
30	For any thing that may befawle,	*Regardless of; befall*
	Syt not by hym, ne stand thou nought	*Sit*
	Yn sych place ther synne mey be wroght.	*where sin; done*
	What man that thee doth wedde with rynge,	*Whatever*

	Loke thou hym love aboven all thinge;	*love him*
35	Yf that it forteyne thus with thee	*If it happens*
	That he be wroth, and angery be,	*angry*
	Loke thou mekly answere hym,	*submissively*
	And meve hym nother lyth ne lymme;	*neither provoke him in any way*
	And that schall sclake hym of hys mode	*mitigate his anger*
40	Than schall thou be hys derlynge gode.	*darling good*
	Fayre wordes wreth do slake;	*Fair words diminish wrath*
	Fayre wordes wreth schall never make,	
	Ne fayre wordes brake never bone,	*Nor; ever break bones*
	Ne never schall in no wone.	*dwelling*
45	Be fayre of semblant, my dere doughter,	*fair; appearance*
	Change not thi countenans with grete laughter	*your countenance*
	And wyse of maneres loke thou be gode,	*with regard to manners*
	Ne for no tayle change thi mode	*gossip; your demeanor*
	Ne fare not a thou a gyglot were,	*act not as if you were a loose woman*
50	Ne laughe thou not low, be thou therof sore.	*loudly; sorry*
	Luke thou also gape not to wyde,	*yawn (gape); too wide*
	For anything that may betyde.	*happen*
	Suete of speche, loke that thow be	*Sweet; speech*
	Trow in worde and dede; lerne thus of me.	*True*
55	Loke thou fle synne, vilony, and blame,	*flee sin*
	And se ther be no man that seys thee any schame.	*i.e., starts rumors*
	When thou goys in the gate, go not to faste,	*walk on the path; too fast*
	Ne hyderwerd ne thederward thi hede thou caste.	*one way or the other; looking*
	No grete othes loke thou swere:	*cursing*
60	Byware, my doughter, of syche a maner!	*Beware*
	Go not as it wer a gase	*if you were a goose (frivolous person)*
	Fro house to house, to seke the mase	*idle diversion*
	Ne go thou not to no merket	*market*
	To sell thi thryft, bewer of itte.	*material wealth; beware*
65	Ne go thou nought to the taverne,	
	Thy godnes for to selle therinne;	*betray*
	Forsake thou hym that taverne hanteth,	*those who; haunt*
	And all the vices that therinne bethe.	*reside within*
	Wherever thou comme at ale other wyne,	*or wine*
70	Take not to myche, and leve be tyme;	*too much; leave on*
	For mesure therinne, it is no herme,	*moderation; harm*
	And drounke to be, it is thi schame.	*drunk; shame*

How the Goode Wife Taught Hyr Doughter

	Ne go thou not to no wrastylynge,	*wrestling matches*
	Ne git to no coke schetynge,	*cock shooting*
75	As it wer a strumpet other a gyglote,	*or a whore*
	Or as a woman that lyst to dote.	*is like a fool*
	Byde thou at home, my doughter dere.	*Stay*
	Thes poyntes at me I rede thou lere,	*about men I advise you to learn*
	And wyrke thi werke at nede,	*when needed*
80	All the better thou may spede	*succeed*
	Y swere thee, doughter, be heven Kynge,	*promise; by*
	Mery it is of althynge.	
	Aquyente thee not with every man.	*Acquaint yourself*
	That inne the stret thou metys than;	*you meet*
85	Thof he wold be aqueynted with thee,	*Though; acquainted with you*
	Grete hym curtasly, and late hym be.	*Greet; courteously*
	Loke by hym not longe thou stond,	*stand*
	That thorow no vylony thi hert fond	*through; villainy; heart found*
	All the men be not trew	*true*
90	That fare spech to thee can schew.	*fair speech; show*
	For no covetys no giftys thou take,	*covetousness; gifts*
	Bot thou wyte why: sone them forsake.	*Unless you know; quickly*
	For gode women, with gyftes	
	Me ther honour fro them lyftes,	*Men; steal*
95	Thofe that thei wer all trew	*Though; true*
	As any stele that bereth hew,	*steel; i.e., is polished*
	For with ther giftes men them over gone.	*overwhelm*
	Thof thei wer trew as ony stone,	*i.e., worthy*
	Bounde thei be that giftys take:	*Obligated*
100	Therfor thes giftes thou forsake.	
	Yn other mens houses make thou no maystry;	*attempt; mastery*
	For drede, no vylony to thee be spye.	*fear; witness*
	Loke thou chyd no wordes bolde,	*quarrel*
	To myssey nother yonge ne olde	*mis-say (slander) neither*
105	For and thou any chyder be,	*if you; troublemaker*
	Thy neyghbors wylle speke thee vylony.	*slander you*
	Be thou not to envyos,	*too envious*
	For dred thi neyghbors wyll thee curse,	*fear*
	Envyos hert hymselve fretys,	*Envious; itself disturbs*
110	And of gode werkys hymselve lettys.	*itself hinders*
	Houswyfely wyll thou gone	

221

On werke deys in thine awne wone.   *own dwelling*

Pryde, rest, and ydellschype,   *idleness*

Fro thes werkes thou thee kepe;   *[Away] from; activities; keep yourself*

115   And kepe thou welle thy holy dey,   *day*

And thy God worschype when thou may,   *worship*

More for worschype than for pride;   *honor*

And styfly in thy feyth thou byde.   *steadfastly; faith; abide*

Loke thou were no ryche robys;   *wear, fancy clothes*

120   Ne counterfyte thou no ladys   *copy; ladies*

For myche schame do them betyde   *befall*

That lese ther worschipe thorow ther pride.   *lose; honor*

Be thou, doughter, a houswyfe gode,   *good housewife*

And evermore of mylde mode.   *of humble spirit*

125   Wysely loke thi hous and meneye,   *look [after]; household servants*

The beter to do thei schall be.   *to serve [you]*

Women that be of yvell name,   *bad reputation*

Be ye not togedere in same   *together in company (i.e., avoid them)*

Loke what moste nede is to done.   *See*

130   And sette thi mené therto ryght sone.   *assign your servants*

That thinge that is before done dede,   *before it is needed*

Redy it is when thou hast nede.

And if thy lord be fro home,   *i.e., husband; away from*

Lat not thy meneye idell gone   *Let; your servants go idle*

135   And loke thou wele who do hys dede,   *his work*

Quyte hym therafter to his mede;   *Give him; reward*

And thei that wylle bot lytell do,   *but little*

Therafter thou quite is mede also.   *cancel his reward*

A grete dede if thou have to done,   *task*

140   At the tone ende thou be ryght sone;   *At one end*

And if that thou fynd any fawte,   *fault*

Amend it sone, and tarrye note.   *do not hesitate*

Mych thynge behoven them   *Many things behoove*

That gode housold schall kepyn.   *household*

145   Amend thy hous or thou have nede,

For better after thou schall spede;   *fare*

And if that thy nede be grete,

And in the country courne be stryte,   *grain; straight*

Make an houswyfe on thyselve,   *i.e., do the work*

150   Thy bred thou bake for houswyfys helthe.   *bake bread; well-being*

222

Amonge thi servantes if thou stondyne,
Thy werke it schall be soner done
To helpe them sone thou sterte,
For many handes make lyght werke.

155 Bysyde thee if thy neghbores thryve,
Therfore thou make no stryfe,   *do not begrudge them*
Bot thanke God of all thi gode
That He send thee to thy fode;   *sustenance*
And than thow schall lyve gode lyfe,

160 And so to be a gode houswyfe.
At es he lyves that awes no dette,   *ease; owes; debt*
Yt is no les, withouten lette.   *lie, without a doubt (truly)*
Syte not to longe uppe at evene,   *Sit*
For drede with ale thou be oversene   *fear; intoxicated*

165 Loke thou go to bede bytyme;   *on time*
Erly to ryse is fysyke fyne.   *Early to rise; good medicine*
And so thou schall be, my dere chyld,
Be welle dysposed, both meke and myld,   *disposed*
For all ther es may thei not have,   *ease*

170 That wyll thryve, and ther gode save,   *their wealth*
And if it thus thee betyde,   *happens*
That frendes falle thee fro on every syde,   *friends fall away*
And God fro thee thi chyld take,
Thy wreke one God do thou not take,   *grievance on*

175 For thyselve it wyll undo,
And all thes that thee longe to
Many one for ther awne foly   *Many [a] one; own folly*
Spyllys themselve unthryftyly.   *Defeat; unwisely*
Loke, doughter, nothing thou lese,   *lose*

180 Ne thi housbond thou not desples.
And if thou have a doughter of age,   *i.e., marrying age*
Pute here sone to maryage;   *Offer her*
For meydens, thei be lonely
And nothing syker therby.   *lack certainty as a result*

185 Borow thou not, if that thou meye,   *may*
For drede thi neybour wyll sey naye;
Ne take thou nought to fyrste,   *[what is] lent on credit*
Bot thou be inne more bryste.   *Unless; need*
Make thee not ryche of other mens thyng,   *men's money*

223

190   The bolder to spend be one ferthyng.   *by one farthing*
         Borowyd thinge muste nedes go home,   *be returned*
         Yf that thou wyll to heven gone.   *heaven go*
         When the servantes have do ther werke,
         To pay ther hyre loke thou be smerte,   *pay their hire; prompt*
195   Whether thei byde or thei do wende   *stay before; leave*
         Thus schall thou kepe them ever thi frende,   *your friends*
         And thus thi frendes wyll be glade
         That thou dispos thee wyslye and sade.   *yourself; seriously*
         Now I have taught thee, my dere doughter,
200   The same techynge I hade of my modour: *mother*
         Thinke theron both nyght and dey,
         Forgette them not if that thou may,
         For a chyld unborne wer better   *is better unborn*
         Than be untaught, thus seys the letter.   *goes the proverb*
205   Therfor Allmyghty God inne trone,   *throne*
         Spede us all, bothe even and morne;   *Protect; evening*
         And bringe us to Thy hyghe blysse,
         That never more fro us schall mysse!"

         Amen, quod Rate

Select Bibliography and Notes to
How the Goode Wife Taught Hyr Doughter

Manuscripts

Bodleian Library MS Ashmole 61 (*SC* 6922), fols. 7a–8b (c. 1500). [Base copy text for this edition.]

Emmanuel College Cambridge MS I. 428 (James 106), fols. 48b–52a (c. 1350).

Trinity College Cambridge MS 599 (R. 3.19), fols. 211a–213a (c. 1500).

Lambeth Palace Library MS 853, pp. 102–12 (c. 1430). [In stanzas with refrain.]

Huntington Library MS HM 128 (Ashburnham 130), fols. 217a–220a (c. 1450).

Early Printed Editions

Madden, Sir Frederick, ed. *How the Goode Wif Thaught Hir Doughter*. London: C. Whittington, 1838.

Stow, John. *Certaine Worthy MS Poems of Great Antiquitie*. London, 1597; rpt. 1812.

Editions

Coulton, G. G. *Social Life in Britain from the Conquest to the Reformation*. Cambridge, Eng.: Cambridge University Press, 1918; rpt. 1919, 1938, 1968.

Furnivall, Frederick J., ed. *Queene Elizabethes Achademy: A Booke of Precedence, etc., with Essays on Early Italian and German Books of Courtesy*. EETS e.s. 8. London: N. Trübner, 1869. Pp. 44–51.

———. *The Babees Book, Aristotle's ABC, Urbanitatis, Stans Puer ad Mensam, The Lytille Childrenes Lytil Boke, The Bokes of Nurture of Hugh Rhodes and John Russell, Wynkyn de Worde's Book of Kervynge, The Booke of Demeanor, The Boke of Curtasye, Seager's Schoole of Vertue, etc. etc. with some French and Latin Poems on Like Subjects and Some Forewards on Education in Early England*. EETS o.s. 32. London: N. Trübner & Co., 1868. Rpt. New York: Greenwood Press, 1969. Pp. 36–47.

Hindley, Charles D., ed. *The Old Book Collector's Miscellany*. London: Reeves & Turner, 1871.

Mustanoja, Tauno, ed. *The Good Wife Taught Her Daughter, The Good Wyfe Wold a Pylgremage, The Thewis of Gud Women*. Helsinki: Suomalaisen Kirjallisuuden Scuran, 1948.

Partridge, John, ed. *The Hystorie of the Moste Noble Knight Plasidas and Other Rare Pieces*. London: J. B. Nichols & Sons, 1873.

Modernizations

Rickert, Edith, ed. *The Babees Book: Medieval Manners for the Young Now First Done into Modern English from the Texts of Dr. F. J. Furnivall*. London: The Ballantyne Press, 1908. Rpt. London: Chatto & Windus, 1923. Pp. 31–42. [A modernized version.]

Walsh, James J., ed. *A Golden Treasury of Medieval Literature*. Boston: The Stratford Co., 1930.

Related Studies

Ashley, Kathleen M. "Medieval Courtesy Literature and Dramatic Mirrors of Female Conduct." In *The Ideology of Conduct: Essays on Literature and the History of Sexuality*. Ed. Nancy Armstrong and Leonard Tennenhouse. New York: Methuen, 1987. Pp. 25–38.

Ashley, Kathleen M., and Robert L. A. Clark, eds. *Medieval Conduct*. Minneapolis: University of Minnesota Press, 2001.

Bornstein, Diane. *Mirrors of Courtesy*. Hamden, CT: Archon Books, 1975.

———. "As Meek as a Maid: A Historical Perspective on Language for Women in Courtesy Books from the Middle Ages to Seventeen Magazine." In *Women's Language and Style*. Ed. Douglas Butturff and Edmund L. Epstein. Akron: L & S Books, 1978. Pp. 132–38.

———. "Women's Public and Private Space in Some Medieval Courtesy Books." *Centerpoint: A Journal of Interdisciplinary Studies* 3 (1980), 68-74.

Hanawalt, Barbara A. *Growing Up in Medieval London: The Experience of Childhood in History*. Oxford: Oxford University Press, 1993.

Notes to *How the Goode Wife Taught Hyr Daughter*

Nicholls, Jonathan. *The Matter of Courtesy: Medieval Courtesy Books and the Gawain Poet.* Suffolk: D. S. Brewer, 1985.

Sponsler, Claire. *Drama and Resistance: Bodies, Goods, and Theatricality in Late Medieval England.* Minneapolis: University of Minnesota Press, 1997. [See especially ch. 3: "Conduct Books and Good Governance." Pp. 50–74.]

Stiller, Nikki. *Eve's Orphans: Mothers and Daughters in Medieval English Literature.* Westport, CT: Greenwood Press, 1980.

Notes

Abbreviations: **B**: Bodleian Library MS Ashmole 61 (*SC* 6922), fols. 7a–8b; **F**: Frederick J. Furnivall (1869); **E**: Emmanuel College Cambridge MS I. 428 (James 106), fols. 48b–52a; **H**: Huntington Library MS HM 128; **La**: Lambeth Palace Library MS 853; **TM**: Tauno Mustanoja.

1   *Lyst and lythe a lytell.* An exhortation to the audience to pay attention. TM suggests that this text is authored by a male cleric. Diane Bornstein disagrees: "The poem has a rough rhythm, simple rhyme scheme, Anglo-Saxon vocabulary, and a popular proverbial tone. . . . The poem may represent the traditional lore that a mother passed on to her daughter, put into written form or dictated to a scribe by a woman with some literary skill. If it was written by a man, he effectively answered the persona of a woman of the lower middle-class" ("Women's Public and Private Space," p. 64). The MS is highly abbreviated; "and" appears as an ampersand which F has transformed, as have I. He has also accounted for other abbreviations and added final -*e* where the meter seems to call for it. Many of these emendations have been retained.

8   *shalt.* B: *sh.* The gap following *sh* in *shalt* is filled in by F. Many such lacunae in B are filled in by F.

11   *tythes.* Regular payment of tithes to the parish church was expected not only of the head of the household but of individual members of the parish.

16   *stowarde.* Stewards were important to medieval society and its literature, serving as surrogates for an absent lord. The introduction of the steward's position as one requiring complete trust will play out later in the poem when the daughter is told that a wife is expected to serve as household manager in the absence of her husband. This also suggests that the household has some wealth.

20   *meke and myld.* This is an oft-used phrase with a range of meanings, many of which are gender specific. The MED defines *meke*, for instance, as: "gentle, quiet,

227

unaggressive; of a woman: modest; of eyes: soft"; when combined with *myld*: "full of loving kindness, benevolent, kind, sweet." Chaucer defies gender distinctions in his description of the knight in the Prologue to the *The Canterbury Tales*:

> And though that he were worthy, he was *wys*,
> And of his port as meeke as is a mayde. (I[A]68–69)

21   *And bydde thy bedes aboven alle thinge*. The beads referred to here are typically used in prayer.

22   *With sybbe ne fremde make no jangelynge*. F reads *frennde* ("friend") for *fremde* ("stranger"). The admonition (lines 19 ff.) alludes to the Pauline injunction in 1 Corinthians 14:35 that women refrain from speaking in church.

33   *wedde with rynge*. The ritual of the wedding ring provided a visible sign of betrothal, a symbol of a private vow made public. La adds *bifor God*.

37   *Loke thou mekly answere hym*. F's gloss on this — "do not answer him" — suggests that *mekly* be understood as an injunction against a woman's vocal response in this social situation. However, as the note to line 20 above suggests, to be meek is to assume a range of postures, most of which imply humility.

38   *lyth ne lymme*. "Body joint nor limb," i.e., anywhere, completely.

41–44   *Fayre wordes*. The three *fayre worde* sayings here are clearly proverbial, though not cited by Whiting, who lists five other "fair word" proverbs (see W581–85).

46   *Change not thi countenans with grete laughter*. The wife's admonition against uncontrolled laughter reflects proper constraints upon female behavior. "A wyf sholde eek be mesurable in lookynge and in berynge and in lawghynge, and discreet in alle hire wordes and hire dedes," says Chaucer's Parson (*CT* X[I]936). Restraint in laughter is a sign of modesty in a woman; loud laughter is the opposite, suggestive of scorn, ridicule, or lack of sexual restraint. It is one quality of the unruly woman that the narrator of Dunbar's *The Tretis of the Twa Mariit Wemen and the Wedo* finds threatening. Chaucer says of the Wife of Bath: "Wel koude she laughe and carpe" (*CT* I[A]474), suggesting her sanguine irrepressibility; and of herself she observes, "As helpe me God, I laughe whan I thynke" (*CT* III[D]201). In The Miller's Tale the frisky Alisoun counsels Nicholas, prior to her humiliation of Absalon: "Now hust, and thou shalt laughen al thy fille" (*CT* I[A]3722), and then laughs herself in one of the most famous lines in Middle English: "'Tehee!' quod she, and clapte the wyndow to"

(I[A]3740). Criseyde, filled with thoughts of Troilus, laughs immoderately when Pandarus makes jokes about his role as go-between: "And she to laughe, it thoughte hire herte brest" (*Troilus and Criseyde* 2.1108). Moderate laughter can be a sign of allurement, as in Swete Thought's soothing of the lover by speaking of "[h]ir laughing eyen, persaunt and clere" (*The Romaunt of the Rose*, line 2809). But such laughter may likewise suggest comeliness and self-assurance, as in *The Book of the Duchess*, line 850, where the Good Fair White "[l]aughe and pleye so womanly." Strong women like St. Cecile in Chaucer's The Second Nun's Tale or St. Margaret in the St. Katherine Group may laugh in the face of the tyrant or the fiend, thus humiliating him, but these women are not the models the good wife would invoke for her impressionable daughter.

52   *betyde*. B: *betytde*.

55   *blame*. B: *blane*.

61   *gase*. "Goose." Or possibly a "gad about," or "gaze about."

69   *other*. B: *or*. The poet/scribe (Rate) consistently abbreviates this term.

73   *Ne go thou not to no wrastylynge*. Wrestling matches were the province of men and as such were considered inappropriate entertainment for unmarried women.

74   *Ne git to no coke schetynge*. B: *fygntyng*. F glosses this sport as "cock fighting" and notes that four dashes under *schetynge* indicate "an intension to erase" the word. The sport here, however, is not roosters fighting one another in a ring surrounded by spectators (see MED *sheting* ger. [b]). Rather, it is a sport requiring the shooting of the rooster with an arrow. Other MSS readings clarify: *Go thou noght to wraxling, no scheting ate cok.*

75   *strumpet*. B: *strmpet*.

83   *every*. B: *ever*.

99   *Bounde thei be that giftys take*. There is implicit obligation in the receiving of gifts against which the author warns. It is similar to feudal obligation when the status of the giver is higher than that of the recipient.

105 ff.   After line 106 there is a drawing of a fish (pike?) extending the width of the leaf and marking the bottom of the folio. The poem continues at the top of the next folio.

110   *werkys*. B: *werky*.

113   *ydellschype*. B: *ydellschy*.

116   *when*. B: *whe*.

130   *mené*. B: *men*. There is a significant difference implied by the emendation. The household servants (*mené*) over which the daughter is expected to rule are made up of both men and women. This MS omits a mother's responsibility to beat her children as expressed in La:

> And if thei children been rebel, & wole not them lowe,
> If ony of hem mys dooth, nouther banne hem ne blowe,
> But take a smert rodde, & bete hem on arowe
> Til thei crei mercy, & be of her gilt aknowe. (Lines 201–04)

In general the Bodleian (Ashmole) text is more gentle in its attitudes toward child-rearing.

148   *courne*. This term refers not to the plant with ears native to North America, but rather is the word for grain. F notes that in the Lambeth MS 853, the basis for the *Babees Book*, the word is "time" as it is in the manuscripts printed in E and H:

> And yf thin nede beo gret, and thin time streit.
> And yif thi nede be grette, and thi tyme streite.

There is an alteration in meaning between the terms grain and time, suggesting on the one hand that the time to make bread is when the grain is ready to harvest while on the other, the time to make bread is when there is need for it.

154   *For many handes make lyght werke*. A proverbial expression that first appears in the Middle English romance *Bevis of Hampton*, where it is used to emphasize how even the giant, Ascopard, needs assistance from ordinary men in combat.

161   *awes*. B: *awe*.

171–74   *And if it thus thee betyde*. These lines are omitted in E and H. Interestingly, Rate (see note to line 209) omits a particularly striking quatrain on how a mother should discipline her children. See explanatory note for line 130.

183–84   *For meydens, thei be lonely / And nothing syker therby.* The bias suggesting that women, particularly young women, are phlegmatic hints at an underlying negative view of women in general. The passage may also provide further evidence for male authorship (see note to line 1).

199   *Now I have taught thee, my dere doughter.* As in The Wife of Bath's Prologue, the tradition of women passing on women's knowledge is carried out privately between mother and daughter in the domestic environment: "I bar hym on honde he hadde enchanted me — / My dame taughte me that soutiltee" (III[D]575–76).

204   *thus seys the letter. Letter* might mean "script," or "source," but the sense seems to be proverbial, though not cited in Whiting. F (p. 47), using La as his principle source, reads: *Betere were a child vnbore / þan vntauȝt of wijs lore, / mi leve child.*

209   *Amen, quod Rate. Rate* is taken to be the name of the scribe. F reads *Kate.*

How the Goode Man Taght Hys Sone

Lystenyth all and ye shall here,   *Listen; hear*
How the gode man taght hys sone;
Take gode tente to thys matere,   *Pay attention*
And fonde to lerne hyt, yf ye conne,   *try; learn it; can*
5   Thys songe by yong men was bygonne,   *for; made*
To make them trysty and stedfaste;   *trustworthy*
But iarne that ys ofte tyme evell spon,   *[a] yarn (story); poorly told*
Evyll hyt cometh owt at the laste.   *Useless; end*

A wyse man had a feyre chylde,   *handsome*
10 Was wele of fiftene wyntur age,   *fifteen years old*
That was bothe meke and mylde,   *Who*
Fayre of body and of vysage,   *appearance*
Gentyl of kynde and of corage.   *nature*
For he schulde be hys fadurs heyre,   *father's heir*
15 Hys fadur thus in hys langage   *his [own] words*
Taught hys sone, bothe wele and feyre,   *his son; well; wisely*

And seyde: "Sone, kepe thys worde in hert,   *heart*
And thynke theron to thou be deed,   *until; dead*
Every day the fyrste werke   *activity [that you do]*
20 Loke thys be done in every stedd: *See to it [that]*
Fyrste see thy God in forme of bredd,   *bread*
And serve Hym wele for Hys godenes.
And aftur that, sone, be my redd,   *by my advice*
Go to thy worldely besynes.   *business*

25 "Fyrste worschyp thy God on the day,   *I.e., first thing in the morning*
And, sone, thys schalt thou have to mede: *sustain you*
Skylfully whatso thou pray,   *whatsoever*
He wyll thee graunt, withowten drede,   *bequeath; without a doubt*
And sende thee all that thou haste nede,   *have need for*
30 As far as mesure longyth to strecche.   *measure; stretch*

Thy lyfe in mesure that thou lede,   *I.e., the length of your life*
And of the remenunt thou ne recche.   *remainder; do not reach*

"And, sone, thy tonge thou kepe also,   *i.e., hold your tongue*
And be not talewyse in no way;   *insolent*
35   Thyn owen tonge may be thy foo.   *enemy*
Therfore beware, sone, y thee pray,   *aware*
Where and when, sone, thou shalt say,
And by whom thou spekyst oght;   *to whom you are speaking*
For thou may speke a worde today,
40   That seven yere aftur may be forthoght.   *seven years later; regretted*

"Therfore, sone, bewar be tyme,   *aware in time*
Desyre none offyce for to bere,   *no official position*
For of thy neghburs maugreth thyn,
Thou must them bothe dysplese and dere,
45   Or ellys thyselfe thou must forswere   *compromise yourself*
And do not as thyn offyce wolde,   *your position demands*
And gete thee maugreth here and there,   *ill-will*
More then thanke a thousandefolde.

"And, sone, yf thou wylt leve at eese,   *live; ease*
50   And warme among thy neghburs sytt,   *comfortably*
Let no newfangylnes thee pleese,
Oftyn to remeve nor to flytt.
For yf thou do, there wantyth wytt,
For folys they remeve all to wyde;
55   And also, sone, an ell sygne ys hyt: *ill sign*
A man that can nowhere abyde.

"And, sone, of oon thyng specyally y thee warn,   *one*
And of my blessyng take gode hede,
Loke thou use nevyr comynly the taverne,   *See to it that*
60   And also dysyng y thee forbede.   *dicing (i.e., gambling)*
For these two thyngs, withowten drede,
And comyn women, as y leve,   *common; believe*
Maken yong men evyll to spede,
And bryngyth them often to myschefe.   *lead; trouble*

65   "And, sone, the more gode thou haste,   *goodness you have*
            The rather bere thee meke and lowe.
            Lagh not to moche, for that ys waste,   *Laugh; much*
            For folys byn by laghyng knowe.   *fools are known by laughing*
            And, sone, paye wele that thou doyst owe,   *pay well (in a timely fashion)*
70   So that thou be of dettys clere.   *clear of debts*
            And thus, my lefe chylde, as y trowe,   *dear child*
            Thou mayste thee kepe fro all daunger.   *harm*

            "And loke thou wake not to longe,   *stay up too long*
            Neydur use no rere sopers to late;   *Nor let no last meal of the day be too late*
75   For were thy complexion never so stronge,
            Wyth surfett thou mayste fordo that.   *excess*
            Of late wakyng fallyth often debate,   *quarrels*
            On nyghtys for to sytt and drynke.
            Yf thou wylt rewle wele thyn astate,   *i.e., take care of your body*
80   Betymys go to bedd and wynke.   *sleep*

            "And, sone, as fer forthe as thou may,   *far away*
            On none enquest loke that thou come,   *quest (pilgrimage)*
            Nor no false wytnesse bere away
            Of no mannys mater all ne some;   *man's business*
85   For bettur were thee be defe and dome,   *better to be mute*
            Then for to be on any enqueste,   *quest*
            That afturward myght be undurnome;   *undertake*
            A trewe man had hys quarell leste.   *lost*

            "And, sone, yf thou wylt have a wyfe,
90   Take hur for no covetyse,   *not out of desire of possessions*
            But loke, sone, sche be thee lefe;   *be loved of you*
            Thou wysely wayte and wele avyse,   *wisely wait; be well advised*
            That sche be gode, honest, and wyse.
            Thogh sche be pore, take thou non hede,
95   For sche schall do thee more servyse,
            Then schall a ryche, withowten drede.   *rich [woman]; doubt*

            "For bettry hyt ys in reste and pees,
            A messe of potage and no more,
            Then for to have a thousand messe   *meals*

100	Wyth grete dysese and anger sore.	
	Therfore, sone, thynk on thys lore:	
	Yf thou wylt have a wyfe wyth ese,	*with means*
	By hur good sett thou no store,	
	Thogh sche wolde thee bothe feffe and sese.	*[Even] though; [bring] you; fief; seizin*

105	"And yf thy wyfe be meke and gode,	*meek*
	And serve thee wele and plesauntly,	
	Loke that thou be not so wode,	*angry*
	To charge hur then to owtragely;	*punish her; too outrageously*
	But thou fare with hur esely,	*deal; justly*
110	And cherysch hur for hur gode dede;	*cherish her*
	For thyng overdon unskylfully	*done to excess*
	Makyth wrath to growe where ys no nede.	

	"I wyll neyther glose ne paynte,	*gloss nor paint*
	But warne thee on another syde:	*point*
115	Yf thy wyfe come to make a playnte	*complaint*
	On thy servauntys on ony syde,	*Against*
	Be not to hasty them to chyde,	*too; chastise*
	Nor wrath thee not, or thou wyt the sothe;	*anger you; before*
	For wemen in wrath they can noght hyde,	
120	But soone they can reyse a smoke.	*complain*

	"Nor, sone, be not jellows, y thee pray,	*jealous*
	For yf thou falle yn yelesye,	*into jealousy*
	Let not thy wyfe wyt be no way,	*know of it*
	For thou may do no more folye.	
125	For and thy wyfe may onys aspye,	*once realize*
	That thou hur anythyng mystryste,	*mistrust her [in] anything*
	In despyte of thy fantesye,	*fancy*
	To do the worse ys all hur lyste.	

	"Therfore, sone, y bydd thee,	
130	Wyrche with thy wyfe, as reson ys;	
	Thogh sche be sirvunt in degree,	*servant*
	In some degre sche fellowe ys.	*is an equal*
	Laddys that are weddyd, so have y blys,	*Lads who*
	That cannot rewle ther wyvys aryght,	*rule; wives in the right way*

135   That makyth wemen, so have y blys,

        To do often wronge, in plyght.   *under stress*

        "Nethur, sone, bete not thy wyfe, y rede,   *beat; counsel*

        For therin may no helpe bee.

        Betyng may not stonde in stede,   *Beating; help*

140   But rather make hur to despyse thee.   *despise you*

        With lone awe, sone, thy wyfe chastyse,

        And let feyre wordes be thy gerde;   *support*

        Lone awe ys the beste gyse,   *strategy*

        My sone, to make thy wyfe aferde.   *afraid*

145   "Nodur, sone, thy wyfe thou schalt not chyde,

        Nor calle hur be no fowle name,

        For sche that schall lye be thy syde,   *lie by your side*

        To calle hur foule hyt ys thy schame.

        When thou thyn own wyfe wyll dyffame,   *defame (i.e., slander)*

150   Well may another man do soo.

        Softe and feyre men make tame

        Harte, bukk, and wylde roo.   *Stag; buck; doe*

        "Also, sone, pay wele thy tythe,   *tithe*

        And pore men of thy gode thou dele;

155   And loke, sone, be thy lyve,

        That thou gete thy soule here some hele.

        Thys worlde hyt ys full fekyll and frele,   *fickle; free*

        All day be day hyt wyll enpayre;   *impair*

        And so, sone, thys worldys weele   *i.e., commonweal*

160   Hyt faryth but as a cheryfeyre.   *cherry fair*

        "For all that ever man doyth here   *i.e., in this life*

        Wyth besynesse and travell bothe,

        All hyt ys, withowten were,   *without doubt*

        For owre mete, drynke, and clothe.   *food; clothing*

165   More gettyth he not, withowten othe,   *unquestionably*

        Kynge or prynce whethur that he bee;   *whether he is*

        Be hym lefe or be hym lothe,   *fairminded; loathsome*

        A pore man hath as moche as hee.   *has*

"And many a man her gedryth gode   *here accumulates wealth*
170   All hys lyfetyme for other men,
That he may not, be the Rode,   *by the Cross*
Hymselfe oonys ete of an henne.
But be he dolvyn in hys denne,
Another shall come at hys laste ende,
175   Schall have hys wyfe and catell then;   *chattel*
That he hath gaderyd, another shall spende.

"Therfore, sone, be my counsayle,   *counsel*
More then ynogh thou nevyr coveyte.
Thou wottyst not when dethe wyll thee assayle;   *know; death; assail*
180   Thys worlde ys but the fendys beyte.   *fiend's bait*

"For dethe, sone, ys, as y trowe,   *I know*
The moost thyng that certeyn ys;
And none so uncerteyn for to knowe,   *what is not known*
As ys the tyme of dethe, ywys.   *time of death*
185   And therfore, sone, thynke on thys   *think about this*
And all that y have seyde beforne.   *heretofore*
And Jhesu brynge us to Hys blys,
That for us weryd the crowne of thorne."   *Who; wore*

Select Bibliography and Notes to
How the Goode Man Taght Hys Sone

Manuscripts

Cambridge University Library MS Ff. 2. 38, fols. 53a–54a (c. 1500).

British Library MS Harley 5396, fols. 297a–300b (c. 1475).

British Library MS Harley 2399, fols. 61a–63a (c. 1500).

Bodleian Library MS Ashmole 61 (*SC* 6922), fol. 6a–6b (c. 1500). [Base text for this edition.]

Lambeth Palace Library MS 853, pp. 186–92 (c. 1430).

Balliol College Oxford MS 354, fols. 157a–158b (early sixteenth century).

Editions

Fischer, Rudolf., ed. *How the Wise Man Taught Hys Sone*. Erlangen: A. Deichertsche Verlabsbuch, 1889. [Contains three MSS, including Cambridge University Ff. 2. 38.]

Furnivall, Frederick J., ed. *The Babees Book*. EETS o.s. 32. London: N. Trübner, 1868. [Based on Lambeth 853.]

———. *Queene Elizabethes Achademy: A Booke of Precedence, etc., with Essays on Early Italian and German Books of Courtesy*. EETS e.s. 8. London: N. Trübner, 1869. [Based on Bodleian 6922.]

Ritson, Joseph, ed. *Pieces of Ancient Popular Poetry: From Authentic Manuscripts and Old Printed Copies*. London: C. Clarke, for T. and J. Egerton, 1791; rpt. 1833, 1884.

———. *Ancient Popular Poetry: From Authentic Manuscripts and Old Printed Copies*. Edinburgh: Privately printed, 1884. [Based on Harley 5396.]

Didactic Prose and Exempla

Modernizations

Rickert, Edith, ed. *The Babees Book: Medieval Manners for the Young Now First Done into Modern English from the Texts of Dr. F. J. Furnivall.* London: The Ballantyne Press, 1908. Rpt. London: Chatto & Windus, 1923. Pp. 43–46. [A modernized version.]

Walsh, James. J., ed. *A Golden Treasury of Medieval Literature.* Boston: The Stratford Co., 1930.

Related Studies

Ashley, Kathleen M., and Robert L. A. Clark, eds. *Medieval Conduct.* Minneapolis: University of Minnesota Press, 2001.

Bornstein, Diane. *Mirrors of Courtesy.* Hamden, CT: Archon Books, 1975. [Background.]

Ferster, Judith. *Fictions of Advice: The Literature and Politics of Counsel in Late Medieval England.* Philadelphia: University of Pennsylvania Press, 1996. [Background.]

Dronzek, Anna. "Gendered Theories of Education in Fifteenth-Century Conduct Books." In Ashley and Clark. Pp. 135–59.

Hanawalt, Barbara A. *'Of Good and Ill Repute': Gender and Social Control in Medieval England.* Oxford: Oxford University Press, 1998. [Contains useful discussion of advice manuals and codes of conduct for children.]

———. *Growing Up in Medieval London: The Experience of Childhood in History.* Oxford: Oxford University Press, 1993.

Nicholls, Jonathan. *The Matter of Courtesy: Medieval Courtesy Books and the Gawain-Poet.* Suffolk: D. S. Brewer, 1985.

Orme, Nicolas. *From Childhood to Chivalry: The Education of the English Kings and Aristocracy 1066–1530.* London and New York: Methuen, 1984. [Discusses advice tradition, including mirrors for princes.]

240

Notes to How the Goode Man Taght Hys Sone

Notes

Abbreviations: **B**: Bodleian Library MS Ashmole 61 (*SC* 6922), fols. 6a–6b; **F**: Frederick J. Furnivall; **Fi**: Rudolf Fischer; **H**: British Library MS Harley 5396, fols. 297a–300b; **La**: Lambeth Palace Library MS 853, pp. 186–92; **MS**: Cambridge University Library MS Ff. 2. 38, fols. 53a–54a.

The unique title for MS is: *Here foloweth how the goode man taght hys sone.* The other five replace "good" with "wise."

1   *Lysteneth all and ye shall here.* Conventional exhortation to the audience. Also found in romances of the period, perhaps as a reminder of their origins in an oral storytelling tradition. Here, the exhortation has the effect of capturing an audience's attention before the narrator/poet launches into his didactic treatise, which itself underscores issues of listening and speaking.

3   *Take gode tente.* Another exhortation to pay attention. B reads: *Take god hede.*

4   *fonde to lerne.* The emphasis on learning in relation to the "song" suggests an acute awareness of the didactic value of entertaining fiction.

10   *Was wele of fiftene wyntur age.* The age of fifteen seems to mark a conventional rite of passage into the adult masculine world. Children were imagined to reach an age of reason by their seventh year. Romance heroes experience significant changes in the course of their lives at these ages (e.g., Bevis of Hampton, Eglamour, Gowther, Amis, Amiloun, and Horn). Female saints also undergo a significant challenge at age fourteen or fifteen.

11   *meke and mylde.* A conventional expression suitable for school boys, but sometimes used to describe a man whose peaceful nature exceeds his martial prowess.

15   *in hys langage.* The variant in H — *With good ensaumple and faire langage* — suggests judicious discourse told carefully by an exemplary parent. The wisdom of the "wise" man is proven by the approbation of his pedagogical methods stated in the next line: "Taught hys sone, bothe wele and feyre." B reads *His fader þus on þis langage / Tauȝht his sone wele and feyre.* La reads *With good ensaumple and faire langage / His fader tauȝt him weel and faire.*

241

31   *Thy lyfe is mesure that thou lede.* I.e., the quality of your life is measured by the way you lead it.

33   *And, sone, thy tonge thou kepe also.* The injunction to watch what one says was ascribed to the wisdom of Solomon by medieval writers and applied to both sexes. Proverbial wisdom plays a significant part in this conduct treatise. See Whiting T372 and T374.

47   *maugreth.* The MED cites a range of meanings for *maugre* n. 1.: "(a) blame, reproach; ?ingratitude; ill-will, resentment; wrath, hostility; also, a rebuke; (b) shame, dishonor, disgrace; (c) a fault or an offense."

51   *Let no newfangylnes thee pleese.* The conventional notion of community stability so important to medieval writers is emphasized here as well. The dictate promoted by the father indicates the mistrust with which novelty and its potential threat to that stability was viewed.

57   *specyally.* Fi omits in his edition.

59   *Loke thou use nevyr comynly the taverne.* Compare to *How the Goode Wife Taught Hyr Doughter*: "Forsake thou hym that taverne hanteth, / And all the vices that therinne bethe" (lines 67–68). Medieval taverns were locations not only for drinking but for vices such as gambling and prostitution. The daughter of the Goode Wife is also warned to stay away from these establishments, as well as to avoid wrestling matches and cockfighting, activities not mentioned for a young man to avoid.

    comynly. Fi omits in his edition.

67   *Lagh not to moche.* Compare to *How the Goode Wife Taught Hyr Doughter*. While young women are cautioned to restrict laughter in order to avoid looking immodest, young men are cautioned to restrict laughter in order to avoid looking foolish. Troilus' post-mortem laughter indicates a retrospective understanding of his foolishness in love.

74   *use no rere sopers.* Compare to Robert Mannyng of Brunne's *Handlyng Synne* (ed. Idelle Sullens [Binghamton, NY: Medieval & Renaissance Texts & Studies, 1983]):

        Rere sopers yn pryuyte.
        Wyþ glotonye echoune þey be,

And þyr ys moche waste ynne,
And gaderyng of oþuer synne. (Lines 7261–64)

See also Lydgate's "A Dietary and a Doctrine for Pestilence" in *Minor Poems* (see entry in Select Bibliography to *Payne and Sorowe of Evyll Maryage*, p. 215):

Suffre no surfitis in thyn hous at nyht,
War of rer sopers and of gret excesse. (Lines 137–38)

76   *surfett*. MS: *furfett*; H: *surfett*. Since the MED does not list *furfett*, it is more likely than *surfett* is intended. The stanza (i.e., lines 73 ff.) is somewhat different in La:

And sonne, sitte not up at euen to longe,
Neither vse no rere souperis late;
Þou3 þou be boþe hool an strong,
Wᵗ such outrage it wole aslake;
And of late walking comeþ debate,
And out of tyme to sitte & drink,
Þerfore be waar & keep þi state,
And go to bedde bi tyme, & wynke.

81–88   No equivalent to this stanza is found in B or La.

92   *Thou wysely wayte and wele avyse*. This advice seems to contradict those who say that the average age of marriage was fourteen for boys and twelve for girls and seems commensurate with romance heroes and heroines who typically marry later in life.

97   *reste and pees*. Another conventional expression, also found in *Ratis Raving*, an instruction manual of the late fifteenth century, Chaucer, various hymns to the Virgin, and Barbour's *Legends of the Saints*. See the MED.

104   *feffe and sese*. Whatever property came into a woman's possession or provided for her was to be brought to the marriage as a dowry.

108   *To charge hur then to owtragely*. The issue of how a husband should treat his wife is important in the late Middle Ages. A husband/father had the legal right to "correct" the behavior of his wife and children in any way he deemed fit. Harsh chastisement was common as a form of discipline underwritten by the proverb ascribed to Solomon: "Spare the rod and spoil the child." Robert Mannyng of Brunne explains in *Handlyng Synne*:

Man or womman þat haþ a chyld,
Þat wyþ vnþewes wexyþ wyld,   *bad manners*
Þat wyle boþe mysseye and do,
Chastysement behouyþ þar to.
But ȝe hem chastyse at ȝour myght,
ȝe falle ellys for hem yn plyght.
Better were þe chyld vnbore
Þan fayle chastysyng & seþen lore.
Þus seyþ þe wys kyng salomoun
To men and wymmen eurychoun:
"Wyle ȝe þat ȝoure chylder be aferd,
ȝeuyþ hem þe smert ende of þe ȝerd
And techeþ hem gode þewes echoun,   *manners*
ȝyt dur ȝow breke hem no boun." (Lines 4851–64)

In *Stans Puer ad Mensam*, Lydgate (*Minor Poems*, p. 743–44) advises:

In childeris werre now myrthe, not debate,
    In her quarell is no great vyolence;
Now pley, now wepyng, selde in an estate;
    To her pleyntes yeve no gret credence;
    A rod refourmeth al her insolence;
In her corage no rancour doth abyde;
Who spareth the yerde, al vertue set asyde. (Lines 85–91)

120   *reyse a smoke.* This seems to be an idiomatic expression meaning to make a public
          complaint.

121–44   Three stanzas on the treatment of wives are bawdlerized or omitted in H and B. The
          five stanzas on treatment of one's wife in F's version of La (lines 73–112) avoid the
          topic of disciplining her and rather stress kindness: if she displeases be "softe &
          faire" (line 103) rather than defaming or shaming her with "vilouns name" (line 98).

131–32   *Thogh sche be sirvunt in degree, / In some degre sche fellowe ys.* Scriptural edicts
          established a marital hierarchy that subordinated women and children to fathers/
          husbands who legally presided as the head of the household. Scriptural edicts also
          supported companionate marriage which afforded wives a status commensurate with
          her husband's, at least in theory.

141   *lone awe.* This expression, repeated in line 143, links love and fear; *awe*, meaning
          "dread" and "terror," also means "reverence" and "veneration." *Lone* could also be
          an error for *love*.

...

157   *fekyll and frele.* The mutability of the material world, or in Chaucer's words its "lack of stedfastnesse," is a common theme in medieval thought as expressed earlier in line 51, when the father cautions against "newfangylnes."

160   *Hyt faryth but as a cheryfeyre.* The cherry fair was a celebration held in orchards during the cherry season. Such an event is alluded to in *Sir Cleges* when the hero brings a basket of cherries out of season and thus held to be miraculous to the king as a gift. Reference to the occasion appears twice in John Gower's *Confessio Amantis* (ed. G. C. Macaulay, EETS e.s. 81–82 [London: K. Paul, Trench, Trübner & Co., ltd., 1900–01]) in a discussion of teachers of religion and morality:

> Thei prechen ous in audience
> That noman schal his soule empeire,
> For al is bot a chirie feire. (P.452–54)

> Somtime I drawe into memoire
> Hou sorwe mai noght evere laste;
> And so comth hope in ate laste,
> What I non other fode knowe.
> And that endureth bot a throwe,
> Riht as it were a cherie feste. (6.886–91)

165   *withowten othe.* A conventional expression found in a number of romances and didactic works which emphasize the importance of verbal commitments.

180 ff. There are four lines missing at the end of this stanza. In H the equivalent stanza reads:

> And therfore do thou bi my councelle,
> And take ensample of othir men,
> How litil her good dooth hem availe
> Whanne their be dolven in her den,
> And he that was not of hys kyn
> Hath his wiif, and al that there is.
> Sonne, kepe thee out of deedly synne,
> And asaye to gete thee paradiis. (Lines 129–36)

182   *The moost thyng that certeyn ys.* Fi has *The moost certeyn thyng that ys.*

Select Secular Lyrics

In Praise of Women

I am as lyght as any roe   *swift; deer*
To preyse women wher that I goo.   *wherever*

To onpreyse women yt were a shame,   *unpraise*
For a woman was thy dame;   *mother*
5   Our Blessyd Lady beryth the name
Of all women wher that they goo.

A woman ys a worthy thyng —
They do the washe and do the wrynge: *do the wash; wringing*
"Lullay, lullay," she dothe thee synge,   *sing to/for you*
10 And yet she hath bot care and woo.   *woe*

A woman ys a worthy wyght,   *person*
She servyth man both daye and nyght,
Therto she puttyth all her myght,
And yet she hathe bot care and woo.

Abuse of Women

Of all creatures women be best: *are*
   Cuius contrarium verum est.   *Of whom the opposite is true*

In every place ye may well see,
That women be trewe as tirtyll on tree,   *turtledove*
5   Not lyberall in langage, but ever in secree,   *excessive; secrecy*
And gret joye amonge them ys for to be.
   Cuius contrarium verum est.

247

The stedfastnes of women will never be don,
So jentyll, so curtes they be everychon,   *each and every one*
10   Meke as a lambe, still as a stone,
Croked nor crabbed fynd ye none!   *Cross; crabby*
        Cuius contrarium verum est.

Men be more cumbers a thowsandfold,   *burdensome*
And I mervayll how they dare be so bold,
15   Agaynst women for to hold,
Seyng them so pascyent, softe and cold.   *seeing; patient*
        Cuius contrarium verum est.

For tell a women all your cownsayle,   *counsel*
And she can kepe it wonderly well;
20   She had lever go quyk to hell,   *rather go alive*
Than to her neyghbowr she wold it tell!
        Cuius contrarium verum est.

For by women men be reconsiled,
For by women was never man begiled,
25   For they be of the condicion of curtes Gryzell   *courteous Griselda*
For they be so meke and mylde.
        Cuius contrarium verum est.

Now say well by women or elles be still,
For they never displesed man by ther will;
30   To be angry or wroth they can no skill,   *have*
For I dare say they thynk non yll.
        Cuius contrarium verum est.

Trow ye that women list to smater,   *Believe you; like; gossip*
Or agaynst ther husbondes for to clater?   *chatter noisily*
35   Nay, they had lever fast bred and water   *fast [on]*
Then for to dele is suche a mater.
        Cuius contrarium verum est.

Thowgh all the paciens in the world were drownd,
And non were lefte here on the grownd,   *on earth*

40 Agayn in a woman it myght be fownd,
     Suche vertu in them dothe abownd!
          Cuius contrarium verum est.

     To the tavern they will not goo,
     Nor to the ale-hows never the moo,
45   For, God wot, ther hartes wold be woo,   *God knows; woeful*
     To spende ther husbondes money soo.
          Cuius contrarium verum est.

     Yff here were a woman or a mayd,
     That lyst for to go fresshely arayed,   *desired; smartly dressed*
     Or with fyne kyrchers to go displayed,   *kerchiefs*
50   Ye wold say, 'they be prowde!' It is yll said.
          Cuius contrarium verum est.

     Explicit

The Trials of Marriage

What, why dedyst thou wynk whan thou a wyf toke?
Thou haddest never mor ned brodde to loke!   *eyes wide open*
A man that wedyth a wyfe whan he wynkyth,
But he star afterward, wonder me thynkyth!   *stares*

Against Hasty Marriage, I

Know or thow knytte; prove or thow preyse yt.   *before; wed; praise*
Yf thou know er thou knyt, than mayst thou abate;   *stop*
And yf thou knyt er thou knowe, than yt ys to late.   *too*
Therfore avyse thee er thou the knot knytte,   *yourself before*
5   For "had y wyst" commeth to late for to lowse yt.[1]

---

[1] *For "had I known" comes too late in order to loosen it (the nuptial bond)*

249

Against Hasty Marriage, II

Man, bewar of thin wowynge   *your wooing*
For weddyng is the longe wo.   *woe*

Loke er thin herte be set;   *before*
Lok thou wowe er thou be knet;   *woo; you wed*
5   And if thou se thou mow do bet,   *may do better*
Knet up the heltre and let her goo.   *Tie; halter*

Wyvys be bothe stowte and bolde,   *strong*
Her husbondes aghens hem durn not holde;   *Their; dare*
And if he do, his herte is colde,
10   Howsoevere the game go.   *However*

Wedowis be wol fals, iwys,   *Widows; for sure*
For they cun bothe halse and kys   *can; embrace; kiss*
Til onys purs pikyd is,   *one's purse picked*
And they seyn, "Go, boy, goo!"

15   Of madenys I wil seyn but lytil,
For they be bothe fals and fekyl,   *fickle*
And under the tayle they ben ful tekyl;   *ticklish (loose)*
A twenty devel name, let hem goo!   *them*

A Young and Henpecked Husband's Complaint

How! Hey! It is non les,   *lie*
I dar not seyy quan che seyst "pes!"   *I dare not speak when she says "peace!"*

Yyng men, I warne you everychon: *Young*
Elde wywys tak ye non;   *Old wives (i.e., widows)*
5   For I myself have on at hom —   *one*
I dar not seyn quan che seyst "pes!"   *when she*

Quan I cum fro the plow at non,   *When; noon*
In a reven dych myn mete is don;   *filthy dish; food*

250

I dar not askyn our dame a spon —	*[for] a spoon*
10 I dar not seyn quan che seyst "pes!"	

If I aske our dame bred,	*[for] bread*
Che takyt a staf and brekit myn hed,	*She; breaks*
And doth me rennyn under the bed —	*makes; hide (run)*
I dar not seyn quan che seyst "pes!"	*speak when she says*

15 If I aske our dame fleych,	*[for] meat (flesh)*
Che brekit myn hed with a dych,	*dish*
"Boy, thou art not seyn woryth a reych!"	*rush*
I dar not sey quan che seyst "pes!"	

If I aske our dame chese	*[for] cheese*
20 "Boy," che seyst, al at ese,	
"Thou art not worth half a pese!"	*pea*
I dar not sey quan che seyst "pes!"	

A Henpecked Husband's Complaint

Care away, away, away —
Care away for evermore!

All that I may swynk or swet,	*work for; sweat*
My wife it wyll both drynk and ete;	*eat*
5 And I sey ought she wyl me bete —	*If; anything to the contrary; beat*
Carfull ys my hart therfor!	*Full of care*

If I sey ought of hyr but good,	*anything; her*
She loke on me as she war wod,	*as [if] she were crazy*
And wyll me clought abought the hod —	*clobber; head*
10 Carfull ys my hart therfor!	

If she wyll to the gud ale ryd,	*good ale[house] ride*
Me must trot all be hyr syd;	*I; by her side*
And whan she drynk I must abyd —	*wait*
Carfull ys my hart therfor!	

15   If I say, "It shal be thus,"
       She sey, "Thou lyyst, charll, iwous!   *You lie, churl, certainly*
       Wenest thou to overcome me thus?"   *Do you expect; oppose*
       Carfull ys my hart therfor!

       Yf ony man have such a wyfe to lede,   *deal with*
20   He schal know how *judicare* cam in the cred; *sentencing (condemnation)*
       Of hys penans God do hym med!   *penance; reward*
       Carfull ys my hart therfor!

Old Hogyn's Adventure

       Hogyn cam to bowers dore —   *bedchamber door*
         Hogyn cam to bowers dore,
       He tryld upon the pyn for love,   *wiggled up and down; latch-pin*
         Hum, ha, trill go bell —
5   He tryld upon the pyn for love,
         Hum, ha, trill go bell.

       Up she rose and lett hym yn —
         Up she rose and let hym yn,
       She had a-went she had worshipped all her kyn,[1]
10   Hum, ha, trill go bell —
       She had a-went she had worshipped all her kyn,
         Hum, ha, trill go bell.

       When thei were to bed browght —
         Whan thei were to bed browght,
15   The old chorle he cowld do nowght,   *could; nothing*
         Hum, ha, trill go bell —
       The old chorle he cowld do nowght,
         Hum, ha, trill go bell.

       Go ye furth to yonder wyndow —
20   Go ye furth to yonder wyndow,

---

[1] *She thought she had "honored" all her "family"*

And I will cum to you within a throw,
    Hum, ha, trill go bell —
And I will cum to you withyn a throw,
    Hum, ha, trill go bell.

25   Whan she hym at the wyndow wyst —   *When she realized he was at the window*
    Whan she hym at the wyndow wyst,
She torned owt her ars and that he kyst,   *kissed*
    Hum, ha, trill go bell —
She torned owt her ars and that he kyst,
30   Hum, ha, trill go bell.

Ywys, leman, ye do me wrong —   *Truly, my love*
    Ywis, leman, ye do me wrong,
Or elles your breth ys wonder strong,   *breath*
    Hum, ha, trill go bell —
35   Or elles your breth ys wonder strong,
    Hum, ha, trill go bell.

Explicit

I Have a Gentle Cock

I have a gentil cok,   *noble, well-bred*
Crowyt me day;   *[Who] crows for me in the morning*
He doth me rysyn erly,   *causes me to rise early*
My matyins for to say.   *matins*

5   I have a gentil cok,
Comyn he is of gret;   *He comes from a great lineage*
His comb is of reed corel,   *red*
His tayil is of get.   *tail; jet [black]*

I have a gentyl cook,
10   Comyn he is of kynde;   *good birth*
His comb is of red corel,
His tayl is of inde.   *indigo*

His legges ben of asor,   *azure*
So gentil and so smale;   *graceful; slender*
15 His spores arn of sylver qwyt, *spurs; bright (white) silver*
Into the wortewale.   *Up to the root*

His eynyn arn of cristal,   *eyes; crystal*
Lokyn al in aumbry;   *Set; amber*
And every nyght he perchit hym *perches himself*
20 In myn ladyis chaumbyr.   *lady's chamber*

Select Bibliographies and Notes to Select Secular Lyrics

Select Bibliography to In Praise of Women

Manuscript

British Library MS Harley 4294, fol. 81a (early sixteenth century).

Printed Editions

Adamson, Margot Robert, ed. *A Treasury of Middle English Verse*. London: J. M. Dent & Sons, 1930. [A modern translation.]

Chambers, E. K., and F. Sidgwick, eds. *Early English Lyrics: Amorous, Divine, Moral and Trivial*. New York: October House, 1966; rpt. 1967.

Davies, R. T., ed. *Medieval English Lyrics: A Critical Anthology*. London: Faber & Faber, 1963. [Listed under the title "Women are Worthy."]

Greene, Richard Leighton, ed. *The Early English Carols*. Oxford: The Clarendon Press, 1935; rpt. 1977.

Kaiser, Rolf, ed. *Medieval English: An Old and Middle English Anthology*. West Berlin: Rolf Kaiser, 1954. [Listed under the title "To Onpreyse Wemen yt were a Shame."]

Luria, Maxwell S., and Richard L. Hoffman. *Middle English Lyrics; Authoritative Texts, Critical and Historical Backgrounds, Perspectives on Six Poems*. New York: W. W. Norton, 1974.

Robbins, Rossell Hope, ed. *Secular Lyrics of the XIVth and XVth Centuries*. Oxford: Clarendon Press, 1952.

Tydeman, William, ed. *English Poetry 1400–1580*. New York: Barnes & Noble, 1970.

Select Secular Lyrics

Wright, Thomas, and James Orchard Halliwell, eds. *Reliquiae Antiquae. Scraps from Ancient Manuscripts, Illustrating Chiefly Early English Literature and the English Language.* 2 vols. London: John Russell Smith, 1845. Vol. 1, p. 275.

Indexed in

Brown, Carleton, and Rossell Hope Robbins, eds. *Supplement to the Index of Middle English Verse.* Lexington: University of Kentucky Press, 1965.

Utley, Francis Lee, ed. *The Crooked Rib: An Analytical Index to the Argument about Women in English and Scots Literature to the End of the Year 1568.* Columbus: Ohio State University Press, 1944.

Notes to *In Praise of Women*

Abbreviations: **Ro**: Rossell Hope Robbins; **Gr**: Richard Leighton Greene; **C&S**: E. K. Chambers and F. Sidgwick; **L&H**: Maxwell S. Luria and Richard L. Hoffman; **MS**: British Library MS Harley 4294, fol. 81a; **Ty**: William Tydeman; **Ut**: Francis Lee Utley; **Wr**: Thomas Wright and James Orchard Halliwell.

1–2   *I am as lyght as any roe / To preyse women wher that I goo.* The first two lines constitute the burden or refrain which is customarily repeated after every stanza. As many scholars suggest, the burden marks a generic relation of lyrics to carols, both of which were sung as well as accompanied by dance. Secular lyrics often emerge from the oral tradition, though, as Ro notes, "there are a few literary pieces which have had some influence on the shaping of a literary corpus. These include pieces found in MS Harley 2253, the Vernon MS, two items in St. John's College Cambridge MS 259, Cambridge University MS Addit. 5943, Sloane MS 2593, and pieces in two late Scottish texts" (p. 237), many of which are listed in Robbins' *Index* (see above). Gr notes a similar text from the Vernon MS called *Deo Gracias II*, edited by Carleton Brown in *Religious Lyrics of the Fourteenth Century,* second edition (Oxford: Clarendon Press, 1957), p. 138:

> Though I beo riche of gold so red,
> And liht to renne as is a ro. (Lines 9–10)

3   *To onpreyse women yt were a shame.* The poet takes an apparent stand against the anti-feminist slander more typical of popular lyrics and folk song, arguing that

everyone is born of woman, including saints. Ro remarks: "The tendency seems to have been to divert the praise of women in general to the particular praise of the Blessed Virgin as the exemplar of women. The poems praising a mistress have little to do with these general praises — 'they do the wash and do the wring' is a conception not known in courtship and wooing" (p. 237). Ty sees the lyric as representing "the other side of the anti-feminist debate," and notes that "as is usual in this kind of retort, the virtues of the Virgin Mary are advanced to strengthen woman's claim to respect from her husband and men in general" (p. 187). Ut is somewhat skeptical about the poet's sincerity and points out the ambiguity of line 8: "They do the washe and do the wrynge." He explains: "the" may be the article, it may mean "for thee," or it may be accusative and mean simply "thee" (p. 272). It may be possible to read the three instances as dative forms: "do thee washe . . . do thee wringe . . . [and] do thee singe" (in each instances the MS reads "the"); the sense being, women "do the washing for you and the wringing, and she sings lullabies to/for you." This maintains the syntactic parallels where the article does not, in that the syntactic shift to "she does the singing" in line 9 otherwise makes little sense. L&H read the first two instances as articles (p. 40) and the third as the pronoun "thee," which breaks the syntactic parallel. The syntactic parallel is already broken, however, by the shift from "they" in line 8 to "she" in line 9. The woman's doing *the* wash and *the* wringing makes good sense, though the tone of the poem certainly suggests that the lines are being addressed to a somewhat jaded male, as the dative pronouns would make more clear.

8   *They do the washe and do the wrynge.* The domestic economy suggested here is of the lower classes and offers support for claims of the lyrics' "popular" origin. That women do laundry, both the washing and the wringing, challenges contemporary stereotypes of medieval people as disinterested in personal hygiene. There may also be an echo of Lydgate's "A Mumming at Hertford" printed in *The Minor Poems of John Lydgate*, ed. Henry Noble MacCracken, EETS o.s. 192 (London: Oxford University Press, 1934), p. 680:

> Whoo cane hem wasshe, who can hem wring alsoo?
> Wryng hem, yee, wryng, so als God us speed.
> Til that some tyme we make hir nases bleed,
> And sowe hir cloothes whane they beothe to-rent,
> And clowte hir bakkes til somme of us beo shent. (Lines 190–94)

Ut notes that: "when Chaucer's Clerk concluded his counsel to archwives with 'And lat hym care, and wepe, and wrynge, and waille' he touched the spark of the Merchant's married discontent, and the great debate over marriage began to rise to the status of a holocaust" (p. 272). See also note to line 3.

9   *Lullay, lullay*. The woman's singing belies the hard life she lives which is acknowledged by the lyricist in the next line: "And yet she hath bot care and woo." The allusion to song is another means by which the genre announces its intrinsic link to popular song. As Gr suggests: "The burdens of the lullaby carols form a class by themselves. Their characteristic feature is a free use of the soothing onomatopoeia 'lullay.' This is, of course, in imitation of real folk lullabies" (p. cxlii).

11   *A woman ys a worthy wyght*. Despite the implication of strength conveyed in the word *wyght*, the rhyme of "myght" (line 13) with "nyght" (line 12) suggests that a woman's energy seems to be directed toward sexual service.

12   *She servyth man*. Ro adds an indefinite article before *man* to render it singular. However, since the woman here represents all women such a distinction is not needed.

       nyght. MS: *nygh*. I have followed Ro's emendation to restore the end rhyme.

Select Bibliography to Abuse of Women

Manuscripts

Balliol College Oxford MS 354, fol. 250a (early sixteenth century).

Bodleian Library MS Engl. Poet. e. I (*SC* 29734), fols. 55b–56a (c. 1480).

Printed Editions

Davies, R. T., ed. *Medieval English Lyrics: A Critical Anthology*. London: Faber & Faber, 1963. [Entitled "What Women are Not."]

Dyboski, Roman, ed. *Songs, Carols and Other Miscellaneous Poems, from the Balliol MS. 354, Richard Hill's Commonplace-Book*. EETS e.s. 101. London: K. Paul, Trench, Trübner & Co., 1908; rpt. 1937.

Flügel, Eward. "Liedersammlungen des XVI. Jahrhunderts, Besonders aus der Zeit Heinrichs VIII." *Anglia* 26. Halle: Max Niemeyer, 1903. Pp. 94–285.

Greene, Richard Leighton, ed. *The Early English Carols*. Oxford: The Clarendon Press, 1935; rpt. 1977.

———. *A Selection of English Carols*. Oxford: Clarendon Press, 1962.

Kaiser, Rolf, ed. *Medieval English: An Old English and Middle English Anthology*. West Berlin: Rolf Kaiser, 1954.

Luria, Maxwell S., and Richard L. Hoffman. *Middle English Lyrics; Authoritative Texts, Critical and Historical Backgrounds, Perspectives on Six Poems*. New York: W. W. Norton, 1974.

Robbins, Rossell Hope, ed. *Secular Lyrics of the XIVth and XVth Centuries*. Oxford: Clarendon Press, 1952.

Wright, Thomas, ed. *Song and Carols: Now, First Printed, from a Manuscript of the Fifteenth Century*. London: Printed for the Percy Society by Richards, 1847.

Indexed in

Brown, Carleton, and Rossell Hope Robbins, eds. *The Index of Middle English Verse*. New York: Columbia University Press, 1943. [Index #1485]

Utley, Francis Lee, ed. *The Crooked Rib: An Analytical Index to the Argument about Women in English and Scots Literature to the End of the Year 1568*. Columbus: Ohio State University Press, 1944. [Index # 136]

Notes to Abuse of Women

Abbreviations: **Dy**: Roman Dyboski; **Gr**: Richard Leighton Greene (1962); **L&H**: Maxwell S. Luria and Richard L. Hoffman; **MS**: Bodleian Library MS Engl. Poet. e. I (*SC* 29734), fols. 55b-56a; **Ro**: Rossell Hope Robbins; **Ut**: Francis Lee Utley.

2   *Cuius contrarium verum est.* "Of whom the contrary is true." This refrain or burden, repeated after every stanza, negates what precedes. Ro notes: "As with poems attacking marriage and poems treating of love in a mocking fashion, so here in poems of attacks on womankind, there are two main classes: popular poems and sophisticated

poems. In the minstrel collection, Bodl. MS Eng. Poet. E. I, a MS containing the popular songs of the day, collected to meet a genuine popular demand, and not collected because they appealed to the interests of a single literate poetaster, there are many attacks on women. . . . These poems quickly developed stereotyped conventions, and the sophisticated attacks parallel the set descriptions of the beloved and of the routine love epistle" (p. 239). Gr's comment is also worth noting: "[T]he regular return of the constricting or 'destroying' burden makes the carol-form a good one for the employment of this particular type of humour. One can see the possibilities of mirth raised by its performance before women who might not at first understand the Latin of the burden" (p. 240). Ut calls the work an "ironic defense" (p. 165).

The Latin line employed here recalls Chaucer's Chanticleer whose assertion to Pertelote is made under the assumption that neither hens nor women could understand Latin:

> For al so siker as *In principio,*
> *Mulier est hominis confusio* —
> Madame, the sentence of this Latyn is,
> "Womman is mannes joye and al his blis." (VII[B²] 3163–66)

To this Pertelote might respond: *Vir est feminae confusio.* There were women who could read and write Latin well in the Middle Ages. Hildegard of Bingen and Heloise are among the better-known examples.

4   *tirtyll.* The reference is to the turtledove, a symbol of fidelity and affection used frequently in courtly literature.

5   *Not lyberall in langage.* That women could not keep a secret or that they gossiped at every opportunity is a stereotype, reiterated frequently in anti-feminist literature. The counter-stereotype based upon the ideal of the Virgin Mary, i.e., that women are patient, meek, silent, soft, and innately circumspect, seems to be negated by the repetition of the burden after every stanza.

      secree. MS: *secrete.* Ro's emendation retains the end rhyme as well as the sense.

25   *curtes Gryzell.* If these secular lyrics derive from the oral, popular tradition as Ro suggests, then the reference to patient Griselda suggests that the negative feminine stereotype is culturally predetermined.

33   *list to smater.* See Chaucer's The Parson's Tale for a similar sentiment: "[T]hise olde dotardes holours, yet wol they kisse, though they may nat do, and smatre hem" (X[I]857).

34   *Or agaynst ther husbondes for to clater.* The rhetorical question is answered in the next line. The stereotype of woman as gossip resonates in Mirk's *Festial*: "A mayden ys lytyll worthe that . . . ys a claterer, a jangular, a flyter" (lines 229–33).

38   *paciens.* A virtue thought to be feminine.

43   *To the tavern.* Women were cautioned not to go to taverns since they were imagined to be places of iniquity and prostitution. See *How a Goode Wife Taught Hyr Doughter.* Gr notes that "[T]he love of women for the ale-house and the conversation there is one of the most frequent objects of derision among their satirical critics" (p. 240). Perhaps a more sympathetic view may be found in *A Talk of Ten Wives on Their Husbands' Ware*, also known as "The Gossips' Meeting," included in this volume.

49   *fyne kyrchers.* The admonition against ostentatious dress, particularly for women, is commonplace. Sumptuary laws of the time imposed dress codes on the general population in order to define people by class. The puritanical tone evinced here is typical of much homiletic material of the time.

Select Bibliography to The Trials of Marriage

Manuscript

Bodleian Library MS Engl. Poet. e. I (*SC* 29734), fol. 26a (c. 1480).

Printed Editions

Luria, Maxwell S., and Richard L. Hoffman. *Middle English Lyrics; Authoritative Texts, Critical and Historical Backgrounds, Perspectives on Six Poems*. New York: W. W. Norton, 1974.

Robbins, Rossell Hope, ed. *Secular Lyrics of the XIVth and XVth Centuries*. Oxford: Clarendon Press, 1952.

Wright, Thomas, ed. *Songs and Carols: Now, First Printed, from a Manuscript of the Fifteenth Century*. London: Printed for the Percy Society by Richards, 1847.

Indexed in

Brown, Carleton, and Rossell Hope Robbins, eds. *The Index of Middle English Verse.* New York: Columbia University Press, 1943. [Index # 2049, 3919, 2056, 1354]

Notes to The Trials of Marriage

Abbreviations: **Ro**: Rossell Hope Robbins; **Wr**: Thomas Wright.

1   *thou wynk whan thou a wyf toke.* The wink is significant, setting up the subject of marriage; the rhetorical question constructs a silent dialogue between the married man and the speaker. Ro notes that the first printing of this brief admonitory lyric appears in Wright's *Songs and Carols* "as part of a 'carol' with the burden 'man be war or thou knyte the fast'" (p. 239).

2   *ned brodde to loke.* The implication that the man about to be married needs to enter into the relationship with his eyes wide open is consistent with the sentiment of other admonitory pieces cautioning men to prudence, which, as a symbolic figure, has three sets of eyes, looking simultaneously to the past, the future, and the present. There is an analogous passage printed in *Reliquiae Antiquae* which is included in a longer, macaronic poem Wr entitles "Memorial Verses" (vol. 1, p. 289):

> I winked, I winked when I a woman toke,
> Sore me for-thinked, that I so moche wynked,
> For had I never more nede than nowe for to loke.

4   *wonder me thynketh.* The sense may be the speaker's own wonderment as well as a "marvel" or "amazing happening." The wink of an eye suggests that what is being undertaken is not to be understood as a binding, serious event.

Select Bibliography to Against Hasty Marriage, I

Manuscript

Bodleian Library MS Digby 196 (*SC* 1797), fol. 20a (late fourteenth century).

Printed Editions

Greene, Richard Leighton, ed. *The Early English Carols*. Oxford: The Clarendon Press, 1935; rpt. 1977.

Luria, Maxwell S., and Richard L. Hoffman. *Middle English Lyrics; Authoritative Texts, Critical and Historical Backgrounds, Perspectives on Six Poems.* New York: W. W. Norton, 1974.

Robbins, Rossell Hope, ed. *Secular Lyrics of the XIVth and XVth Centuries.* Oxford: Clarendon Press, 1952

Indexed in

Brown, Carleton, and Rossell Hope Robbins, eds. *The Index of Middle English Verse*. New York: Columbia University Press, 1943. [Index #1829]

Notes to Against Hasty Marriage, I

1   *Know or thow knytte*. Like the proverbial axiom, "look before you leap," the opening line suggests caution. Likewise *prove or thow preyse yt* suggests that the relationship should be experienced, the potential bride known before the bridegroom consents rendering the nuptial ceremony legal and binding. Compare the Wife of Bath's amusing tripping up of her old husband as she puts her wares out for trial, according to the principles of premarital "use" of the wares, as advocated by the "olde dotard shrewe" (*CT* III[D]291) himself. See *CT* III(D)285–92.

5   *had y wyst*. The narrator seems to speak from experience. The sense is that foresight is too often missing before irreversible mistakes are made. Hence "had I only known beforehand" becomes a wistful lament.

Select Bibliography to Against Hasty Marriage, II

Manuscript

British Library MS Sloane 2593, fol. 9b (c. 1440).

Printed Editions

Greene, Richard Leighton, ed. *The Early English Carols*. Oxford: The Clarendon Press, 1935; rpt. 1977.

Luria, Maxwell S., and Richard L. Hoffman. *Middle English Lyrics; Authoritative Texts, Critical and Historical Backgrounds, Perspectives on Six Poems*. New York: W. W. Norton, 1974.

Robbins, Rossell Hope, ed. *Secular Lyrics of the XIVth and XVth Centuries*. Oxford: Clarendon Press, 1952.

Wright, Thomas, ed. *Songs and Carols: Now, First Printed, from a Manuscript of the Fifteenth Century*. London: Printed for the Percy Society by Richards, 1847.

Notes to Against Hasty Marriage, II

1–2   *Man, bewar of thin wowynge / For weddyng is the longe wo.* The burden, repeated after every stanza, reinforces the cautionary sentiment. Because marriage was considered to be a monogamous, lifetime commitment, it was not to be entered into without careful forethought.

6   *Knet up the heltre.* The verb *knet*, in this line, means to hang or put aside. The *heltre* is a common piece of saddlery used to restrain large farm animals.

11   *Wedowis be wol fals, iwys.* The admonition against widows is based upon the assumption that widows seeking remarriage were doing so under false pretenses, i.e., not for love, but for other reasons, such as financial security or sexual satisfaction. Chaucer's Alisoun of Bath is a good example of the widow who has made her living by marrying older men for their wealth and younger men for their sexual stamina, while the widow of The Nun's Priest's Tale suggests that a widow's life could be autonomous yet subject to poverty. Widows had more freedom under the law than wives since they were not bound to obey a husband (see Dunbar's *The Tretis of the Twa Mariit Wemen and the Wedo*), but their financial status was often tenuous and dependent on the charity of others. For several perspectives on this matter, see Sue Sheridan Walker, ed. *Wife & Widow in Medieval England* (Ann Arbor: University of Michigan Press, 1993), and Louise Mirrer, ed. *Upon My Husband's Death: Widows in the Literature & Histories of Medieval Europe* (Ann Arbor: University of Michigan Press, 1992).

15   *Of madenys.* The description — "bothe fals and fekyl" (line 16) — marks another feminine stereotype of the deceptive, lascivious female.

Select Bibliography to *A Young and Henpecked Husband's Complaint*

Manuscript

British Library MS Sloane 2593, fols. 24b–25a (c. 1440).

Printed Editions

Chambers, E. K., and F. Sidgwick, eds. *Early English Lyrics: Amorous, Divine, Moral and Trivial.* New York: October House, 1966; rpt. 1967.

Greene, Richard Leighton, ed. *A Selection of English Carols.* Oxford: Clarendon Press, 1962.

———. *The Early English Carols.* Oxford: The Clarendon Press, 1935; rpt. 1977.

Luria, Maxwell S., and Richard L. Hoffman. *Middle English Lyrics; Authoritative Texts, Critical and Historical Backgrounds, Perspectives on Six Poems.* New York: W. W. Norton, 1974.

Wright, Thomas, ed. *Songs and Carols: Now, First Printed, from a Manuscript of the Fifteenth Century.* London: Printed for the Percy Society by Richards, 1847.

Indexed in

Brown, Carleton, and Rossell Hope Robbins, eds. *The Index to Middle English Verse.* New York: Columbia University Press, 1943. [Index #4279]

Utley, Francis Lee, ed. *The Crooked Rib: An Analytical Index to the Argument about Women in English and Scots Literature to the End of the Year 1568.* Columbus: Ohio State University Press, 1944. [Index #401]

Notes to A Young and Henpecked Husband's Complaint

Abbreviations: **Gr**: Richard Leighton Greene (1962).

1–2   *How! Hey! It is non les, / I dar not seyy quan che seyst "pes."* The burden repeats after every stanza, giving the henpecked husband the last word.

2   *che*. The scribe writes *ch* for the "sh" sound throughout the poem. N.b. "fleych," "dych," "reych" ("flesh," "dish," "rush") in lines 8, 15–17.

        seyst. MS: *sey3t*. The scribe uses *3t* for *st* in the refrain throughout the poem.

4   *Elde wywys*. This refers both to the age and status of the potential spouse. While society ridiculed May/December marriages, i.e., older men and younger women, such unions were tolerated, even sought out. Two of Chaucer's most memorable characters — January of The Merchant's Tale and John the Carpenter of The Miller's Tale — have younger wives who cuckold them. The idea of an older woman with a younger man, according to Gr was probably more common in the Middle Ages than in modern times: "[T]he frequency of early widowhood and the great importance of marriage in relation to matters of property were contributing causes" (p. 24). See also Chaucer's The Wife of Bath's Prologue, where her three good husbands are wealthy, old, and at death's door.

7   *plow at non*. This reverses the sentiment of the *Ballad of a Tyrannical Husband*. Both works are oriented toward the concerns of working classes, however.

12   *brekit myn hed*. There are depictions of the husband-beating wife in various other venues, such as misericords and the margins of manuscripts, the *Luttrell Psalter,* for instance.

17   *Boy, thou art not seyn woryth a reych*. According to Gr this phrase is a "common expression of worthlessness" (p. 241). See *A Selection of English Carols*.

Select Bibliography to A Henpecked Husband's Complaint

Manuscript

Bodleian Library MS Engl. Poet. e. I (*SC* 29734), fols. 23a–23b (c. 1480).

Notes to *A Henpecked Husband's Complaint*

Printed Editions

Auden, W. H., ed. *The Oxford Book of Light Verse*. Oxford: The Clarendon Press, 1938.

Chambers, E. K., and F. Sidgwick, eds. *Early English Lyrics: Amorous, Divine, Moral and Trivial*. New York: October House, 1966; rpt. 1967.

Fitzgibbon, H. M., ed. *Early English and Scottish Poetry, 1250–1600*. London: W. Scott, 1888.

Greene, Richard Leighton, ed. *The Early English Carols*. Oxford: The Clarendon Press, 1935; rpt. 1977.

Luria, Maxwell S., and Richard L. Hoffman. *Middle English Lyrics: Authoritative Texts, Critical and Historical Backgrounds, Perspectives on Six Poems*. New York: W. W. Norton, 1974.

Masters, J. E., ed. *Rymes of the Minstrels*. Shaftsbury: High House Press, 1927.

Robbins, Rossell Hope, ed. *Secular Lyrics of the XIVth and XVth Centuries*. Oxford: Clarendon Press, 1952.

Wright, Thomas, ed. *Songs and Carols: Now, First Printed, from a Manuscript of the Fifteenth Century*. London: Printed for the Percy Society by Richards, 1847.

Indexed in

Brown, Carleton, and Rossell Hope Robbins, eds. *The Index of Middle English Verse*. New York: Columbia University Press, 1943. [Index #210]

Utley, Francis Lee, ed. *The Crooked Rib: An Analytical Index to the Argument about Women in English and Scots Literature to the End of the Year 1568*. Columbus: Ohio State University Press, 1944. [Index # 20]

Notes to *A Henpecked Husband's Complaint*

Abbreviations: **MS**: Bodleian Library MS Engl. Poet. e. I (*SC* 29734), fols. 23a–23b; **Ro**: Rossell Hope Robbins.

1–2   *Care away, away, away — / Care away for evermore*. The burden depicts a carefree sentiment that contrasts sharply with what follows. Many scholars have placed this work in the category of *chanson de mal marié*.

3   *All that I may swynk or swet*. The sense is that everything the husband works for will be squandered and/or consumed by his wife at the local pub.

10   *Carfull ys my hart therfor*. MS: *carfull*. Ro adds the rest of the refrain — *ys my hart therfor!* — in the last line of this and subsequent stanzas.

11   *gud ale ryd*. The restrictions against respectable women frequenting taverns are many. See the Wycliffite treatise, *Of Weddid Men and Wifis and of Here Children Also*, and *How the Goode Wife Taught Hyr Doughter*.

20   *judicare*. Latin verb meaning "to judge, condemn, sentence, pronounce." The Latin term is functioning idiomatically as a noun — thus the nominal forms of my gloss.

Select Bibliography to Old Hogyn's Adventure

Manuscript

Balliol College Oxford MS 354, fol. 249b (early sixteenth century).

Printed Editions

Dyboski, Roman, ed. *Songs, Carols and Other Miscellaneous Poems, from the Balliol MS. 354, Richard Hill's Commonplace-Book*. EETS e.s. 101. London: Kegan Paul, Trench, Trübner & Co., 1908; rpt. 1937.

Flügel, Eward. "Liedersammlungen des XVI. Jahrhunderts, Besonders aus der Zeit Heinrichs VIII." *Anglia* 26. Halle: Max Niemeyer, 1903. Pp. 273–74.

Greene, Richard Leighton, ed. *The Early English Carols*. Oxford: The Clarendon Press, 1935; rpt. 1977.

Luria, Maxwell S., and Richard L. Hoffman. *Middle English Lyrics; Authoritative Texts, Critical and Historical Backgrounds, Perspectives on Six Poems*. New York: W. W. Norton, 1974.

Notes to Old Hogyn's Adventure

Robbins, Rossell Hope, ed. *Secular Lyrics of the XIVth and XVth Centuries*. Second edition Oxford: Clarendon Press, 1955.

Tydeman, William. *English Poetry 1400–1580*. New York: Barnes & Noble, 1970.

Notes to Old Hogyn's Adventure

Abbreviations: **Gr:** Richard Leighton Greene, *The Early English Carols*; **Ty**: William Tydeman.

The rhythms of song resonate in the regularity of repeated lines. In the absence of a burden, this lyric is in closer generic alignment with a chant or litany. Gr sees the omission as an indication of shifting genres: "Omission of the burden, while fundamentally more serious in that it changes the piece from a carol to an ordinary poem or song, yet may be superficially less noticeable, for no rime-pattern stanza is affected thereby" (p. cxxxiv).

1   *Hogyn cam to bowers dore.* As Ty notes, "the word 'bower' has many senses but they are usually associated with sexual encounters of this kind" (p. 190). The title of the piece in Ty's edition of songs and carols — "Old Hogyn and His Girl" — reminds us that titles are often editorially determined and vary among the many anthologies of medieval works.

2   The repeated lines have a choric, performative effect, like lining in a congregational (or tavern) meeting, as the leader pronounces a line and the audience repeats it. I have indented such lines.

4   *Hum, ha, trill go bell.* In the absence of a burden this line, repeated throughout the poem, retains the sonorities of minstrelsy. The *bell* perhaps refers to the lock cylinder in which the pin resides.

5   *He tryld upon the pyn for love.* The courtly serenade depicts the lovesick Hogyn rattling the latch of the door while singing his love song for admittance to his lady's chamber. This action parodies the conventional lover who trills upon his stringed instrument in an attempt to persuade his lady to admit him. Chaucer's Absolon in The Miller's Tale is a good example:

    This parissh clerk, this joly Absolon,
    Hath in his herte swich a love-longynge

That of no wyf took he noon offrynge;
For curteisie, he seyde, he wolde noon.
   The moone, whan it was nyght, ful brighte shoon,
And Absolon his gyterne hath ytake;
For paramours he thoghte for to wake.
And forth he gooth, jolif and amorous,
Til he cam to the carpenteres hous
A litel after cokkes hadde ycrowe,
And dressed hym up by a shot-wyndowe
That was upon the carpenteris wal.
He syngeth in his voys gentil and smal,
"Now, deere lady, if thy wille be,
I praye yow that ye wole rewe on me,"
Ful wel acordaunt to his gyternynge. (I[A]3348–63)

9   *She had a-went she had worshipped all her kyn.* Ty notes that Hogyn must be "a person of some worldly substance, like old January" (p. 190).

13–18   The humor of the stanza lies in its irony. Though the old churl gains entry into his beloved's bedchamber he cannot gain entry elsewhere — *The old chorle he cowld do nowght* (line 17).

19   *Go ye furth to yonder wyndow.* Ty sees the motivation as not quite clear "Is the girl offering a farewell kiss through the window?" (p. 190). Given the lover's impotence in line 15, perhaps this is sweet revenge for the lady.

27   *She torned owt her ars and that he kyst.* The motif of the misplaced kiss is most famously captured by Chaucer in The Miller's Tale:

Derk was the nyght as pich, or as the cole,
And at the wyndow out she putte hir hole,
And Absolon, hym fil no bet ne wers,
But with his mouth he kiste hir naked ers
Ful savourly, er he were war of this. (I[A]3731–35)

Select Bibliography to I Have a Gentle Cock

Manuscript

British Library MS Sloane 2593, fol. 10b (c. 1440).

Notes to I Have a Gentle Cock

Printed Editions

Chambers, E. K., and F. Sidgwick, eds. *Early English Lyrics: Amorous, Divine, Moral and Trivial*. New York: October House, 1966; rpt. 1967.

Chaucer, Geoffrey. *The Nun's Priest's Tale*. Ed. Kenneth Sisam. Oxford: The Clarendon Press, 1927.

Cook, Albert Stanburrough. *A Literary Middle English Reader*. Boston: Ginn & Co., 1915; rpt. 1943.

Davies, R. T., ed. *Medieval English Lyrics: A Critical Anthology*. London: Faber & Faber, 1963.

Duncan, Thomas, ed. *Medieval English Lyrics 1200–1400*. London: Penguin Books, 1995.

Luria, Maxwell S., and Richard L. Hoffman. *Middle English Lyrics; Authoritative Texts, Critical and Historical Backgrounds, Perspectives on Six Poems*. New York: W. W. Norton, 1974.

Robbins, Rossell Hope, ed. *Secular Lyrics of the XIVth and XVth Centuries*. Oxford: Clarendon Press, 1952.

Silverstein, Theodore, ed. *Medieval English Lyrics*. London: Edward Arnold, 1971.

Tydeman, William. *English Poetry 1400–1580*. New York: Barnes & Noble, 1970.

Wright, Thomas, ed. *Songs and Carols: Now, First Printed, from a Manuscript of the Fifteenth Century*. London: Printed for the Percy Society by Richards, 1847.

Indexed in

Brown, Carleton, and Rossell Hope Robbins, eds. *The Index of Middle English Verse*. New York: Columbia University Press, 1943. [Index #1299]

Notes to I Have a Gentle Cock

Abbreviations: **Da**: R. T. Davies; **Du**: Thomas Duncan; **L&H**: Maxwell S. Luria and Richard L. Hoffman; **MS**: British Library MS Sloane 2393; **Si**: Theodore Silverstein.

1   *I have a gentil cok*. MS: *cook*. L&H use this poem as the title piece for their section on erotic love, pp. 77–91. The lyric parodies love songs usually directed toward a

271

lady. Da points out the relation of this poem to a popular nursery rhyme, "Goosey, goosey gander": "this rhyme includes the words 'in my lady's chamber', and the earliest record of it does not include the last four lines of the rhyme, as generally known, with their reference to the old man" (p. 334):

> Goosey, goosey, gander,
> Whither shall I wander?
> Upstairs, downstairs
> And in my lady's chamber.

See *The Oxford Dictionary of Nursery Rhymes*, ed. Iona and Peter Opie (Oxford: Clarendon Press, 1952; rev. ed. Oxford and New York: Oxford University Press, 1997).

4   *matyins*. Early morning devotions.

5–8   The description of the rooster is in the manner of *effictio*, the conventional head to toe assessment usually of a lady. Chaucer uses a similar device to describe Chanticleer in The Nun's Priest's Tale:

> His coomb was redder than the fyn coral,
> And batailled as it were a castel wal;
> His byle was blak, and as the jeet it shoon;
> Lyk asure were his legges and his toon;
> His nayles whitter than the lylye flour,
> And lyk the burned gold was his colour.
> This gentil cok. . . . (VII[B²]2859–65)

Si notes the similarity to Latin description of *gallus* in works such as Alexander Neckam's *De Natura Rerum* (p. 129).

11   *corel*. MS: *scorel*.

12   *inde*. Indigo was originally a blue dye from India.

15   Du notes that "in the Sloane lyrics the variation of 3- and 4-stress lines is not uncommon" (p. 246).

      His spores arn of sylver qwyt. The rooster seems to wear the "spurs" of a knight.

19–20   *And every nyght he perchit hym / In myn ladyis chaumbyr*. The last two lines function as a couplet would in one of Shakespeare's sonnets, adding information that both clarifies and contradicts the sentiment expressed in preceding lines. Du points out the sexual innuendo in comparison to the nursery rhyme.

Glossary

abbregement (n.) *reduction*
affray (n.) *outcry, disturbance*
ancille (n.) *slave*
and (conj.) *if; and*
apparailes (n.) *activities, festivities*
appeyren (v.) *to make worse*
askanuns (adv.) *as though*
asken of (v.) *to require*
astaunchen (v.) *to quench, appease*
asterten (v.) *to escape*
availe (n.) *benefit, advantage*
availlen (v.) *to afford help*
avaunten (v.) *to boast*
avow (n.) *vow*

behesten (v.) *to promise*
besteren (v.) *bestir*
bocche (n.) *a botch, a swelling*
borowen (v.) *to save (used in oaths)*
brent (pp.) *burnt*
buffard (n.) *dullard*

casten (v.) *to arrange, plot*
cely (adj.) *hapless, wretched*
cherisshen (v.) *to hold dear (sexual)*
chevysaunce (n.) *agreement, arrangement*
cirurgian (n.) *surgeon*
colour (n.) *pretext, trick*
compassen (v.) *to surround*
confortatife (n.) *medicine*
contenaunce (n.) *(1) behavior; (2) abstention from sexual intercourse*

coorbed (adj.) *stooped*
coragen (v.) *to encourage or embolden*
countertaile (n.) *tally stick kept by a creditor*
cowherand (adj.) *reluctant, cowering*
crevil (n.) *itch*

daunten (v.) *to subdue*
del (n.) *sorrow*
descryven (v.) *to describe*
dighten (v.) *to prepare, arrange*
dismayen (v.) *to discourage*
dreimod (adv.) *sadly*
dreye (n.) *trouble*

enderdai (n.) *other day*
enditen (v.) *to write*
enduen (v.) *to invest*
erdely (adj.) *earthly*
eren (v.) *to plough*
ernde (n.) *errand*
esuen (v.) *to follow*
eyren (n. pl.) *heirs*

fage (n.) *trick*
fagen (v.) *to flatter, to trick*
failen (v.) *to be missing*
fayne (adv.) *gladly*
feat (adj.) *comely*
fere (n.) **in fere** *together*
feynen (v.) *to pretend*
fiere, fyere (adj.) *fiery*
fles (n.) *flesh, meat*

273

flyten (v.) *to argue, fight*
foreward (n.) *contract*
forholen (v.) *withheld*
forshape (v.) *transform, change*
forthynketh (v.) *thought; regret*
frusshen (v.) *to rub*
fullen (v.) *fulfill*

gossiprede (n.) *spiritual kinship, relationship between godparents and godchildren*
governaunce (n.) *behavior, manner*
grith (n.) *peace*
guyse (n.) *manner*
gyly (adj.) *deceitful*

habbe (v.) *have*
halsen (v.) *to embrace by the neck*
hende (adv.) *noble*
henten (v.) *to seize*
hernde (n.) *business*
hethen (adv.) *hence*
hetten (v.) *to hit*
hevinlie (adj.) *celestial; splendid*
hoe (pronoun) *she*
hounbind (v.) *unbind*
houncurteis (adj.) *uncourteous*
hounlawe (adv.) *unlawful*
hounsele (n.) *grief*
hovyd (v.) *halted*

i-lore (pp.) *lost*
inow (adv.) *enough*
iunesse (n.) *youth*
iuvencle (n.) *a calf; a young woman*
iwis(se) (adv.) *certainly, indeed*

juparté (n.) *problem*

kelen (v.) *to cool*

letten (v.) *to delay*
leve (adj.) *beloved*
leven (v.) *to remain*
lewde (adj.) *stupid, foolish; lower class, common*
listen (v.) *to be pleasing*
lore (n.) *lesson, law*

male de flank (Fr.) *sickness of the side of the body*
meet (adj.) *suitable, fitting*
mekil, mekle (adj.) *much, great*
messaventer (n.) *misadventure*
mete (n.) *reward; food, meat*
meven (v.) *to bring forward (an argument), to broach*
mihte of mayntenaunce (ger.) *the keeping of retainers*
mokadour (n.) *handkerchief*
mone pynnes (n.) *mouth pins (teeth)*
mowen (v.) *to be able*
myschaunce (n.) *misfortune*

norturen (v.) *to discipline*

onpurveyen (v.) *not to be provided with or for*
onthryvethen (v.) *not to prosper*
onwis (adv.) *mistaken*
ounderfost (v.) *receive*

palle (n.) *rich fabric*
pank (n.) *inordinate sexual desire*
parformen (v.) *to work out*
pelouhe, pelow (n.) *pillow*
perveyaunce (n.) *provision*
perveyen of (v.) *to provide with*

Glossary

pilch (n.) *fur coat*
playne (adj.) *undisturbed, smooth*
pleasieren (v.) *to give pleasure*
popholy (n.) *hypocrisy*
potent (n.) *crutch*
prevy (adj.) *private*

quair (n.) *book*
quelle (v.) *kill*
querte (adj.) *healthy*

racle (adj.) *rash*
rage (n.) *passion, madness*
ravisshen (v.) *to carry off by force (usually a woman)*
read (n.) *advice*
remewen (v.) *to block (a payment)*
rew (v.) *pity*
roggen (v.) *to pull*
rotour (n.) *one who plays the rote; a lecher*
routhe (n.) *pity*
rownen (v.) *to whisper*
rustiler (n.) *a small amount*
rybaudy (n.) *obscenity, lechery*

sad (adj.) *serious, steadfast*
scathe (n.) *injury*
scient (adj.) *wise, knowledgeable*
seethen (v.) *to boil*
semblable (adj.) *similar*
semyng (ger.) *appearance*; **to one's semyn** *in one's judgment*
shon (n.) *shoes*
siche (adj.) *such*
siker (adv.) *truly*
skil(le) (n.) *reason; craft*
slo (v.) *slay*
sop (n.) *morsel*

spectacle (n.) *glasses*
standen (v.) *to stand*; **standen so** *to be thus*
steed (n.) *place*
stounde (n.) *time*
stynten (v.) *to top*
sudary (n.) *handkerchief*
suen (v.) *to follow*
suithe (adv.) *quickly*
sumdele (adv.) *somewhat*
swelten (v.) *to grow faint*
sweme (n.) *sorrow*
swemeful (adj.) *sorrowful*
swich (adj.) *such*
swyngylle (v.) *beat, pulverize*

tartaryne (n.) *a silk fabric*
tellen (v.) *to count*
tene (adv.) *cautiously*
tent (n.) *a thought*; **taken tent** *to give a thought to*
theen (v.) *to thrive, prosper*
thenk (v.) *think*
thought (adv.) *although, though*
tikeltylle (n.) *loose woman*
torn (v.) *turn, change*
tothir (n.) *other*
trippes (n.) *dancing*
trowid (v.) *believed, trusted*
turnemente (n.) *contest*

unmete (adv.) *exceedingly*

vengeable (adj.) *needing vengeance, destructive*
vilesse (n.) *vileness*
voyden (v.) *to make void*

wayt (n.) *concealed ambush*

Glossary

wem (n.) *spot, blemish*

wenen (v.) *to expect, to hope*

werer (adj.) *perplexed, anxious, doubtful*

wexen (v.) *to grow*

withseynen (v.) *to contradict*

wode (adj.) *crazy, mad*

wondren (v.) *to wonder*

wrethe (n.) *wrath*

wryen (v.) *to incline, deviate from the proper course*

wright (n.) *carpenter*

wroken (v.) *to avenge; to have sexual intercourse*

wyse (n.) *manner*

wyte (n.) *blame*

wyten (v.) *to know; to accuse*

y-lore (pp.) *lost*

ynow (adv.) *enough*

yurstendai (n.) *yesterday*

ywis(se) (adv.) *certainly, indeed*

Volumes in the Middle English Texts Series

The Floure and the Leafe, The Assembly of Ladies, and *The Isle of Ladies*, ed. Derek Pearsall (1990)

Three Middle English Charlemagne Romances, ed. Alan Lupack (1990)

Six Ecclesiastical Satires, ed. James M. Dean (1991)

Heroic Women from the Old Testament in Middle English Verse, ed. Russell A. Peck (1991)

The Canterbury Tales: Fifteenth-Century Continuations and Additions, ed. John M. Bowers (1992)

Gavin Douglas, *The Palis of Honoure*, ed. David Parkinson (1992)

Wynnere and Wastoure and The Parlement of the Thre Ages, ed. Warren Ginsberg (1992)

The Shewings of Julian of Norwich, ed. Georgia Ronan Crampton (1993)

King Arthur's Death: The Middle English Stanzaic Morte Arthur and Alliterative Morte Arthure, ed. Larry D. Benson and Edward E. Foster (1994)

Lancelot of the Laik and Sir Tristrem, ed. Alan Lupack (1994)

Sir Gawain: Eleven Romances and Tales, ed. Thomas Hahn (1995)

The Middle English Breton Lays, ed. Anne Laskaya and Eve Salisbury (1995)

Sir Perceval of Galles and Ywain and Gawain, ed. Mary Flowers Braswell (1995)

Four Middle English Romances: Sir Isumbras, Octavian, Sir Eglamour of Artois, Sir Tryamour, ed. Harriet Hudson (1996)

The Poems of Laurence Minot (1333–1352), ed. Richard H. Osberg (1996)

Medieval English Political Writings, ed. James M. Dean (1996)

The Book of Margery Kempe, ed. Lynn Staley (1996)

Amis and Amiloun, Robert of Cisyle, and Sir Amadace, ed. Edward E. Foster (1997)

The Cloud of Unknowing, ed. Patrick J. Gallacher (1997)

Robin Hood and Other Outlaw Tales, ed. Stephen Knight and Thomas Ohlgren (1997)

The Poems of Robert Henryson, ed. Robert L. Kindrick (1997)

Moral Love Songs and Laments, ed. Susanna Greer Fein (1998)

John Lydgate, *Troy Book: Selections*, ed. Robert R. Edwards (1998)

Thomas Usk, *The Testament of Love*, ed. R. Allen Shoaf (1998)

Prose Merlin, ed. John Conlee (1998)

Middle English Marian Lyrics, ed. Karen Saupe (1998)

John Metham, *Amoryus and Cleopes*, ed. Stephen F. Page (1999)

Four Romances of England: King Horn, Havelok the Dane, Bevis of Hampton, Athelston, ed. Ronald B. Herzman, Graham Drake, Eve Salisbury (1999)

The Assembly of Gods: Le Assemble de Dyeus, or Banquet of Gods and Goddesses, with the Discourse of Reason and Sensuality, ed. Jane Chance (1999)

Thomas Hoccleve, *The Regiment of Princes*, ed. Charles R. Blyth (1999)

John Capgrave, *The Life of St. Katherine*, ed. Karen Winstead (1999)

John Gower, *Confessio Amantis*, Vol. 1, ed. Russell A. Peck (2000)

Richard the Redeless and *Mum and the Sothsegger*, ed. James Dean (2000)

Ancrene Wisse, ed. Robert Hasenfratz (2000)

Walter Hilton, *Scale of Perfection*, ed. Thomas Bestul (2000)

John Lydgate, *Siege of Thebes*, ed. Robert Edwards (2001)

Pearl, ed. Sarah Stanbury (2001)

Other TEAMS Publications

Documents of Practice Series:

Love and Marriage in Late Medieval London, by Shannon McSheffrey (1995)

A Slice of Life: Selected Documents of Medieval English Peasant Experience, edited, translated, and with an introduction by Edwin Brezette DeWindt (1996)

Sources for the History of Medicine in Late Medieval England, by Carole Rawcliffe (1996)

Regular Life: Monastic, Canonical, and Mendicant Rules, selected with an introduction by Douglas J. McMillan and Kathryn Smith Fladenmuller (1997)

Commentary Series:

Commentary on the Book of Jonah, Haimo of Auxerre, translated with an introduction by Deborah Everhart (1993)

Medieval Exegesis in Translation: Commentaries on the Book of Ruth, translated with an introduction by Lesley Smith (1996)

Nicholas of Lyra's Apocalypse Commentary, translated with an introduction and notes by Philip D. W. Krey (1997)

Rabbi Ezra Ben Solomon of Gerona: Commentary on the Song of Songs and Other Kabbalistic Commentaries, selected, translated, and annotated by Seth Brody (1998)

John Wyclif: On the Truth of Holy Scripture, translated with an introduction and notes by Ian Christopher Levy (2001)

To order please contact:

MEDIEVAL INSTITUTE PUBLICATIONS
Western Michigan University
Kalamazoo, MI 49008–5432
Phone (616) 387–8755
FAX (616) 387–8750

http://www.wmich.edu/medieval/mip/index.html